Beyond Audit

Beyond Audit

Auditing Remotely and Delivering Value

ROBERT L. MAINARDI

WILEY

Published by John Wiley & Sons, Inc., Hoboken, New Jersey.
Published simultaneously in Canada.

For general information on our other products and services or for technical support, please contact our Customer Care Department within the United States at (800) 762-2974, outside the United States at (317) 572-3993, or fax (317) 572-4002.

Wiley publishes in a variety of print and electronic formats and by print-on-demand. Some material included with standard print versions of this book may not be included in e-books or in print-on-demand. If this book refers to media such as a CD or DVD that is not included in the version you purchased, you may download this material at http://booksupport.wiley.com. For more information about Wiley products, visit www .wiley.com.

Library of Congress Cataloging-in-Publication Data is Available:

ISBN 9781119789604 (Hardback)
ISBN 9781119789611 (ePub)
ISBN 9781119789628 (ePDF)

Cover Design: Wiley
Cover Image: Photo by Oliver Buchmann on Unsplash
Author Photo: Courtesy of the author

SKY10025129_022321

To my parents, Angelo and Lucy, who watch over me. I hope they are proud of the son, brother, friend, and father they raised. And to my children, Robert and Gabrielle, I will never stop loving and supporting you … always believe in yourselves.

Contents

Preface

FOR OVER THREE DECADES, I have been actively working in an internal audit department or partnering with them to create the most effective and efficient audit operations. That operational efficiency measure has given way to determining if these departments are truly focusing on the most critical risks their company is, might be, or could be facing. Too often, internal audit departments get caught in a "drone army" mentality and focus on moving the audit coverage forward without building any additional business process knowledge or providing guidance to improve the overall business process. While coverage is important and should be considered, examining all aspects of an internal audit operation will prove to be invaluable.

At the time this book was written, companies and their employees are developing plans in the hopes of resuming normal business operations and activities. This is an excellent opportunity for internal audit departments to pause and consider not only how effectively they execute their corporate responsibilities, but also how much risk permeates in each phase of their audit process as well as their entire audit methodology and the successful compliance and execution of same. Throughout this book, there are references to the Beyond Audit methodology, which has been developed to provide insight, guidance, techniques, suggestions, and templates to improve your current audit methodology. Additionally, it will introduce the Audit Risk Barometer, which was created to allow audit departments to independently and objectively assess their operations through a review of six individual and distinct categories and deliver an overall audit process risk assessment to focus and create targeted action plans to address opportunities for improvement. The risk barometer facilitates an in-depth view of your current audit function from the current methodology to the delivery of your audit products, which generates the detailed support for the overall risk score and blueprint to address the most impactful enhancements to improve the audit function.

This book addresses the need for internal audit departments to focus on improving their own process in the new remote audit environment to ensure they are working in partnership with the business owners to gain a clear understanding of the business objectives and gather all pertinent information and data to provide value-based recommendations which result in real change. The only way to facilitate change is to ensure that the audit department recognizes the critical skills required to be successful in the execution of remote audits and continues the development of those skills to improve audit performance.

It should be noted that at the conclusion of each chapter, there will be a link provided that will allow the reader to view a video summary of a particular skill, technique, or template discussed in the chapter and or an interview with a subject matter expert examining the concept that was detailed in the chapter.

Chapter 1 provides a discussion regarding the current state of internal audit departments around the globe and the corresponding challenges they are encountering when trying to execute and complete their audit plan, often with only virtual access to their business partners. It also explains the critical role the business partner plays throughout an audit and how internal audit needs their participation.

Chapter 2 takes an in-depth look and analysis of being assigned to a remote audit, especially for the first time, and all the challenges that executing a remote audit engagement will present through each phase of the audit. Included in the discussion will be suggested targeted techniques that provide the audit team with the tools to stay on track and produce value focused results and an introduction to the importance of the internal audit and business partner relationship.

Chapter 3 outlines how to successfully market the internal audit department to ensure all business partners understand what internal audit does and, more importantly, why they do it. More than ever in this remote audit environment, a clear communication of internal audit's mission statement, purpose, and partnership will be required to complete the audit engagement requirements.

Chapter 4 introduces the Beyond Audit Learning Map and personal development plan process as well as the critical skills necessary for every auditor to develop and foster to be successful at their level in the department. And while communication will always be a critical skill for auditors to continually develop, there are seven other skills discussed to consider in any development plan.

Chapters 5 through 8 provide the methodology details for the three main audit phases: (1) planning, (2) fieldwork, and (3) reporting, plus the action plan implementation phase to facilitate change in the business process. Each chapter defines the phase and the specific objectives and corresponding requirements needed to comply with the audit methodology.

Chapter 9 presents and explains the audit dashboard process from the objective of the dashboard, to development, to reporting, to required actions needed to address gaps identified using audit performance data. Also included in the dashboard discussion are techniques to identify specific metrics to be tracked from your existing audit methodology and the corresponding metric criteria requirements to score metric performance.

Chapter 10 is dedicated to the critical role that communication plays in the internal audit department especially when operating in a remote environment. The topics covered include the communication model and the significant challenges that the message medium plays in the delivery of information between two parties. In addition, the Beyond Audit Advisor Approach is detailed to provide a suggested technique to produce effective communications.

Chapter 11 introduces the Audit Risk Barometer, which is an unfiltered, honest assessment of the internal audit department's operations as it relates to six individual categories. This self-assessment process takes the participants through a review of descriptive statements in each category, which are compiled for a total category score. The category scores are then totaled to calculate the internal audit's overall risk score. Three different risk scores alert the internal audit team as to their department's strengths and weaknesses.

Chapter 12 provides the ideal profile of an exceptional, self-aware, self-validating, high-performance internal audit department by discussing the top 10 characteristics that support this definition of a world-class audit organization. Both hard and soft department characteristics are discussed to create a baseline for audit departments to maintain focus, provide ongoing team and methodology development, and improve service to their business partners.

Chapter 13 discusses the critical and continuous role that training and development play in every internal audit department. While auditors should take responsibility for their own development, the audit department provides support and the proper learning environment to ensure audit development and success. Also included in this chapter is the Beyond Audit Learning Map, which details the suggested courses and topics for beginning auditors to provide a solid foundation to establish their audit skills.

Acknowledgments

EVEN THOUGH THE DEVELOPMENT of this book occurred at such an odd time of isolation, I still had incredible support from so many people. I want to say thank you to all of those people, both professionally and personally, who experienced delays in response but waited patiently as I focused on creating this book.

I owe the biggest thanks to my son and daughter, Robert and Gabrielle, who sacrificed the most during the writing of this book. Even though I could not give them the level of attention they deserved, they still diligently checked in on me to ensure I remembered that I had kids. Even with their busy professional careers, they found time to share with me during my book development and writing breaks, and I deeply appreciated that. You have both turned out to be incredibly successful, and I could not be prouder to tell everyone that you are my children. Stay focused on your goals and never give up.

Thanks as always to my brothers, Jerry, Michael, and Stephen. All three of them provide support for me, whether it is for computer challenges, guidance, or office needs. No matter what, I can count on one of them chipping in to help me address the issue. I know my parents would be proud of how close we have stayed, and I could not be any luckier to have these guys in my life.

As always, a special thank-you to Barumbi for the constant inspiration and support throughout this entire process. From the first book on continuous auditing to now, you have been a constant every single day, and I know I could never replace you. I look forward to continuing to develop new approaches and concepts with you and look forward to collaborating long into the future. I could never replace the perspective, motivation, and insight you share with me. Let us keep this thing rolling.

No acknowledgment would be complete without including Lieutenant Colonel Henry "Pat" Campbell. Pat has been by my side for over 35 years since we met at Penn State, and I could not ask for a better fourth brother. Just like my brothers, I know that I can count on Pat and his wife, Laura, any time I need support or have any other ridiculous request. The two of you are amazing. I appreciate everything we have shared and look forward to seeing you soon. As I have mentioned to you before, I could never thank you enough for the 21 years of service in the US Air Force. The sacrifices you made allow me and countless others to enjoy their lives while you protected ours. I appreciate what you have done, and the sacrifices Laura made while you were away. You inspire me and every person you meet. Love you, brother.

In an unexpected acknowledgment, I must recognize three men that I literally owe for saving my life. How do you recognize and thank someone for keeping you alive and above ground? Words do not really seem like enough, but I will give it a try. To Dr. Martella, Dr. Sacchetti, and Dr. Tarditi, thank you a million times over for identifying, correcting, and providing me the absolute best care in fixing an unknown congenital defect that I was born with and no one, except for you, noticed and replaced just in time. You and your families will always be in my prayers and I am forever in your debt. Thank you so much for allowing me to spend more time with my children. All three of you are amazing and deserve the highest praise.

Thanks to Jonathan Marks, who is a constant source of critical industry, business, and professional knowledge and always dedicates the necessary time to provide insight into any topic. His intellectual property delivers a focused vision for the most effective way to understand and analyze a process. He is not only an invaluable source of intelligence but also a great friend. We have collaborated on many learning events, presentations, and projects, and I look forward to continuing those efforts going forward.

Thanks to my financial team, compiled of one amazing man, John Smith. Mr. Smith, aka Sma Sma Smitty, is not only my business associate but also a great friend. I appreciate the input, guidance, and support you have provided to keep me in the game for over 13 years and am looking forward to our next adventure.

Thank you to my long-time friend, Dino Borghi, at Borghi's by the Bay in Stone Harbor, New Jersey, for always taking care of me, my family, and business associates with unbelievable meals and unmatched service. It is beyond fun cooking and working with you, as well as hanging out to do things we probably should not be doing. If I have to make a bad decision with anyone, you are it. Give me a Hunge. You are the best.

As I acknowledged in my last book, there are so many business partners and audit team members that I have collaborated and worked with over the past three decades, and I truly appreciate all their hard work and contributions. Thank you all for the support and effort that you provided, whether it was to deliver a quality product to improve a business process or enhance the skills of a particular audit team. I look forward to partnering with you again in future endeavors.

About the Author

AFTER TWO DECADES IN the internal audit profession, Robert started his own company in 2007, which partners with internal audit, compliance, fraud, and business professionals to develop and facilitate custom training as well as provide resources and assistance in evaluating, creating, and implementing formal audit methodologies and effective business processes. Prior to starting his company, Robert worked in six different internal audit departments, most recently as the vice president of Internal Audit for the Penn Mutual Life. Prior to joining Penn Mutual, his work history included The Vanguard Group, Aetna, Prudential, Advanta, and GMAC Mortgage.

As a professional keynote speaker and facilitator, Mr. Mainardi leads programs to:

- Develop and maintain world-class internal auditing functions
- Evaluate internal audit risk via the Audit Risk Barometer
- Create, implement, and maintain continuous auditing programs
- Build learning maps to facilitate successful professional development
- Draft, finalize, and issue high-impact audit reports
- Deliver quality and value in a remote audit environment
- Improve communication and client relationship development
- Identify, recruit, interview, and maintain quality audit staff

Mr. Mainardi is an active member of the Institute of Internal Auditors (IIA). He is an internationally recognized featured speaker at accounting, audit, fraud, and other professional association conferences. He received a BS degree from the Pennsylvania State University, where he majored in Accounting and Business Law. He also earned a master's degree in Finance from Temple

University. Plus, he has merited the Six Sigma Green Belt certification from the American Society for Quality, which recognizes the recipient for unique expertise in problem-solving and statistical analysis. He also has earned the Certified Financial Services Auditor (CFSA), Certification in Risk Management (CRMA) designations, and the Qualification in Control Self-Assessment.

1

What Happened

THINK BACK FOR A MOMENT. Do you even remember the beginning of the year 2020, which started with such promise? You probably made a couple of New Year's resolutions. Maybe it was something about your weight, exercise, or even your job. At work maybe you made a commitment to improvement. This was going to be your year – you were going to seek opportunities to lead jobs, take a leadership position, and maybe even get promoted. No matter what goals you set for yourself, you were certain you knew what you needed to do and how you were going to get there. You had a plan.

The one factor every person has to consider when making a plan is to ensure that all possible and potential roadblocks to achieving the goals are identified and considered. Now, while there is no way to consider, document, and explain every reader's personal goals, I can definitely speak on the objectives of an audit department. For more than three decades, I have been a team member in an internal audit department and/or partnering with them to create the most effective and efficient internal audit operation. And while each department is unique, the methods, direction, discipline, execution, and oversight of the operation remains the same. So, let us focus on the audit department and how they entered the year with a plan and an energetic team filled with optimism.

In the same vein that an individual would set yearly goals, so does the audit function. The chief audit executive meets with the leadership team and discusses the company's direction and how the internal audit department is going to partner with each of the business leaders to ensure the operations in every division are being completed in the most effective and efficient manner. And in order to provide that validation, internal audit will ensure that the process design, implementation, execution, reporting, and oversight are producing the intended outcome, no matter if the result is a physical production or a process. The audit chief knows the key to delivering a value product to their clients is to recognize that each process will produce an outcome; however, the internal audit team must verify and validate the outcome is the intended or desired outcome according to the business process requirements. With the stated objective to provide this type of specific value to their clients, audit departments realize the discipline, focus, effort, and dedication it takes to deliver.

 ## AUDIT EXECUTION CHALLENGES

When the audit leadership team reviews all of the pertinent business activity data and comes together to discuss and create the annual plan, they consider the barriers the team will face to produce their quality product. These barriers include, but are not limited to, available hours both from a team and client per-spective, data identification and availability, auditor experience and business knowledge, allocated time, as well as unplanned events. Now, I can assure you that when the audit leadership teams got together to build their 2020 plan, many challenges were discussed that could stand in the way of completing their audit plan. However, having the country shut down due to a virus was definitely not one of them. That being said, the audits that were in progress and the ones that remained on the plan when this pandemic hit the country must be com-pleted. Multiple partners, both internal and external, need and rely on the audit results in order to plan the company objectives moving forward. But how is an audit department that relies on information, communication, and data from its business partners expected to complete the audit assignments when mem-bers of the department are no longer in an office where they can interact and obtain the necessary and critical information required to provide the quality validation of business operations?

As with any unplanned event, barrier, or obstacle, the team must adapt and improvise in order to overcome the challenges encountered and complete the assigned tasks. But how does an audit team or an auditor go about getting the critical information without meeting with the client to explain the needs and requirements in order to complete the job not only effectively but also accurately? Any auditor, whether experienced or not, will tell you that the internal audit and business partner relationship is the key to unlocking access to pertinent data and insight into the business process under review. Why is this relationship so important? The bold fact of the matter is, no one – either at work or in your personal life – is going to give you information regarding what, when, and how they do what they do unless they know and trust you. That is just human nature. And in your work life as an auditor, you already know that you are not going to be a person whom the business teams look forward to seeing on a regular basis. It is a stigma that has followed auditors since the beginning of the profession. In its simplest terms, auditors are there to ask the business personnel questions and verify that they are completing their assigned tasks as described, hopefully, in the policies and procedures. While the task at hand seems simple, any auditor will tell you it is a lot more difficult than it sounds – a prime example of saying it is so much simpler than doing it successfully.

So how does one accomplish this task of information gathering and knowledge development if they are unable to meet with their clients in person? This is where the auditor's job becomes 10 times more challenging than it was before the pandemic. The focus of audit departments worldwide has shifted in the second and third quarter of 2020. It went from analyzing data, partnering with a client to explain deviations, and developing value-added recommendations to identifying new ways to obtain the necessary information to do their jobs.

All internal auditors recognize the value that the business-level data has in the successful execution of audit engagements. Audit teams have become much more aware of how important communication, relationship building, and marketing the audit department has become in this new remote environment. For so long, internal audit departments have not placed enough emphasis on marketing their department in an effort to establish a strong foundation to build business partner relationships. If audit teams thought it was challenging before to get information from their business partners, they now face brand-new hurdles to leap over when it comes to acquiring data and information in this remote audit world.

The change that has been thrust upon the audit industry was not one that could have been predicted, but it certainly must be addressed if audit teams want to be successful going forward. There has been speculation that this remote environment could last through the coming year. If it was not evident before, each corporate executive and members of the corporate committees realize the critical role the audit department plays in the company and how much the business teams, regulatory bodies, external auditors, executives, and investors rely on the information produced and distributed from the audit teams. In order to address the needs of their internal and external clients, audit teams should take a step back and perform a self-evaluation of their internal process to ensure they have the following:

- Communication as the cornerstone of their department
- A commitment to building strong client relationships
- Focus on identifying and gathering data from a pure source
- Test plan developed from the business objective
- A report identifying root cause and linked to specific corresponding actions

This reflection on audit department operations will show the reliance on communication through all phases of an audit from the detailed plan through testing to reporting and action plan development and adoption.

How else would auditors be able to accomplish their assigned tasks if they did not have communicating effectively with clients as the number-one priority regardless of the audit phase or task? Unfortunately, not all audit teams emphasize client relationship development or communication skillsets when it comes to audit execution. Why? There is a misconception that the audit team can and will be given any data or documentation requested as mandated by the audit charter and the audit committee. And while this is true, the charter or committee documentation does not mandate the specifics regarding delivery of the requested data or information.

As every auditor will tell you, the work is never completed as quickly as they would like it. Time is one of the only commodities that no one can get more of – no matter what your position, job, or financial standings. There is nowhere to buy more time, not even on Amazon. If there was an option, everyone would take it. So, in the absence of being able to purchase more time, how do auditors go about getting the information? The key is and always will be their communication skills and relationship building. Remember, it was previously mentioned that the relationship strength is how you unlock the key to information. That strength will be based on the level of trust and experience your client has had with you during previous audit engagements. Here is the best explanation regarding the internal auditor and business partner relationship that provides the most effective illustration of the need for constant focus and development of a successful working relationship.

UNDERSTANDING YOUR ROLE

The analysis and explanation start with a remarkably simple question. As an auditor, could you do your job effectively without your business client? The simple answer to that question is *no*. There is no chance for an auditor to build effective (detailed) business knowledge, understand policies and procedures, document the business objective(s), recognize workarounds, gather pertinent business data, answer process questions, develop a detailed test plan, validate potential deviations from the work standard, identify root causes, create process-based recommendations, generate a clear, concise report, and verify action plan implementation and adoption *without* client participation. It would be a losing battle, not to mention a very time-consuming approach filled with business process assumptions. No auditor would want to generate an audit work file, and especially not an audit report, without having a clear understanding of the business and its corresponding objectives.

Now flip the question around. Could the business team do their job and complete their assigned responsibilities without internal audit involvement? The unfortunate answer to that question is *yes*. Absolutely, without a doubt, the business team could do their job with no internal audit help or intervention. If you asked the business process workers, they would all probably say their preference would be to perform their day-to-day responsibilities and activities without having to deal with anyone from audit. The business teams view internal audit as a nuisance, a bother, and an unnecessary interruption to their work. So, if the business team prefers no outside audit interference, how are auditors to go about breaking down the preexisting barrier that has been in existence forever? The answer is, through a dedicated effort on the part of the auditors to constantly be focused on the relationship.

While this fact of auditor "need" when it comes to client involvement during audits is daunting, there is a glimmer of good news. The need is not an insurmountable barrier but does represent a significant challenge to every auditor. But to overcome this barrier, the auditor will have to recognize and accept one indisputable fact when it comes to the internal audit and business partner relationship. And that fact is, no matter what type of relationship is being discussed – whether it is boyfriend and girlfriend, husband and wife, or auditor and client – there is always one person in every relationship who wants it a little more than the other. Okay. So, what does that mean? It means one person will always work harder and be more flexible to ensure the relationship continues to grow and stay strong. Auditors must realize early on in the relationship development process that we are the party recognizing we will have to work harder and be more flexible than our business partner to ensure the relationship stays strong and intact. What I must clarify for you is in recognition that the auditor must put in more time, effort, and dedication to foster the audit and client relationship. It does not mean in any way shape or form that the auditor should bend the rules or requirements during the audit itself. During the engagement, the auditor should keep the business partner "in the know" and ensure the work, status of project request, completed testing, preliminary results, and any potential issues should be reviewed, discussed, and validated with the business partner to ensure they are never in the dark when it comes to the audit status. While this might seem like common sense, there are often times when auditors forget to communicate the details of potential findings or work statuses. Surprises are fun and usually a good thing, except during an audit. If you want to keep your relationships strong with your business partners, always remember the role that clear, prepared, supported communication plays in developing, fostering, and maintaining relationships. Too often, auditors enter into exchanges (formal meetings or hallway discussions) with clients unprepared. I know this is not something you would do, but let us discuss the potential impact not only on the relationship with your client but also the development of the auditor.

A critical point that must be emphasized here is being prepared. You can never be too prepared for a meeting. Believe me, I know all the excuses for not preparing effectively for a meeting. You could say, I do not want to prepare too much because it will come off disingenuous. That is false. Being prepared does not mean to memorize what you are going to say. If you memorize what you want to say it will come off as fake and robotic. However, if you prepare effectively, it will show you are committed to the topic, understand the details, know where the data originated, and can effectively explain questions regarding the subject matter. If you do not adequately prepare, how will you know when to stop asking questions or when you have the information or data required? The keys to effective preparation for any meeting with a client are understanding the meeting objective and mastering the data to be discussed. With these two keys, any auditor can effectively and confidently communicate with the business partner. So, let's touch on both, briefly, to ensure everyone is on the same page.

CRITICAL MEETING KEYS

You would be surprised how many auditors go into a meeting with a client without a meeting objective. As a thirty-year audit veteran, I will tell you there were times when I relied on my experience to carry me through meetings. Because I have been in hundreds and hundreds of meetings over my career, I would tell myself that I would just "shoot from the hip" and use my "vast" experiences to get through a meeting. What a mistake! As I got older and hopefully wiser, I discovered no amount of experience can replace understanding the meeting objective and being prepared to discuss and drive targeted questions to address the meeting objective. Keep in mind, the meeting objective is the purpose or reason you are having this meeting. *Objective* as a noun will always mean purpose. Put yourself in the business partner's shoes. They will be thinking, why does the auditor want to get together to discuss this topic? When you enter a client meeting and clearly understand the objective, you are focused, recognize the questions needed to effectively facilitate, can keep the meeting on track, and know when sufficient answers and evidence have been given to address the objective. If you enter a meeting without an objective or just with a list of questions, the meeting will feel disjointed, unorganized, and ultimately have a negative impact on the relationship. It relays a sense of unpreparedness to the meeting participants. You may have a list of questions to ask your business partner, but there is always a reason you are asking those same questions.

Starting the meeting by stating the specific objective creates that sense of purpose and communicates to your business partner the need for attending. Once the objective is clear, the discussion and questions that follow must link to the specific meeting objective that was explained at the beginning. This understanding of meeting purpose focuses the auditor and helps direct the conversation in a positive direction to the outcome. At the end of the meeting, there is a sense of conclusion for the information needed as well as completion for that part of the audit. That sense of accomplishment, even the smallest achievements, make a positive impact on your business partner as they see a focused audit team effectively using time to complete the tasks at hand. Additionally, the auditor and audit team project a confident, unified approach as they execute their audit methodology.

The second key is mastering the data. While mastering the data may seem like a simple concept, understanding its value is a must. No matter what the audit assignment or task is, most auditors do not take the necessary time to build their business knowledge. Let's be honest with each other. How many times have you been placed on an audit team but you never looked at the planning documentation to understand the business objective or reviewed the program to ensure you completely understand the section or steps you have been assigned? I will admit it. I have made that error. Auditors do not want to ask questions to other team members; there is a fear it will make them look "not smart." News-flash – questions are one of the greatest tools for an auditor, whether the questions are internal to clarify an assignment, task, test step, or acronym or if it is a targeted question to the business owner. Auditors will not continue to learn unless they ask questions.

So let me get this straight: You are going to enter a business partner meeting without clearly understanding the process, testing, or data you are about to discuss (and question), and you think you will feel confident in that meeting? You think the business partner is going to believe that the audit team is there to provide guidance to assist them in doing their job (achieving the business objective) in the most efficient and effective manner with less rework? Not a chance. When it comes to the data, the auditor must not only understand the details of what information is being questioned (even when the meeting facilitator did not complete the testing in question), but also the source of where the data originated. Too many times, audit and client meetings get sidetracked because the auditor could not explain where the data in question came from.

One of the critical factors when it comes to mastering the data is to ensure and verify that the data source is pure. The best way to define *pure* when it comes to the data source is to validate that the data you have received from the client and are using in the testing *is* the complete, best source of data available. *Complete* means it contains all of the pertinent fields required to complete the business task. Also, verify the data is the most current and up to date available at that time for testing. Once you have confirmed the data source is pure, you can be confident when discussing the data there is no opportunity for the data to be discounted. Auditors must be aware that experienced business owners will respond to issues of potential exceptions or questionable business personnel actions by casting doubt on where the auditor got the data (the source). Do not be blindsided; make sure you have obtained the purest source of data available. The business owner might try to twist the data itself, but there is no hiding from data.

In every one of the meetings you have with the business owner, prepare effectively by confirming the meeting objective prior to the event and mastering the data. Then remember one additional key to effective meeting facilitation and relationship building with your business partner: Never try to defend the questions you are asking. When asking questions or clarifying potential exceptions with your business partner, always use the data to support (not defend) the specific questions being asked. The data will drive the support for your message and will always give you the confidence as you seek clarification for questions posed.

This book has been created based on the Beyond Audit methodology, which has been developed with communication as the foundation to support the learning and execution of internal audit activities from risk-based engagements through to the communication of results to business partners and committees. There are specific excerpts of the Beyond Audit methodology, techniques, and templates mentioned throughout as well as references to access on-demand videos and interviews (www.beyondaudit.org) illustrating critical concepts, techniques, and templates. As you proceed through the pages, there will be discussions of the skills and techniques to ensure the internal audit team can successfully navigate the ever-changing demands and requirements of remote auditing. Included in this remote environment lesson will be how the focused skillset has changed, marketing your revised audit approach, ensuring your audit team understands the internal audit mission and objective, and review of the methodology keys from objective identification to execution, reporting, and action plan adoption. Also, it includes new techniques to not only evaluate your department's efficiency but track audit's progress when it comes to key deliverables. As always, the book will wrap up with education, training, and development suggestions so you can create a high-performing, world-class audit team.

CHAPTER TWO

Understanding the Remote Approach

A NY TIME YOU ARE assigned an audit, the typical steps kick in as you prepare and pull together the planning requirements according to your specific audit methodology. At a minimum, you will establish the audit in your database, select a team (unless you have been assigned one), review previous audit work in the area, and begin the planning phase and all the corresponding requirements. The good news is that all of the standard audit activities you would perform for any audit will remain the same even though you will now be performing this audit remotely. So, what is the big deal? Whether the audit team is executing the audit in the office or within the business unit (the preferred approach) or doing it remotely, the auditor will still have to understand the business process, gather intelligence and data, test the data, and report the results. Simple.

TRADITIONAL VERSUS REMOTE AUDIT

Performing an audit remotely is not as straightforward and simple as you might think. There are thought perspectives that believe remote auditing is actually easier than in-person auditing. Think about that – there are no business disruptions, which are a constant complaint from your client. The audit team can just focus on the job at hand and evaluate the data and process under review.

While that may sound like the utopia of audit (no direct client interaction and just review and testing), that is a bad assumption. Take a moment and consider how challenging it is to get someone from the business team to meet with you or give you inquiry access to their system; why no one from the business team has time to take another auditor through the business process; how long you have to wait for documentation you requested; why no one from the business team has time to discuss potential findings. Now there are exceptions where some audit clients are the most accommodating, open, and forthcoming business partners and will provide the time, data, and information needed to complete any audit request. But make no mistake about it, those types of clients are few and far between. Most clients view audits as a disruption to their day-to-day operations and no business personnel has time to waste educating the audit team on the business operations that the process owners believe the audit team should already know. I know it's an unfair assumption, but it is real.

To emphasize and illustrate the remote audit approach concept, let's discuss how we as traditional auditors can effectively and seamlessly switch gears and go from the in-person approach to a remote evaluation of critical business processes. As in every assigned audit, the auditor should begin with an understanding of the audit objective. Unfortunately, most audit teams get assigned an audit and never bother to review the annual risk assessment to determine why this audit was included in the annual plan. The auditors just figure that the annual planning was completed, and it was decided to include this audit in the current year. What the auditors do not realize is that the information compiled in the annual audit plan provides a solid foundation as to what the business process includes, key personnel, systems utilized in the business process, as well as any potential process risks. Also included in the annual planning documentation is the audit history, which details when the area was last reviewed, what the audit rating (opinion) was, and issues identified that required management action. Auditors might not recognize how valuable this information could be, especially when it comes to auditing remotely. I will admit, not reviewing the annual planning documentation is probably less impactful when executing a traditional audit but it is significantly detrimental when performing a remote audit. Why? you may ask.

Compare the two approaches. In the traditional audit, you will get to meet the key players in person during an opening conference and walkthroughs and review the previous audit report (hopefully) as you plan. Conversely, in a remote audit, you will be given the names of the key players, but never meet, and you will not get to sit face to face with a processor during the walkthroughs and have to sort through those details via policies and procedures and follow-up questions. Definitely not as easy as it may sound. Additionally, by reviewing the annual planning documentation, the auditor receives valuable background information on the business process as well as the context in which the review was completed both from an annual perspective and previous audit. As we discussed in the previous chapter, you can never prepare enough, and in a remote audit, you have to prepare and plan twice as hard as before and be dedicated to the details of your audit methodology. Take my advice on this point and make your remote audit life much easier: Review the annual planning documentation, ask questions to the person who completed it, gain an understand of the business objective(s) and supporting processes, and set an initial scope based on the objective(s) and previous findings from the last audit. This first step in preparing for the remote audit will provide a solid foundation for you to effectively plan and build a test approach to satisfy the audit objectives and deliver a value-added report to your client.

After the review of the annual planning documentation and the audit team identification, it is beneficial to have an internal team meeting with all auditors who will participate on this project. Just like any other meeting, the facilitator (project lead/in-charge) must adequately prepare for this overview meeting with their audit team. Topics to be discussed and explained with include, but are not limited to, the business unit background, business objective(s), proposed initial scope, last audit's report, rating and issues, any open actions, and the reminder to be aware of how important communication is during a remote audit. To clarify these topics, consider business unit background. This information should detail the business unit's location, staff size, turnover statistics, management tenure, volumes for both transaction and dollar (if applicable), and current systems used. When it comes to business objective(s), the auditor has to understand what the purpose of this process under review is. More simply put, the audit team must understand the role this particular business process plays in the organization. Consider what product or information does this group create and is it for internal consumption or is it for the public. If it is for internal usage, another business unit or team is relying on this team's product and decisions will be based on the information provided. And if it is for public consumption, the risks become even higher if the process is not completed timely and accurately. Communication, as you will hear throughout this book, is going to be the cornerstone and foundation for the success of your audit function, especially while executing remote audits. One of the most underrated concepts of communication with audit clients is the fact that solid communication fundamentals start within your own audit team. When the communication requirements are stressed and enforced within your audit team, it becomes immediately transparent with your clients. Another benefit to strong internal communications is it becomes a habit to speak to your co-workers as it pertains to work challenges, client difficulties, or even clarifying questions about the process under review. The audit team should be filled with people who want to share all of their business and company knowledge, audit and business experience, and suggestions on how to handle a difficult task or client. Those individuals who openly share with their teammates create a strong communication base and functional team. Highly communicative teams not only create a strong, unified approach but also develop leadership skills as they continually practice explaining (in detail) how the audit process works, how the business process is focused on completing their assigned tasks, and how this particular business process links to the overall objectives of the company. Communication provides an avenue for ongoing development of business process knowledge that pays dividends no matter what position you have at the company.

 ## RECOGNIZING THE CHALLENGES

Every audit you participate on will have challenges, but the remote audit will exacerbate simple ones into much more difficulties throughout the audit. Regardless of the audit type, the biggest challenge is availability of the client. Whether the clients like it or not, they should be a key participant in every audit due to their knowledge of the process, access and understanding of the data, system knowledge, and overall process experience.

I think many times auditors take for granted the availability of client access when executing a traditional audit. That luxury is missing during a remote audit. I know this may seem like a simple concept, but it plays a huge role when the auditor is trying to complete the planning process and is missing critical data or information to close the loop on one particular process piece. Gone is the time of getting up from your desk and finding someone in the process area to question regarding the missing information. An auditor's ability to follow up, ask qualifying questions, or retrieve missing documentation becomes much more complicated when they do not have immediate access to the business team. And there is no telling when and if your business partner is going to answer the phone to address the next question from their audit counterpart.

Another significant challenge during a remote audit will be obtaining the detailed process steps from start to finish, especially if you are auditing an area never reviewed before. Since there will be no documentation available from the previous audit (completed process map), the auditor will be responsible to obtain this process level information from their business client. Every auditor knows how difficult it is to create a process map from scratch; it takes time to review the most updated policies and procedures, examine supporting process data, understand the systems used, draft an initial narrative, and then meet with the client to clarify the understanding of the process as well as ask any outstanding questions. All these steps are necessary to develop a complete process map. In the nonremote world, you can expedite this process by sitting down and getting a walkthrough of the process with your business partner and asking clarifying question as you go along. However, in the remote audit world, it is not possible to perform a walkthrough over the phone or even in a videoconference. Trust me, it just does not work. That does not leave the auditor with many options other than to dedicated the time and effort it will take to become intimate with the policies and procedures (that you hope exist or are up to date) along with all the other data and information requirements to build a solid narrative of the process to be used to facilitate the phone discussion with the client. The more detailed the understanding of the business process, the more effective the process validation call will go with your client. This type of exercise requires excellent communication skills to ensure the auditor validates the process details and the business partner clearly understands the questions being asked. As you read on, you will see how communication skills are always at the foundation of success for any auditor in every industry.

Understanding the Business Process

Remember during any type of audit, the auditor will be required to perform independent research regarding the business process under review. The key during this research period is to ensure that you are focused on the activities in the area assigned. Do not waste time trying to build an understanding of the processes like the personnel in the business unit. No matter how hard you try and how much time you dedicate to learning any business process, you will never know the detailed workings of the operation like someone who is actually doing the job in the current environment. Your objective during this research period is to ensure that you are reviewing the most up-to-date information available regarding the business operations and are creating a foundation of general knowledge of the process. You will then use your communication skills to fill in the detailed nuances to the process.

The next step in this research part of planning is going to focus on any previous audit activity, external exams or reviews, as well as open and closed action items. The easiest one of these is going to be the previous audit activity. This information is readily available to you along with the supporting evidence and access to the individuals who performed the actual audit. I would suggest reaching out to whoever completed the last review to get their perspective on the area, business personnel, challenges encountered during the audit, and the final report. Discussing these topics with the person directly involved with the project will yield much more valuable information than just reading through the documentation. Plus, it will save you time, and we all know that in every audit, that is a precious commodity.

Another component during this phase that must be included is understanding the rules that the business operation is required to follow. These rules include the established policies and procedures and all federal, state, and local laws. It is important to note, especially during a remote audit, when looking at the policies and procedures that you must be especially aware of the details surrounding workaround scenarios. These types of scenarios include exception processes, manual overrides, management discretion decisions, and supervisory overrides. While all of these exist in most business processes, it is important to ensure that you understand the situations that allowed these types of transactions to occur.

The other critical detail that must be explained is what level of standard, formal documentation is required when one of these workaround processes is selected. Consider, the business team is performing their job by going outside the normal order of processing. The documentation included must clearly explain why this occurred and exhibit some level of approval. Hopefully, all workaround scenarios are fully explained in the policies and procedures and included the required documentation and approval required for each type. The final workaround point to discuss is the validity of this type of transaction. The key distinction in determining the appropriateness of a workaround is pretty straightforward. While workarounds exist and are necessary in business processes because no business process will be the same every day of the year, the validation of workarounds is determined by the control environment. What that means is that a workaround is appropriate if, and only if, it does not bypass a critical control. If a workaround procedure is used to avoid a critical or key control (approval, review, etc.), then it should be flagged and discussed as part of the standard policies and procedures. Keep an eye out for these types of controls and be sure to inquire as to the frequency of their occurrence. This type of information will provide insight to the day-to-day operations.

As you complete your independent research of the business process and prepare to set up a meeting (in our remote audit, this will be a call), you must obtain and verify that you have the appropriate client contact. During the initial stages of a remote audit, you must ensure you have a client contact person who can be reached for any process validation, system access, sample selection, and data and documentation questions. Having an established client contact from audit kickoff will expedite the critical step of information sharing throughout the audit. Be aware and quickly raise the question within your own audit team if you have been assigned a business partner contact who does not have the time, information, or detailed knowledge to effectively and efficiently address specific audit questions. Without an effective business contact, the remote audit will stall on a regular basis. Keep your ears focused on identifying traits of a business contact who is not ready for primetime during your audit.

If your contact is not reachable during normal business hours, is not able to answer process questions without having to validate the information before providing a response, and is consistently missing established deadlines for providing requested data, system access, or samples, you need to discuss the situation with your audit team and determine the root cause. Unfortunately, in these scenarios, it could be the result of a lack of experience or process knowledge or it could be because the business contact was instructed to review all requests and questions with a third party in the business unit to ensure only certain details and data are provided to the audit team. While it is usually a lack of experience or knowledge causing the delays in responding, there have been numerous instances where data and information was being scrubbed before giving it to the audit team. In the end, if your audit planning approach is complete and follows the Objective, Risk, Control process approach to be detailed in Chapter 5, ultimately the data and corresponding testing will validate the control environment and corresponding effectiveness. The only result of delaying the delivery of information to the audit team is expanding the length of the audit. So, when possible, be sure and verify you have a competent, knowledgeable business contact for your remote audit. You can accomplish this by building a rapport with the business contact during your relationship development by asking for their background and tenure in the department. This type of basic business experience knowledge usually provides a good indication of how smoothly information will be exchanged throughout the audit.

RESPONSIBILITY ASSIGNMENTS

Another factor that will contribute to the success of your remote audit will be the assignment of work to be completed in each audit phase. This responsibility is no different in a regular audit, as compared to a remote audit. However, the person responsible for keeping the audit on track should have a heightened awareness of the assigned task, along with the corresponding deadlines for each, as the tasks can get out of control from a delivery standpoint much easier on a remote audit. This is due to the fact that the audit team is usually physically dispersed during the remote audit and task delinquencies can go unnoticed sometimes until it is too late.

To ensure remote assigned tasks keep to their assigned deadlines, the project lead or in-charge has to remain diligent in the tracking and monitoring of the business unit questions, data requests, and audit testing completion. Any delays, missed deadlines, or audit work challenges must be identified proactively and addressed with expediency. Too many times, the audit suffers from a lack of oversight on remote audits because there is a lack of regular and timely communication within the audit team. As previously discussed, remember how critically important it is for the audit team to maintain a high level of communication within the department and during audits to ensure all team members are aware of the deadlines and the urgency to complete assigned tasks on budget.

One caveat must be mentioned when it pertains to assigned budgets. A budget is the documented estimate of time to complete a task, and it is based on either historical data or a projection that was formulated from the testing requirements to be completed. Keep in mind that budget estimates are just a best guess. Although they should be regarded as a guide for how long any audit task or testing should take to complete, budgets can and should be challenged when they appear to be unrealistic. Do not ever rush or force the assigned work just to fit into the budget number. That is a huge mistake. The moment you identify that there is no possible chance that you or any auditor could complete an assigned task under that corresponding budget, say something. Do not try to go faster to make the deadline just for the sake of the deadline. When that happens, whatever work or testing was supposed to be completed will get finished within the budget but will ultimately have exclusions and mistakes, along with a false sense of accomplishment.

One additional tip related to budgets: The moment you are certain there is not sufficient time to adequately complete the assigned task within the budget, reach out to your audit project lead and explain the need for additional time. Make sure you detail the initial budget, data and work required, and the time needed to review and conclude on the data. This will ensure you have considered all aspects of the task and sufficiently supported the need for additional time to complete the work adequately and accurately. In the remote audit environment, the budgets tend to be more aggressive because audit teams believe execution of the planning and fieldwork phase do not need any buffer time built into the assignments because there is no time for chatting about the work or relationship building. It is all about just getting the information and data and doing the work. In actuality, the inverse is true. In a remote audit, it takes more time for auditors to understand the process requirements and data being provided, so more time needs to be allowed for the audit team to ask qualifying questions to ensure the auditors fully understand the process before attempting to evaluate for the planning phase or reperform the process during fieldwork. So, before you begin a task or audit testing, make sure you review the work being assigned, along with the corresponding budget, and determine if the initial budget number matches the work assigned. Auditors should always closely monitor their own work and ensure they are delivering a complete quality product while communicating with the audit project lead on any work challenges and potential deadline extensions. This will assist the project lead in ensuring the business client during this remote audit is up to date on the status of the audit work being completed in their business area.

 ## COMMUNICATING CRITICAL INFORMATION

In an effort to keep your business partner "in the know" during this remote audit, it is paramount to establish regular, formal status meetings through-out the audit. The frequency of these status meetings is usually established in the introduction or kickoff meeting. When I am leading an audit (especially a remote one), I will suggest to my business partner that we should have a weekly status meeting to ensure communication channels between the two teams remain open, clear, and strong. Along with my weekly status meeting request, I provide the need and benefits of the timing. When it comes to the need, auditors have to realize that in any audit, getting the information to do the job requires many requests (usually more than one per need) for information, data, and explanation. To fulfill that need, we can establish a weekly meeting to discuss the status of the audit as well as outstanding requests to date. This meeting provides a perfect forum to facilitate active follow-up and communication of the work in progress, completed, and still to be done. Additionally, auditors benefit by being well informed on any of their work in progress and can communicate it back to their management team, keeping them informed of the audit in progress. When you look at the weekly update meeting from the business team side, tell them this meeting is to provide an up-to-the-moment status on the audit, documentation and data requests, as well as any issues noted to date. Business team management wants to be made aware of the issues because it will provide an arena to clarify and potentially quantify the issues identified in the status memo. Keep in mind that auditors never, ever put an issue in the status memo until and unless it has been validated by the audit team as authentic (poses a risk to the business unit achieving its objective(s)) with someone in the business unit. Auditors do not want to go into a status meeting with an issue that has not been validated because if they are wrong, it will impact their credibility not only in this meeting, but also for the rest of the audit. Each time an auditor brings up any issues from that meeting forward, it will be called into doubt because of a single mistake made in a status update meeting. Ultimately, though, I will leave the status meeting frequency up to my customer. If my clients prefer to have a meeting every two weeks, that is their choice, but I let them know the associated risks. Having a longer time between status meetings does not impact the business partner as much as it does the auditor because they could possibly have to wait 10 days to get an answer or a delivery status on a requested item, which could impact their ability to complete the task and meet the budget.

As referenced in the previous paragraph, to effectively facilitate this audit status meeting, a formal status memo is created by the audit team and provided in advance to their business partner. This allows the business personnel to review the document and prepare any questions regarding its contents and obtain an update on any and all outstanding audit requests. As you complete the audit status template, keep in mind there are a few specific objectives of the template. First and foremost, the status memo provides a percentage completion status of each phase of the audit. It details the planning, fieldwork, and reporting phase completion percentages. This provides your business partner with a snapshot of the audit at any time and helps guide them on the time remaining in an audit (which always seems like it is not soon enough for them). Second, the status memo details any identified and validated issues that have been noted to date. Remember that these items, to appear on the formal status memo, must have been validated with someone in the business processing unit to ensure the audit is interpreting the testing data accurately and fairly. Also, there is a section below each issue requesting a proposed management action. It is proven that the sooner you start discussing the issues and requesting a management response, the more effective the audit report phase. This additional section assists in facilitating a root cause (Chapter 7) discussion and proposed management action to properly address that cause and ultimately the identified issue. Third and just as valuable, the status memo details any outstanding audit requests for documentation, data, or samples. Again, in an effort to facilitate what could be a challenging client discussion, the status memo indicates when the request was made and that it still remains unfulfilled. From the date requested, it is simple to see how long this item has been outstanding and allows the auditor to explain that the work cannot be completed until that information is received. This results in a longer audit, which neither the audit team nor the business client wants. And finally, the status memo outlines the remaining steps in the audit, including, where applicable, the projected target date (i.e., the draft report, final report, survey). Overall, the status memo provides a quick snapshot of the audit status and gives the auditor an effective tool to facilitate the meeting with confidence.

As discussed previously, relationship building is a critical part of any audit and business partner relationship. Auditors leverage this relationship to assist in the facilitation of all phases of an audit, from planning to action plan implementation. We are going to discuss both the relationship values in every phase of the audit and the need for audit to remain focused on relationship building.

With the unplanned emergence of remote auditing due to the pandemic, business partner relationships have become even more important to the success of every audit. These relationships fuel and drive the learning and sharing of critical business process information and required data sharing. As we go through the discussion of each audit phase, consider how focused your audit team is currently on relationship building. Does your team dedicate the time and resources it takes to foster and strengthen the audit and business partner relationship? Is there an interaction with business personnel? Or is the audit team too focused on getting the fieldwork completed and the final report issued so they can move on to the next project? I totally understand. Finishing outstanding audits helps the audit department move the coverage needle and get closer to completing the communicated audit plan. However, being in audit is not solely about completing the audit plan. Also, just because the team finishes the audit plan, does not translate into the audit department adding value to the company and being seen as a true asset to business operations. The audit department should be building on their existing audit knowledge, obtaining a more detailed understanding of the business objectives and corresponding processes, and providing value-added recommendations to their business counterparts linked directly to the achievement of the confirmed business objectives in the most effective and efficient manner. Unfortunately, those critical skills and business knowledge can only be developed from conversations and exposure with the business partners. The business personnel have the detailed information that can assist in auditor development. The knowledge auditors can develop and build on will make them a more valuable partner and asset to the business partners as audits continue to expand in scope and criticality. So, let's first examine each phase of the audit and discuss the role the auditor and business partner relationship plays in the successful completion of planning, fieldwork, and reporting.

To successfully complete any phase of an audit or any project, you must have specific and clear understanding of the objective. Remember, when talking about an objective (as a noun, not an adjective), it means *purpose*. Once you have identified the purpose, you can direct all efforts to building a stronger understanding, work plan, and valued feedback to your business partner to assist them in achieving their goals. Without this knowledge, how would you know what topics to understand, red flags to looks for, data to test, and recommendations to develop?

AUDIT PLANNING

So, let's first start with the audit plan. You have been given an audit and begin to compile critical business process–level information related to a particular business unit, which you may or may not have encountered before. Additionally, it may be the first time the audit department has audited this particular area, so there are no previous audit reports or documentation to provide any background on your new assignment.

How do auditors approach such a task when they are beginning at ground zero when it comes to information on this unknown business function? Most auditors will do the obvious and go straight to the internet and research this particular topic to see what most common information about this process is available. They may go to their favorite audit-related internet site to try and obtain more information or possibly "canned" audit programs related to their assignment.

Keep in mind that after your online research efforts are complete, the information you have obtained is only a general overview and does not in any way, shape, or form represent the business processes within your company. Every company and its corresponding business support processes have specific requirements that are unique to their way of doing business. And those unique business characteristics can only be learned from the business personnel and not the internet. Thus, there is a mandatory need to establish a good working relationship with the business partner to gain a baseline understanding of the function. If this truly is a business function the audit department has never reviewed, it is going to be critical for the lead auditor to ensure they explain to their business contact the audit department objectives and how an audit works. Again, while this may seem like an easy task, the audit leadership team must ensure all auditors have the same knowledge of the audit function and deliver a consistent message to audit clients regarding audit's mission and the required steps necessary to complete an audit. This will guarantee that all audit clients are receiving the same message regarding the audit process and the need for business partner involvement throughout the audit to ensure its success.

While auditors need to acquire business process knowledge during the planning phase, they must recognize completing the task does not mean acquiring the same knowledge as the business processing personnel. Too many times, auditors in the planning phase exhaust the full planning budget diving too deep into the intimate details of a business process. Getting "buried in the weeds," for a lack of a better phrase, usually means the audit team has gone too far into the business process minutia, which, in the end, will not increase the value of audit testing or the final report. During the planning phase, it is important to remain focused on the key business processes, which drive the achievement of the business deliverables (objectives). This is accomplished by reviewing the business developed policies and procedures, available flowcharts, and process walkthroughs with business personnel. The auditor should use every meeting and interaction with business team members to strengthen and foster the audit and business partner relationship. Auditors should spend more time with their business partners explaining the learning approach an audit requires and the corresponding reasons why it is so important. Let your business partners know how important the information sharing (and learning) is to an auditor during the planning phase as it sets the direction and focus of the upcoming audit. Additionally, all knowledge gained will be used in the development of the audit testing. With the proper business knowledge sharing, the audit planning documentation can be executed with minimal issues, questions, and business personnel disruption. Sufficiently detailed planning documentation will provide a solid foundation for the audit testing to be developed and executed, again, with minimal disruption to the client. This type of approach seems pretty standard. Meet with the client; gain an understanding; share information regarding the audit process; and learn as much as you can during planning. Appears to be pretty straightforward and simple. No – imagine trying to accomplish all of these things over the phone or video call without being able to sit down in the same room with the person and facilitate these critical discussions. I do not care how good a communicator you may be. Executing these discussions remotely poses significant barriers to success, not to mention an increased time commitment. If an initial planning meeting with a client to explain the audit process, introduce the team, and discuss the initial scope usually takes about an hour, consider doubling that budget at a minimum if you are doing it remotely. And I am going to assume, if this is a new client who has never been audited, the budget will be more than double. I am not suggesting the time commitment is not worth it. On the contrary, I believe it is not just worth it – it is mandatory. Do not skimp or rush through the audit department overview (or any other parts) during the introduction meeting with your client, because this meeting not only sets the tone for the current audit but is also the foundation for the audit and business partner relationship.

AUDIT FIELDWORK

After the planning phase comes the audit fieldwork. During this phase, the auditors must continue to work the audit and business partner relationship each time client documentation or data is requested, clarification of a business process step is required, or validation of a potential deviation from the business processing standard is noted. In each one of the previously listed incidences, the auditor is going to be required to communicate directly with the client to obtain the information or gain an explanation of an unknown. This creates the perfect opportunity for the auditor to build additional rapport with the business partner in an effort to gain trust to strengthen the bond between the two. Think about not only how critical these interactions are with the client but also how difficult these can be to execute when it is being done remotely. Being in audit over 30 years, I can attest to how challenging the fieldwork phase is, especially when additional information, data, or detailed explanations are needed to complete a test. Now complicate that need with the facts of the client not being readily accessible or the questions requiring answers are difficult. That is what remote auditors are facing on a daily basis.

During these remote audits, auditors may not know if a client is available for questions or willing to answer the phone when it rings. And if the client does answer, will the client have the time to discuss and explain the challenges the auditor is facing, or will a new meeting have to be scheduled to address the issues? Everyone in business knows how difficult it is to schedule business meetings with representatives from multiple units. While this type of situation will not stop the audit from progressing, it will impact the timing of the audit testing and will result in the auditors having to reacquaint themselves with the test requirements. All of these situations affect the timing of the targeted audit completion.

Also, remember to prepare for this impromptu follow-up meeting with the client, as the auditors must be ready with the exact topics, questions, and data which are to be discussed in this call. If the auditor is not adequately prepared for this call, I can guarantee you three things:

1. The call will not sound professional.
2. The audit client will not be happy with the interruption and lack of respect regarding effective use of their time.
3. The auditor will not receive all of the information required to complete the testing and possibly forget an item, which will require another call.

All three of these outcomes damage the audit and business partner relationship, and in established relationships create unnecessary erosion. It may not seem like a significant issue at the time, but the repeated calls or interruptions due to a lack of preparation on the auditor's part will create stress on the relationship, which impacts the audit team's ability to access critical information to complete the audit in a timely manner (close to the allotted budget) and establish a productive communication channel to facilitate issue validation, root cause, recommendations, and action plan discussion needed to deliver a value in the final audit report.

AUDIT REPORTING

The relationship building in the audit report phase could be considered the pinnacle of the audit and business partner relationship due to the impact of the interaction between the two groups during this final phase of the audit. Think about how much back-and-forth there can be when the draft report is being created. The audit status memo that was mentioned previously in this chapter, along with the benefits it has, not only in the development of the client relationship but also in the report generation process, can and will be relied on heavily to effectively support the final audit product. For the audit report to truly be value-added, it must include specific, tangible, and data-supported issues identified by audit and validated by business personnel. The process of acquiring the data and verifying the veracity of the included report issues relies on a productive and amicable relationship between the auditors and the business team. In this situation, the strength of the relationship drives a more efficient audit process and a collaborative effort to generate the draft audit report as well as the final product to be distributed to the executive team. With a strong relationship, the report generation discussion will be based on agreed-upon data and facts and not subjective opinions and perspectives.

Over the past three decades of keynote addresses, conference workshops, and training events all over the world, I have always stated one undisputable fact about myself and my experience being an internal auditor: I was never the smartest or best auditor on the team, but I focused on building my business knowledge, observing successful audit and business personnel, executing assigned work to the best of my ability, and learning from my mistakes. In the end, however, I always credited my success of going from a staff auditor to a vice president of audit and facilitating training for over 30 years to my ability to communicate and build relationships both inside and outside of audit. Successful relationships will provide you with benefits ranging from learning from co-workers to successful partnerships with business unit personnel to add value. Use relationships to not only further your personal development, but also positively impact the effectiveness and efficiency of business processes you encounter throughout your career.

 AUDIT WRAP-UP

The final point to review before we leave the audit approach discussion during a remote audit is the wrap-up phase. This is not usually considered an official audit phase, as most groups consider the audit to only consist of planning, fieldwork, and reporting. Now, I know how it feels when the audit report gets finalized and distributed. There is a definite sigh of relief that the audit is complete, and you have almost certainly moved on to the next project on the list. But is the audit really complete and over? The answer to that is no. There is file clean-up, survey distribution, lessons learned, and annual risk assessment updating (if required). File clean-up includes an internal review to ensure all audit sections are complete with the proper testing referencing and required sign-offs are evidence on all work performed. Lessons learned is an audit team–only meeting where the participants on the remote audit discuss critical aspects of the audit, such as how well did we plan, use technology where applicable, develop audit testing linked to the business objective, and productively foster the audit and business relationship. The lessons learned can be compared and used in unison with the audit client survey results to identify gaps in the audit process and suggest audit methodology revisions to strengthen audit execution.

While these items in wrap-up phase are for the most part an internal exercise for the audit team, the audit survey process is still a critical outstanding item that impacts the audit and business partner relationship. The survey itself should have a targeted distribution. Many times, audit teams make the mistake of sending the survey out to the executive over the business process that was just examined and possibly including the business manager over the unit. However, if the audit team truly wants to solicit feedback on how well the audit was planned, the fieldwork was executed, and the report was generated, then you should be reaching out to the key business personnel contacts that the audit team interacted with during this challenging remote audit. Simply sending the audit survey to the executive or manager over the area being audited is not going to provide you with an honest assessment of how well the audit went or how effective communication was throughout the audit. That is going to require a different distribution to unfiltered feedback on audit's performance during this remote review.

Audit surveys should be limited on the number of questions asked but require two responses to each question. The response should first require how important the item referenced in the question was to the business partner and, second, determine how well the audit succeeded in that effort. Additionally, the survey should include specific questions related to not only to the effectiveness of audit's communication but also the frequency of said communications. Communication will always be at the foundation for success for auditors and should be recognized as the cornerstone in your department and a mandatory core competency for every audit team member. The communication cornerstone concept will be discussed in Chapter 10. Without effective communication, audit execution and success, especially on remote reviews, will not be effective and will take much longer to complete.

CHAPTER THREE

Marketing the Internal Audit Department

CREATING YOUR AUDIT BRAND

When you work in an internal audit department, it does not matter what types of audits you execute, where you are located, the tenure of the leadership team and staff, how long your department has been established at the company, or how exceptional you believe your street credibility is with the business unit partners. You still need to market your audit department.

The fundamental question that every audit department should be asking themselves is, Do our clients know what we do and why we do it? Each time I facilitate training on marketing the audit department, I ask this very question, and the response is consistent. Not everyone in the company understands what audit's objectives really are, and most business partners just seem to tolerate the inconvenience of interruption to their operations when audit comes to town to review the business operations.

Trust me on this point: Audit departments do not want to engage with their business partners in the situation where the business personnel do not understand what audit does, why audit is in their operation, or how this particular business unit was selected for an audit in the first place. When the business unit lacks a fundamental understanding of the internal audit process, the audit and relationship starts off in a very strained position. Now, complicate this situation with a *remote* audit in which the auditors and business partners will not be meeting in person, and you begin to recognize the enormous hurdles that auditors must overcome to adequately communicate the purpose and details of the process to create a clear path for mutual understanding of how the audit will be executed. This further illustrates the critical need for the audit team to leverage their communication skills to be successful.

So, let us take the difficult task of marketing the audit department step by step. The first question you are probably thinking about is why it is such a difficult task. Marketing the audit department is difficult because throughout history, audit departments have carried a bad reputation of being nothing but an impediment for the business trying to complete its day-to-day responsibilities. From the business perspective, an audit is a disruption to daily operations because the auditors have to learn the business, ask questions, get system access, do process walkthroughs, ask more questions, pick samples, execute testing, find discrepancies, ask even more questions, and then issue a report stating what the business does poorly. Keep in mind, that is the business *perspective*, and while it does outline, at a high level, the general audit process, the audit is not actually much of a distraction to daily business operations. But you can understand why it is so challenging to try and market the audit process to a business owner when *audit* comes with all of these preconceived notions of being a disrupting force. Truth be told, effective audit departments communicate at a high level and leverage the minimal client meetings to obtain critical process information and data to complete the audit without bothering business personnel. The 10 characteristics of an effective department will be revealed and discussed in Chapter 12. But for now, the focus is on effectively marketing your audit department.

 DEFINING INTERNAL AUDIT

The first step in effectively market anything is to ensure you can define what it is you are trying to market. It is not possible to sell (market) a process to a business partner unless you can explain what it is that you are trying to get someone to accept. And if this process does not have a corresponding value to your partners, they will not want anything to do with it. Without any solid, detailed explanation, any potential business partner will not be interested in what you are selling. Got it? For auditors to be able to market their process, it has to be clearly defined.

What is the definition of internal audit? Well, there are two ways to define audit, and we are going to review both of them to ensure you have the correct perspective when speaking about the audit department. First, internal audit can be defined from the "book" perspective. Internal audit is an independent, objective process that can provide consulting services and process validation reviews focused on improving business operations and adding value. The focus for the audit department is to assist the organization's business units to achieve their objectives in the most efficient and effective manner with the least amount of rework. Internal audit is designed to partner with business unit personnel to facilitate a formal review process methodology to identify, examine, and evaluate the business objectives and corresponding risks, controls, and oversight within each operation. Now, that is what I call a comprehensive definition of internal audit! I *know* every person who sees this definition will want to immediately incorporate it into all of their internal audit marketing materials. The facts are stated and there is a clear definition and distinction of what audit is doing on a day-to-day basis to make every business process a world-class operation (and the envy of all their peers). If it was not clear enough in those last couple of sentences, that was sarcasm. Does the previous explanation define what internal audit represents? Yes, but unfortunately with these "book"-type definitions, it might only be clear to someone who has a baseline understanding of internal audit. For business personnel, while the explanation sounds official and uses the standard business terminology, it still might not convey the true objective of internal audit and how it affects the business units within the company.

While I believe the previous paragraph clearly depicts and explains internal audit's primary objective, it does not consider what I call the *terminology gap* when discussing key components of the internal audit function. As auditors, we can sit around a table and discuss risk and controls for hours and completely understand what each of us is talking about. However, the business owners and their teams are not familiar with these terms as it applies specifically to their own processes. This gap in an equal understanding of the internal audit foundational concepts creates a basic misperception when business teams are trying to understand what internal audit is going to be examining in the day-to-day operations of the business unit. Internal audit must ensure all of the auditors on the team can effectively articulate the internal audit objective and the associated terms like *risk, control,* and *oversight*. While the Beyond Audit Objective, Risk, and Control methodology will be discussed in detail in Chapter 5, it is important to spend a moment discussing it here. As a member of the audit team, being able to understand and explain these three terms is crucial to communicating the internal audit objective as well as building a strong, honest, and upfront foundation for the relationship with the business client.

INTERNAL AUDIT'S THREE PILLARS

The three pillars of *risk, control,* and *oversight* form the basic structure of any effective risk-based audit methodology. It is critical that all internal audit team members have a clear and consistent understanding and the ability to define them to a client in nonaudit terms. So, let's briefly discuss each one, starting with risk.

Risk is the probability that an event or action will adversely impact the organization or business unit. Now that may seem like a good explanation of risk to an auditor, but business personnel do not speak in these terms. This definition seems too formal and comes off as the auditor lecturing the business partner, creating an environment equal to a teacher and a student. The key to any introduction or interaction with a client should feel like two people discussing a process – more importantly, the business process being examined. The auditor should try to turn every meeting with the client into a conversation about the business process and focus on developing a relationship that does not feel so much like an examination of what the business does not do well but an interaction between two people where the business representative is the process expert and the other person is there to learn how the process works from start to finish. Trying to communicate with this objective in mind will promote a healthy relationship foundation and that encourages the exchange of process-based knowledge instead of a judgment examination of the business process. As the business process knowledge sharing meeting continues, the auditor can work with the client to discuss risks without giving the formal definition to explain it. Any time the topic of risk comes up with a business partner, one of the first things the business partner will say is "losing money is a big risk for us." While that may sound valuable to an auditor, losing money is not actually a risk. It is an impact of a risk happening in the business process. Think of it like this: A particular business risk was realized, and it cost the company money. So, remember, losing money may sound like a process risk but it is an impact of a risk and not a risk itself. Auditors must educate their business partner on risk being a barrier to the business team being able to accomplish their day-to-day activities to meet their business objectives. Risks do not represent impacts to the business process but impediments to doing their jobs.

When it comes to *control,* no business team is sitting in their offices looking for ways to add new controls to their process to strengthen the environment of their business operations. Most business units are wondering how they can do what they do faster so they can get more business and process more transactions. And in the business effort to go faster and process more transactions, it creates an environment that is ultimately not well controlled. As the auditor introduces the control concept, it should be linked to the idea of removing any barriers that could impede the business process from being completed in the most effective and efficient manner.

The control concept is then easily linked to the business *oversight* concept. Business oversight focuses on the information the business leadership team receives indicating that all business process components are operating as intended. As stated previously, there will be a deep dive on the three audit concepts of risk, control, and oversight in Chapter 5.

Once the auditor has cleared the first hurdle of explaining the key concepts of what audit does, it is important to clarify *why* audit does it. Most business teams can say they understand what the audit is trying to accomplish but will follow that up with "the business process works fine without any help from audit." This is where the auditor must be able to articulate the two potential outcomes of an audit that, in the end, are designed to benefit their business partner. One of the outcomes of an audit is that the audit results will show the business process has been effectively designed, built, implemented, executed, and accurately reported. These five factors of the business process, when done correctly, will produce the expected results. Keep in mind, every process will deliver a result. The key, which must be verified through data examination and effective reporting, is whether the business process achieves the intended result. The examination of the data and reporting should be done on an ongoing basis by the business unit and is the same information the audit team will examine during their review. The other outcome of an audit is that after a detailed review of the data and validation with the business partner, the audit reveals a breakdown(s) in the business process that does not produce the intended results. This breakdown is going to be directly linked to one of the five factors from design to reporting, and it is the job of the auditors, in partnership with their business partner, to identify the root cause (to be discussed in Chapter 7) of where the process breakdown occurred. It is always critical to ensure the business partner is involved in all aspects of the audit process. Once the business partner has obtained a clear understanding of what audit does, along with the two potential outcomes explaining the audit objective, the auditor can now detail what the business partner can expect in an audit from start to finish.

EXPLAINING THE AUDIT PHASES

The most important part of marketing the audit department is to deliver an unfiltered account of what the business partner is to expect in the three main phases of an audit – planning, fieldwork, and reporting. It is critical to provide perspective on the internal audit department before diving into the details of the three phases of an audit. Most importantly, explain that every audit department, like other business units, must adhere to standards and methodology requirements. It is not necessary to get into the details of the Institute of Internal Audit (IIA) standards, but it does help in building rapport with the audit client to state the audit department has guidelines to adhere to, just like the business unit, in completing their job. In addition to the standards are the specific audit methodology requirements, and it helps to explain these regarding the three main phases. This type of discussion gives the business partners the background knowledge to help them understand where the audit department is coming from during the review. This information is even more important during a remote audit because the client is only going to be getting requests from the audit department and may not understand why the audit team keeps asking for additional information. However, if the business partner understands the three main phases of an audit, it will make the request and delivery of information during the audit go much more smoothly.

Even before drilling down into the phase details with the client, the auditor can provide perspective of the internal audit department by informing the client of the different types of reviews audit can perform. This not only provides perspective on internal audit, but also plants the seed for future reviews that could be performed at the client's request. Let your business partner know that the audit department offerings include risk-based audits, continuous audits, operational reviews, and partnering on significant business projects or system implementations. The key on any audit is to let the business partner know that audit is a *partner* to the business and not just a group tasked with examining existing business operations. Again, the auditor should focus on building the relationship with every client on every job. It is even more critical during a remote audit to offer audit assistance to the business operation's team with any challenges they could be facing in this remote operational environment. Additionally, the auditor always wants to focus on internal audit's mission to consistently provide value on each engagement. That value is in process valuation and improvement, independent assessment, the risk and control knowledge sharing, and data-driven recommendations. All of these value points are linked to assisting the business units to meet their objectives consistently.

Another point to share with your business partners to provide insight to the audit operations is to explain how the audit selection process works. Many, if not all, business partners have no idea how their business process has been selected for an audit. Business management can get the wrong impression of an audit if they believe the audit is a result of the business struggling or making mistakes. That could not be further from the truth, and audit selection can explain and relieve that fear. Without getting into the details of the annual risk assessment with your client, the auditor can explain that each business process is evaluated annually to determine the corresponding process risk in an operation. All processes reviewed during the annual risk assessment are given a corresponding risk rating and then compared with other business processes to determine which audits to perform in any given year. Additionally, the frequency since the last audit is considered during the development of the annual audit plan. Obviously, there is more to it than just the rating and audit frequency but there is no need to get into all of the details. The goal of this discussion is to provide insight into how audits are identified and selected each year.

Now that the internal audit background foundation has been discussed, the three main phases of the audit can be described to your business partner to complete the marketing discussion. The first thing I do when explaining the three phases of the audit methodology is to indicate the percentage of time spent on each one. Beginning with planning, the details should include that this is where the highest percentage of time is spent (40–50 percent) in order for the auditor to gather the appropriate level of process knowledge and corresponding data as the testing plan is developed to examine the most critical areas of the business process. The reason the planning phase requires the majority of the budgeted time for the project is because this phase establishes the direction for all subsequent testing to be performed in order to draw the value-based conclusion. The planning phase identifies the most critical processes in the business unit under review. These processes will drive the deliverables linked to the business objectives. Let your business partner know that the audit team is aware of the time and effort required by the business personnel to complete all of their associated tasks but the audit team is only going to focus (perform detailed testing) around the most significant activities as determined during the planning phase through discussions with the client. Remind your client that the audit team will not select the areas to test without verifying the critical role each process plays in the business process achievement of their objectives. Given the enormous amount of time it takes the audit team to understand the business process, review reports, gather data, and hold discussions with the client, especially on a remote assignment, it should be obvious why the planning phase would take up the largest percentage of time in the execution of a risk-based audit.

While every internal audit department recognizes the planning phase should receive the majority of the audit budget, most audit teams do not spend the appropriate amount of time planning, especially if it was an audit that was completed in the past. Why? Usually, it is because of one of two reasons. First, the audit department, having documentation of the last completed audit, believes it would be more beneficial to save time by rolling forward the last approach and getting the current audit done more quickly so as to move on to the next project. And second, audit departments believe they can learn the process "on the fly" and develop a more intimate knowledge of the process requirements through executing the testing (fieldwork) and can thus save the time taken from planning and put it into the fieldwork phase. Neither of these reasons are correct and definitely do not increase the value of the audit results. As a matter of fact, rolling forward the previous testing performed may work, but with the way business processes evolve and adapt to current needs and requests, the details of the process are usually never the same as in previous years. Thus, using the roll-forward planning method may seem smart at the time when in actuality more time will be wasted during testing trying to determine why there are so many deviations from the testing standard. And using the fieldwork phase of audit to understand the process not only results in a slower understanding of the critical process, which requires testing, but also includes support processes that would not have been tested if the required planning had been completed. In the end, the audit team should dedicate the necessary time and effort in the planning phase to identify and understand the critical points of the audit process so that testing can be targeted and streamlined.

From the audit methodologies I develop for my clients, it indicates that the planning phase is complete once the audit program has been drafted, reviewed, and approved by the audit team. That means all the business knowledge, policy reviews, data gathering, flowcharts, and risk assessments have been completed and the most critical business processes have been identified. It is at that point the specific audit steps for validation of the business processes can be drafted. The audit program is created to only test the required steps in the identified critical business processes. That is not to say there aren't other activities occurring in the business unit under review, but the scope of this audit does not include them. This targeted testing approach is why the fieldwork phase of the audit should comprise about 30–40 percent of the budget. That should be sufficient time to execute the program and leave time to clarify the results. There should not be a need for the audit team to spend more time on the fieldwork phase, unless it still includes time dedicated to understanding the business process that should have been handled in the planning phase.

The final phase to explain to your client is going to be the reporting phase. While I recognize that many audit departments seem to spend a significant amount if not a majority of the budget in this phase, that doesn't have to be the case. Most departments overcomplicate the reporting process. If the planning and fieldwork phase are executed in the manner described in the previous paragraphs, I can assure you that your department can reduce the amount of time currently being spent in the reporting phase on every audit, even if it is not a remote review. Depending on how your audit methodology is constructed, the reporting phase of an audit should require about 10–30 percent of the associated budgeted time.

Aside from verifying that your audit methodology adheres to the planning and fieldwork suggestions listed above, here are three tips to help facilitate a smoother report generation phase:

1. *Your audit methodology should include a standard audit report template.* Included with this template should be instructions on how to effectively document the required fields in the template, along with an example of a well-written, concise, clear, constructive audit report.
2. *Keep the partner informed.* It is critical that throughout the audit process, especially during a remote audit, the audit team keeps their business partner informed not only of the status of the audit, but also all validated deviations from the processing standard that have been identified during the audit testing that could be included in the final audit report. This consistent and clear communication will ensure there are no surprises for the client when the draft report is created since all potential reporting items have been communicated and explained in advance (via the audit status report).
3. *Request business action plans throughout the audit.* This will help expedite the audit report generation process.

These three simple actions will provide time-saving opportunities for any audit department to expedite the report phase of their audit methodology.

For complete transparency regarding the audit process, do not forget to communicate to the client that even when the audit is completed, the audit and business teams will stay in contact through the implementation and adoption (Chapter 8) of all agreed-upon action plans detailed in the final audit report. To accomplish this final task of the audit, there will be regular communications to ensure the action plans to address any deviations from the business process standards are appropriately designed and implemented to close any exposures noted. The communication frequency for the business unit's action item follow-up is usually completed on a monthly basis. Most internal audit departments log, track, and report action item follow-up to business unit management and the executive team to ensure these critical items receive the proper attention even after the audit is completed and the final audit report has been distributed. This wrap-up phase of the audit provides the internal audit team an opportunity to continue to foster and maintain the audit and business unit relationship.

 DISPELLING THE MYTHS

Before closing the topic of remote internal audit marketing or audit department marketing in general, I wanted to share the most common audit perception myths and their associated realities (Table 3.1) in an effort to help audit departments remove the existing stigmas that have been linked to internal audit departments over the past three decades since I first started auditing.

TABLE 3.1 Auditor Perceptions: Myths and Realities

Auditor Myth	Auditor Reality
Police officer	Partner
Crusader	Change agent
Enforcer	Efficiency expert
Assassin	Advocate
Stressor	Solver
Rebel	Risk expert
Disrupter	Driver
Criticizer	Coach
Problem	Provider
Watchdog	Winner

Too often, internal audit teams are seen as the enemy because they are too often portrayed as police officers, enforcers, or watchdogs over the business processes – eager to find infractions and pounce on the guilty offenders. In the auditor's fantasy scenario, however, *no* exceptions are noted because exceptions represent a significant increase in work. The objective of internal audit is to work with clients on every audit to increase business knowledge and provide value to the business partner. At no time is the internal audit department's goal to review a process in an effort to identify problems.

In fact, the audit department has been established to partner with the business unit teams to support them in any way to make their tasks as efficient and effective as possible. Contrary to popular belief, the audit department would prefer to *not* identify deviations from the business processing standards because auditors know the significant amount of work those items require to validate, document, research, and close. Auditors should strive to constantly improve their business knowledge, be problem solvers who help resolve minor issues, provide guidance, and recommend solutions to increase the business process efficiency and effectiveness. They are not and do not want to be a disruption in the day-to-day business operations or create problems or stress for their business partners. No auditor I have ever met, worked with, or taught wants to be seen as an opposing force to the business partners. In the end, internal auditors and business unit personnel all work for the same company and should be working in unison to create the most effective and efficient processes to assist the business unit in meeting their established objectives.

So remember, communicating with your business partners, especially during a remote audit, requires dedicated time, effort, and resources to properly explain who audit is, what audit does, how audit executes their duties, and how important it is to be viewed as a partner to the business unit. Consistently marketing the internal audit department will provide significant dividends to both audit and their business partners.

Successfully marketing the audit department is not something that happens within the week or month when your audit team decides to begin to focus on the marketing components listed in this chapter. For any process change, this effort takes time and requires that all internal audit department members, not just the leadership team, are aware and committed to the steps necessary to accomplish the marketing objectives. This task has received much more focus and attention since the emergence of remote audits. While it might be easier during the remote audits to send emails, instant messages, or texts, or to make calls to gather information and data to complete assigned audit tasks, those communication mediums do absolutely zero to market the internal audit department and the corresponding services and value it can provide. When audit departments start receiving calls from business unit management asking for audit representation on a project team, for a specific audit to be started, for an operational review to be facilitated, or an opinion on a simple process enhancement, internal audit will know not only that their marketing efforts are beginning to change the misconceptions regarding audit activities but also that the internal audit department is gaining credibility across the company.

4

Building an Effective Audit Team

THERE ARE MANY SUGGESTIONS of how internal audit can be more effective, but as previously discussed, having a well-developed, detailed audit methodology has to be the foundation for your audit team to be as effective and efficient as possible. Additionally, the internal audit department must operate as a team when it comes to marketing their services and staying focused on communicating at a high level to create and maintain business partner relationships. These concepts may seem simple and very straightforward, but bringing them from a concept to a reality on a consistent basis is a significant challenge. To make this happen, every auditor throughout the audit team must have the audit knowledge and skills to perform the associated responsibilities. These skills will range from basic audit methodology understanding to building and managing an effective team that is recognized throughout the company as a high-value partner. The big question facing audit teams around the world is how to ensure their audit team has the skills necessary to be successful. The answer is to start with the Learning Map process.

BEYOND AUDIT LEARNING MAP

The Learning Map process is a customized document that details the expected results and core competencies for every level or job position within an internal audit department (Figure 4.1). This document is created from each internal audit's services offered as well as the specific audit methodology requirements. As you are aware, each audit department around the world has unique requirements to their services provided and the corresponding techniques utilized to satisfy each deliverable. In order for the Learning Map process to be effective, it must detail the particular skills needed to successfully navigate the requirements of each position within the internal audit department. Regardless of title or level, the Learning Map will guide each auditor to the skills necessary to exceed the position requirements. The Learning Map has a simple but effective structure, and when followed provides consistent results across an audit team. The map itself begins by detailing the expected results and core competencies (skills and behaviors) required to be successful at the specific level and then is followed by the corresponding learning to achieve these desired outcomes. The learning can be training, self-study, shadowing a coworker, and practice activities that once completed will provide the foundation to achieve the necessary result. The learning can be either an internal or external source, but whatever method is suggested, the auditor can

Expected Results	Competency	Topic	Activity	Resource	Ext Course/ Activity
Complete audit fieldwork	Functional and Technical Expertise	Audit methodology review	Walkthrough of audit methodology with senior staff or senior auditor	Internal audit methodology	Team development and sharing
		Risk-based auditing	Review workpapers and audit phase checklists	Department guidelines and phase requirements	New team training - Department and audit system overview
		Flowcharting basics	Draft flowcharts for assigned business unit processes	Various online and external offerings	Visio basics
		Feedback Fundamentals	Integrate feedback received through audit senior and manager review comments	Audit team	Intro to audit training
		Writing Techniques	Ensure communications are clear, concise, and meet department standards	Self-review, supervisory review, and approval	Writing basics

FIGURE 4.1   Beyond Audit Learning Map

be certain the training has been reviewed, previously attended, and proven effective. There are no education suggestions contained in the Learning Map that have not been previously reviewed and approved. Keep in mind that the training suggestions are ones that have been the most effective at developing the necessary internal audit skills required to successfully execute the corresponding audit methodology. This match between process requirements and specific learning should not be taken lightly, as the Learning Map creation process is not completed quickly. The map development requires a dedicated effort to understand the methodology requirements and a detailed understanding of the internal auditor levels and their corresponding roles in the audit methodology execution. Once the roles and responsibilities for each audit level have been identified and documented, then a brainstorming session is completed to determine the necessary skills and behaviors needed to ensure the auditor can accomplish the expected results. The map development steps in that order will result in Learning Maps for the audit department to follow. An additional benefit received from a Learning Map process is the guarantee that all internal audits, at every level, are held accountable and evaluated for the same tasks. This makes team evaluation and development an easier process for internal audit management while building team confidence at the same time.

An excerpt of the Beyond Audit beginning auditor Learning Map template is shown in Figure 4.1 for a department that executes risk-based audits. This template can be utilized in any internal audit department for risk-based audits or any other audit service offerings. Keep in mind, one Learning Map will be created for every level or position in the audit department from beginning auditor up to and including the chief audit executive. The most important concept of the Learning Map development process is to ensure the creator identifies, validates, and understands the roles and responsibilities of each position in the department to include in the corresponding Learning Map. This is crucial to the success of Learning Map incorporation into an audit department due to the fact that this document will be used as the source in which all internal audit team member performance is measured and evaluated. The benefit to incorporating this document into an audit department is that it provides the audit team with the specific skills and behaviors needed to succeed and progress in the department and ensures all auditors are being measured against the same criteria. The entire audit management team will also find a benefit when the year-end evaluation process begins, and they can use the Learning Map to maintain objectivity and link performance to specific targeted behaviors illustrated throughout the year.

SKILLS FOCUS IN THE REMOTE ENVIRONMENT

In 2020, the largest adjustment made to Learning Maps was the incorporation of remote-type skills that each audit position will have to ensure they focus on to be successful in this revised audit operating environment. While the same skills may already be identified and included in an internal auditor's responsibilities, it is important to enhance those skills and detail the specific behaviors required for successful execution. Here we discuss some of the critical skills that will need additional details to ensure successful remote audit performance.

Communication

The first skill, and probably the one with the biggest need for enhanced detail inclusion, is *communication*. And while communication is going to be discussed in Chapter 10, it is important to note performance enhancements considerations in terms of the Learning Map. Communication is a competency linked to the targeted result of keeping both the audit team and business unit management informed of the remote audit progress. Without effective communication to either of these two parties, there is an opportunity for incorrect assumptions to be made about every facet of the audit, including, but not limited to, audit status and potential reportable issues noted to date. The audit team does not want the audit or business management team to dedicate time, effort, or resources to an audit item that may not have been fully validated or confirmed. In order to avoid such a mistake, it is critical for the remote audit team to focus on continued, detailed, and regular communications with all parties involved in the audit process.

Communication, regardless of the audit environment you are in, will always be linked to the success of the individual auditor and audit team performance. And while most audit departments talk about communication being one of the critical skills every auditor should focus on developing, it is not a skill that is consistently listed in their Learning Maps (if they use them) or an item in their review performance checklist.

For the record, communication should not be just a checklist item on a review or auditor performance worksheet. Communication is the prominent skill that should be reviewed, explored, and discussed with each internal audit team member with related specific examples of successes and failures (opportunities for improvement) noted throughout an audit or even the year. Ask yourself two simple questions: Does the communication skill get a sufficient amount of attention across our audit department within each level as well as in the department as a whole? Is our audit department putting the right amount of emphasis on this critical skill to ensure the success of the audit team and audit execution? Most of the audit teams I work with agree that communication is critical, while at the same time admitting they do not drive the importance of the critical skill as much as they should. Audit teams should take the time to remind each other of the need for high levels of communication, especially in the remote environment, and hold each other accountable to communicate at a high level both inside and outside the audit department.

Here are a few points to consider when examining the dedication to communication within your own internal audit department when it comes to participating on a remote engagement. First, identify the business unit contact who will be the primary business representative receiving and handling all audit communications related to the engagement. This is the foundation piece for establishing a clear communication channel throughout the audit and is an essential piece in the development of your audit and business partner relationship. Since the audit team will not be onsite during this project, identifying this business partner liaison for the audit team will help ensure that audit-specific requests are directed to the responsible business partner.

On the surface, selecting a business partner to work with the audit team during a remote project does not seem to be that challenging a step. That would not be a smart assumption. Identifying the right business partner who recognizes the importance of this role (which they will maintain from start to finish) requires a dedicated effort. It is not as simple as picking someone who works in the business unit under review. Because of the focus, significance, and demand on audit communications required in a remote audit, the business partner should be someone with experience, knowledge (process and supporting system), and a process detail understanding. With this business profile, the audit can leverage the business partner's skillset, not only to expedite audit requests because the partner knows exactly where to go to get the corresponding information but also potentially to address and answer direct process-related questions without having to reach out to any other business process personnel. Once the auditor identifies the appropriate business partner, the audit team can utilize this resource throughout the audit to assist in completing the assigned tasks. The correct selection of a business partner for a remote audit directly impacts the effectiveness and efficiency of the project.

Reflect for a moment on a typical audit project and the time and effort it took to request and receive any business-related documents, policies and procedures, data, or selected samples. In your experience, was it easy to obtain business documentation when it was requested? When the audit department asks for something, do they get it immediately with no questions asked? Unlikely. The challenge that audit departments have faced since I began auditing in 1986 has been getting documentation to review and understand the process and acquiring a sample selection to validate the process accuracy and efficiency. Some business partners are under the mistaken assumption that if they do not provide the documentation and data to be tested, then maybe the audit team will go away and not be able to conclude on the business process adequacy. Well, the business management team eventually recognizes pretty quickly that the audit team *cannot* go anywhere until all of the testing is completed. So, the business data will have to be shared, but no one told the business partner how quickly it had to be shared. Every auditor has at least one client that the auditor would label as "challenging" or "difficult." That translation means getting time, documentation, or data is going to be like pulling teeth. This particular business owner is *challenging*. Now, take the same exact situation of the need to obtain business process information but add another layer of difficulty of being on a remote audit.

Prior to remote engagements, when auditors could not get documentation or information requests fulfilled, they would physically go directly to the business unit and either obtain the requested information or confirm the delivery date of same. Unfortunately for audit teams, the days of direct interaction on every audit assignment are gone. And while I recognize some experts believe that audit life is going to go back to normal in the near future, I do not share that optimism. I think business units are going to request remote audits due to the fact that a remote audit is less disruptive to the day-to-day operations. Audit teams around the globe will have to get acquainted and comfortable with the fact that, more often than not, face-to-face interaction with their business partners will be a thing of the past only referenced in auditing textbooks in the section on history of the vocation. And do not think for a second that a videoconference meeting is the same as meeting with someone in person. It is not. There is no comparison to a face-to-face discussion and nothing will ever come close to delivering the value of that type of meeting. That is why the identification of the key business unit contact is going to be vital to the success of a remote audit. Auditors must not only identify this business asset but also explain the responsibilities of being the liaison on a remote audit. Do not sugarcoat the importance of the role; remember to stress the time-sensitive nature of the requests and delivery of audit requirements to complete the job. As we have discussed previously, honest and upfront communication with your business partner will ensure a more efficient and effective audit execution while continuing to focus on the development and maintenance of the audit and business partner relationships.

Listening

Another skill directly linked to communication but often overlooked and taken for granted is listening. The reason I mention that listening is taken for granted is because every person assumes when someone is speaking, all of the recipients of the message are listening. Listening, however, is one of the most difficult components in communication. And while people say that they are great listeners, that is very seldom true. Listening, like all other critical skills, requires focus, dedication, and development in order to master it.

Contrary to popular belief, listening has nothing to do with hearing. An individual in a conversation can hear what another person is saying and not be listening all at the same exact moment. Consider how many times, both in and out of the workplace, that you have had to repeat what you were saying to another person. If I had a dollar for every time someone said to me, "What did you just say?" or "Could you repeat that?" I would not have to work another day in my life. It is a daily occurrence because – plain and simple – people do not attentively listen unless, of course, it benefits them. So, let's jump right back into the auditor and business partner discussion. In these types of interaction, the audit team is there to review the business process. The audit itself is going to be time consuming, disruptive, and even disturbing to some members of the business processing team. So, when the in-person discussions are being held between the audit and business teams, not every person in attendance is on the edge of their seat hanging on every word being spoken. Hence, there's a need for repetition, examples, and deadlines to be utilized during the conversation.

Now, complicate that same scenario with the conversation being held on the phone or videoconference. As soon as the audit-related conversations are taken out of the office and into a remote situation, the listening component of communications immediately suffers. Remote meetings, while they may seem efficient to discuss the topics, are not effective when it comes to the comprehension and understanding of all parties involved. The bottom line is that it is much harder to listen when the speaker is not directly in front of you, making eye contact, and verifying you understand the message being conveyed. It has been discovered that during remote audits and even business discussions, the focus is on covering (discussing) all of the relative topics on the agenda – if you are actually using one – and not, if ever, validating a clear understanding of the items being discussed. It seems hard to believe that individuals in a remote meeting cannot stay focused for 30 minutes, but it is true.

Remember that there is a very distinct difference between hearing and listening. Hearing is your ears physically hearing words coming from another person in a meeting. Listening is not only your ears hearing the spoken words but your brain actually comprehending what is being said. The key indicator that people in a meeting are only hearing the words and not truly listening is when there are no questions being asked. By the way, asking a question does not mean you are not smart or do not understand the topic being discussed. No, providing questions means you are actively listening and require clarification of the last thing that you have heard. That is why so many speakers and trainers constantly ask their audiences if they have any questions regarding what is being discussed. Auditors during these remote audits must incorporate questions into each meeting to verify the message is being heard and understood, as this is the only medium of communication that the auditor is going have at their disposal during a remote engagement.

One last point when it comes to remote communications and listening: Many times, during the preparation and facilitation of these remote meetings, the auditor believes in the message and that the delivery is clear. However, questions again must be utilized to ensure what is being said is actually what is being heard. I can tell you stories of numerous times when what I was saying was not what was being heard. I thought the message was clear and delivered effectively, but I could tell it was not working. Use clarifying questions to solicit any details or examples of the requests being made. This will eliminate a significant amount of rework and also build on the audit and business team relationship.

Also, do not think the lack of effective listening is only on the part of the business team during these remote discussions, because you would be wrong. There are many times when the communication breakdown is because the audit team did not pick up clear signs and messages in the meeting. This happens because both parties sometimes find these meetings difficult and the audit team is trying to cover all the necessary requests with encountering a huge battle. So, it is possible that the audit team missed a couple of key phrases that would have raised some red flags. For example, when an auditor asks the business partner, "Is this how the transaction is processed?" and the reply is, "That what the policies and procedures require," it seems like a confirmation of the process, but it is not. The business process team said the policy requires those process steps but never acknowledged that is how the transaction is actually completed. Another example is when any confirmation question is asked; for example: "Are the account reconciliations done by the end of the month?" and the response is "usually," "almost always," or "we try to." When any of those responses are given to a confirmation question, that means *no*. Saying "trying" or "usually" (almost always) translates into *no*. But during a remote discussion, I have seen audit teams document the answer as *yes*, and I point out that the business partner never confirmed that processing requirement.

When the audit team is effectively prepared and actively listening, these types of misdirection answers immediately raise a red flag and demand follow-up questions to obtain current process confirmation. Do not get lost in the noise of the conversation or the overwhelming amount of technical information or data being thrown at you during these meetings. Utilize the process knowledge you have gained during the initial planning phase activities to script focused questions related to the achievement of the business objectives being examined. That is why facilitating these meetings, especially in a remote environment, takes experience, skill, and planning. Always be prepared and listen attentively to the responses to direct questions. This will help ensure what the auditor is asking is exactly what is being heard by their business partner peers in the meeting.

 ## REMOTE BUSINESS PARTNER MEETINGS

Here are a few tips for handling remote business client meetings. Although there are no significant differences between the facilitation suggestions for a successful in-person versus remote meeting, it is important to note the techniques to concentrate on during the planning, introduction, execution, and closing of these meetings. Let us start with planning. As mentioned multiple times previously, there is no substitute for being prepared. I realize you will say you are prepared for work, meetings, testing, writing, and all the other audit-related activities, but these remote meetings take focus. And focus is developed through understanding your meeting objective(s). This meeting objective knowledge provides the auditor with the skill to effectively navigate the meeting, communicate the key points, obtain the necessary documents, and quickly identify if and when the meeting gets off topic. The meeting facilitator must be able to explain the objective and this is masterfully accomplished by utilizing a formal agenda distributed in advance to all attendees and having a sufficient level of business process knowledge. Business owners are intelligent and shrewd and can quickly recognize when a person, outside of their processing unit, is trying to discuss business-related operations without the corresponding process knowledge. That lack of knowledge and preparedness will be immediately evident and cause the meeting to fail and the objectives to go unfulfilled. That is not how you want to start building a relationship with your business partner. Take the necessary time to educate yourself on the process details and clearly understand what it is you want to get out of this meeting. The most important parts of the meeting are to restate the meeting objectives at the introduction, inform the participants with an overview of the audit process, introduce the targeted outcomes and deliverables from this meeting, and utilize the agenda to facilitate the discussion.

The audit process overview is invaluable. Whether my business partner has been through multiple previous audits or is a first-time client, I still provide a brief overview of the current audit process. This provides the business partner with baseline knowledge of the audit phases and gives them insight into the corresponding requirements for each phase. Discussing the audit process gives the business partner insight into the deliverables for each audit phase. Just remember to not get lost in the details of the audit process, as it is meant to be an overview, not an onboarding lesson for a new auditor.

Here is a brief outline of remote meeting facilitation tips. To be effective in these ever-changing workplace situations, it is important that the auditor maximize the interaction time with the client and remain vigilant when it comes to gathering pertinent business process information and data. One of the most critical skills to accomplish this is to maintain control of each business client meeting. Now, that is easier said than done, especially given the time pressures being applied on both the business and audit side. There never seems to be enough time in the day, let alone the budget you have been given to execute an audit project. However, it is possible to maintain control of a meeting while simultaneously saving a little bit of time. I know it seems impossible to save time anywhere during the workday, but it can happen if you adequately prepare, build an agenda, and utilize the agenda to stick to the meeting. But hang on, it is not as simple as it sounds.

 ## AGENDAS DRIVE THE MEETING

Preparation has been discussed a few times already, but here is how it applies to the business partner meeting. Preparation in this situation requires the auditor to review the business process policies and procedures, gain an understanding of the business terminology, identify where audit needs additional business process clarification, and document what information needs to be obtained to complete the audit phase steps being discussed in the meeting. These steps are utilized to create the meeting agenda, which is going to be used as a script for the auditor. This script, unlike in a movie, is not supposed to be memorized. It is used by the auditor to go step by step, covering the particular points and needs to ensure the auditor obtains the business process level information and data needed.

When used effectively, the agenda can act as a shopping list for the auditor as well as a constant reminder throughout the meeting to maintain control and to stay on topic.

In a remote meeting environment, it is useful to ask the participants if they have any additions to the agenda (which was distributed in advance of the meeting). Again, this is where details and listening become so important. Notice you are not asking the meeting participants if they have any *changes* to the agenda. It is an audit department–generated document based on information and documentation needed to execute the audit. The business partner is not in a position to alter or delete items from the agenda because that might prevent specific pertinent topics from being discussed at the meeting. How questions are phrased, and the details of those same questions, become critical to ensure the proper exchange of intelligence is occurring.

There is no problem asking if the business partner would like to add anything to the agenda, but they cannot remove any proposed topics that are scheduled to be discussed. The final point about soliciting new agenda items is to remember that any new agenda item suggestions from the meeting participants go at the bottom of the agenda and will be discussed if the meeting time permits. If there is not sufficient time at the end of the meeting, after all audit points have been covered, an additional meeting can be scheduled to cover the new agenda items. At this point, the auditor will know how important the new topics were to the business partner if they are willing to schedule another meeting to cover them. The bottom line, when it comes to the agenda, is that the document was created by the auditors with specific objectives in mind and cannot be altered by the business partner. Additions are always welcome, but deletions are not allowed.

The key to using the agenda without it seeming like you memorized it is to facilitate the meeting going item by item through the agenda. The agenda should be created in the natural order of discussion beginning with the meeting objectives and an audit process overview and then progressing through the business process–related topics which require clarification. This always concludes with next steps, which will be discussed shortly. Relying on the agenda to guide you through the meeting increases the success of the meeting and delivers the audit message in a clear, concise tone. This becomes even more critical in the remote audit because you are not in a face-to-face environment where you can clarify points more easily based on facial expression and utilize more open-ended questions.

The agenda in these situations can also provide an early warning mechanism for the meeting facilitator if it appears the discussion has moved off one of the agenda items. Again, this notification will require active listening on the part of the audit team throughout the entire meeting. But when utilized effectively, the early warning system works. Remember, the business partners are skilled and experienced communicators, and they have the ability to discuss their business process in detail. That skill also allows them to convey business information which may, on the surface, sound valuable but is not specifically addressing the audit question being asked. Skilled communicators can answer a question related to the topic being discussed and at the same time not provide any real benefit to the audit team. Remember when we discussed adequate preparation of the business process details, this is where the auditor, who is actively listening, can restate the question and let the business partner know that the auditor recognizes the answer did not adequately address the question being asked. This is not to be done in a rude manner or with an "I gotcha" type of response. It is just a direct way to convey to the meeting participants that you have effectively prepared and want a direct response to the question asked.

To assist in the facilitation of this remote audit meeting, the preparation must include auditor notes documented on their copy of the agenda so the facilitator recognizes the key points that must be covered during the meeting as well as the information and/or documentation that the auditor will not end the meeting without. These detailed notes serve as a reminder to the remote meeting facilitator of exactly what is needed to satisfy the specific agenda items. As these meetings progress, there are many instances where the discussion becomes very technical or detailed and the facilitator can lose track of the initial question being asked. The agenda notes provide the proper perspective as to the specific information that will satisfy the auditor's request and eliminate unnecessary information from clouding the message or question specifics. Take my advice on this point. After participating in and leading more meetings than I wish to count and facilitating in this new remote environment, I can attest to the fact that no amount of experience allows you to successfully facilitate these meetings without a well-prepared agenda with detailed notes to ensure you stay on track and obtain the necessary information to complete the engagement requirements.

The final point to review regarding remote audit meeting facilitation is closing the meeting. While this may seem like a simple task of asking if there are any other questions before we conclude the meeting, in the remote environment, there are specific points to be articulated before dismissing the participants from the discussion. If you have dedicated the necessary time to prepare and facilitate the meeting, the closing must be as deliberate and strong as the opening. In closing, the auditor will formally ask if there are any outstanding items that should be discussed before the meeting ends. Usually, there are no additional items, which means the meeting summary can be given. In this summary, the agenda items are reviewed along with the corresponding outcome for each one, which is usually either that the information was obtained or there are still outstanding items related to the specific agenda point.

After the agenda summary is completed, the discussion will shift to next steps in the audit process, which include, but may not be limited to, confirmation that the meeting information will be reviewed and incorporated into the steps and the remaining steps of the audit phase being discussed will be outlined. This additional audit phase information will ensure that the business partner is provided a clear and concise status of the audit along with audit work that still needs to be completed. The final point to discuss is a quick review of any outstanding information, documentation, or data, which the business needs to provide to the audit team or vice versa along with the corresponding target delivery dates for each. This is discussed so that there is communicated and documented accountability that makes for more direct follow-up if the targeted delivery date is missed. Upon final review of the meeting summary items, inform all meeting participants that a formal meeting minutes document will be created by the audit team and distributed to everyone on the call. This document will contain the participant list, agenda items discussed, outstanding deliverables from both the audit and business teams with the agreed-upon delivery dates, and next steps in the process. These types of details discussed in the meeting summary and the formal meeting minutes document further build and strengthen the relationship between the audit team and business partner.

 ## AUDIT STATUS MEMOS

Another skill auditors must focus on in the remote audit environment is the strict adherence to the audit status memo process. The audit status memo is the formal document created on a recurring basis that provides an up-to-date status of the audit activity during all engagements. The on-time development and delivery of the status memo is critical to ensuring your business partner is current on the project and issues noted to date (which have been validated)

are communicated timely and business action plans are being developed on an ongoing basis. With no regular face-to-face access with the business partner, the status memo is the only communication medium to inform business personnel of the deviations from the processing standards identified during the audit.

Keep your status memos clear and concise and adhere to the agreed-upon frequency of delivery. It is a good practice to follow up the status memo delivery with a phone call to your business partner to let them know you have delivered the status memo and that the business team can contact you with any questions, clarifications, or details needed to support any items included in the memo.

Also, let them know the audit team will be reaching out to their business partners to obtain proposed management action plans related to the issues noted to date in the status memo. Remind the business partner that just because the issue is noted in the status memo, does not necessarily mean it will be included in the final audit report. It is detailed in the status memo as a result of it being identified during audit testing as a deviation from the business processing standard and subsequently validated with the business processing team. The determination of final audit report inclusion will be discussed with business unit management, and final disposition will be based on overall risk to the achievement of the corresponding business objective.

REMOTE AUDITOR SKILLS PROFILE

Before we close the topic relating to educating the audit team with focused skills for the remote audit environment, there should be a brief examination of the core auditor skills and how the audit team must recognize the need to be vigilant related to utilizing these skills during a remote audit engagement. There are eight skills listed below, which every auditor should possess and continue to develop throughout their audit career. Each one will be briefly explained to provide a foundation for the audit team to review, reference in the department Learning Map, and include in their corresponding personalized development plan.

- Communicator
- Listener
- Sharer
- Thinker
- Doer
- Participator
- Helper
- Defender

In the first four chapters, communication has been a primary focus, and for good reason. In any remote work environment, the success and failure of a project hinges on how information is being shared from the start to the end, including a consistent flow of details throughout, relating to the status of the work assignment. Without a standard and consistent level of communication between the audit team and the business partner, the remote engagement will fail due to the uncertainty of the work that is being performed and the lack of timely information sharing. When communication is not a primary skill, stressed throughout your audit methodology, a consistent unrelated outcome is a dysfunctional audit and business relationship. Even though during the execution of the audit the relationship is at the top of the priority list of the audit team, the relationship ultimately suffers damage that is exceedingly difficult to correct during future audit engagements. Always remember to be transparent with your client in regard to the audit process, individual audit phase requirements, status of work completion, validated issues identified to date, and remaining steps to complete the project. This level of communication will provide a solid foundation for the audit and business relationship as well as create the standard for audit communications on future projects.

As was stressed earlier in this chapter, listening, while inherent in any communication, does not receive the right level of attention during meetings, especially remote ones. It is important to remember that listening is not enough. Auditors, in this new environment, must be active listeners and stay focused on the topic being discussed as well as attentive to the corresponding details. One suggestion to assist with meeting focus is to keep a pen in your hand during the meeting. Being ready to document process details helps with active listening. Try it and see if it helps you remain attentive to the meeting details. Everyone knows it is too easy to let your mind drift or get distracted in a meeting – and that is usually the moment when someone asks for your opinion or when transaction details are being discussed. So, stay at the ready to note key process points and listen attentively from start to finish.

Dedicated internal communication, at all levels, within an audit department ultimately leads to strong external communication with your clients. The key to internal communication success is to have every member of the internal audit team be cognizant of the *sharing concept*. The sharing concept is when auditors freely share their audit and business knowledge, previous experiences, lessons learned from mistakes, suggested audit-related techniques, communication skills, and any other practices they have learned during their own audit tenure that could possibly help a coworker. It is in this type of *development first, competition last* environment that audit teams develop an effective audit staff that inherently builds their team's skillset without even trying. It is the communication, focus, and repetition of these topics that help shape audit skills and shorten the learning curve related to the critical attributes needed to be successful on the audit team. Within a sharing audit department environment, everybody wins, and that ultimately translates into a more credible audit reputation.

While you probably would not associate *thinker* as a critical skill needed within an audit team, it actually plays a critical role in the audit process. People view thinking as an inherent skill that any person in any job would apply on an ongoing basis. But it is the opposite that is true. More than I would like to acknowledge, it is becoming more prevalent that audit departments are doing less thinking and more exercising as the audit methodology is being applied during both traditional and remote engagements. Here is the point I am trying to articulate. Auditors are intelligent, detail oriented, and inquisitive. However, when faced with a large project, lack of sufficient budget, large sample sizes, and the inability to freely access the client to address outstanding questions, auditors can sometimes take on what I call a drone army mentality. The scariest part of the drone army mentality is that it is easy to be consumed by this approach because it expedites the audit phases, especially the planning and fieldwork ones. Let me explain. The drone army mentality changes the audit process from an execution of the audit methodology to an exercise. Meaning, the audit team will leverage and roll forward the planning documentation from the previous audit without really validating and updating any potential business process changes. Then the auditors will do the same with the audit program and execute the same testing as in the previous audit. This type of approach will save numerous hours and generate audit results to satisfy the annual audit plan. What this drone army mentality never requires is creative thinking. There is no need to apply any thinking or consider potential enhancements to the business process even though it could be improved. No. The drone army mentality is about treating the audit requirements as an exercise; you receive your program testing requirements and you complete them as instructed in the documentation. The unfortunate side to the drone army approach is that the audit work completed really is not looking at the business process from a risk perspective or an achievement of business objectives perspective. It is looking at the business process as an exercise in following an existing program and documenting the results. The crucial skill related to being a thinker, especially from an audit perspective, has been removed when this type of mentality is applied. When considering the increase in process risk in a remote business environment, critical thinking would be the number-one skill an auditor would want to apply since there have been significant changes in the processing and oversight requirements in the business process. Instead, thinking is removed, the previous audit approach is applied, and the testing is completed without a single thought given to the enhanced remote processing environment that has been adopted by the business unit. Take the additional time, step back, and think about the new challenges the business operations may be experiencing in the altered, remote environment. Only then can an audit department be confident that the audit results reflect a validation of the current control environment.

The fifth core skill requires the auditor to be a doer. The explanation of this skill is literal. When an auditor is assigned a task or section of the audit program to execute, they complete the assigned responsibilities to satisfy the requirement. Being an effective doer on the audit team does not translate into never asking any qualifying or clarifying questions. If an auditor did not participate on the planning of a particular project, it would be difficult to assume that the doer would not have a single question related to the work that has been assigned. It is possible if they worked on the audit the previous year, they might not have any questions related to the associated tasks. However, I would hope an auditor on a return engagement would question that there were not any changes to the audit program, given the changes in the business process to achieve even the same objectives. While the doer is expected to complete the tasks assigned, it is critical that they raise any challenges or concerns they may have regarding the work, budget, or gathering of corresponding data to complete the tasks. An effective doer on the audit team proactively identifies challenges related to completion of the assigned work and immediately raises questions to avoid significant time wasted.

The next two core skills are participator and helper. And while these two auditor characteristics may sound like synonyms, they have a distinct difference. The participator skill is more strategic and requires thought from the auditor, which must be based on their knowledge of the business process and achievement of the business objectives. Here is what that means. When there is any discussion regarding the business process being audited, the audit team is encouraged to contribute any thoughts related to business process efficiency suggestions, reduction of required rework inherent in the business process, or a more effective way to audit the business process. This contribution does not mean that every auditor in the brainstorming meeting has to speak just to speak. This participator skill is not about repeating the last suggestion someone else made in an effort to make it seem like it is your suggestion because you were the last person to bring it up. This skill is about considering your business process knowledge and applying analytical thought to either improve the existing process or suggest ways to evaluate the business performance more effectively. That is what an effective audit participator does. Conversely, when the core skill of helper is considered, all audit team members must realize that internal audit, more than most business functions, relies on consistent team performance to deliver a quality audit product on every engagement. That being said, auditors must be at the ready to help each other when one team member is struggling with a test or assigned task or if a team member is dealing with a challenging client. In the remote audit environment, auditors are going to encounter more frequent obstacles in completing assigned duties just based on their new operating environment. So, when you see a team member struggling, the helper skill should immediately kick in without any other team member asking for help or telling you to help. Never forget that the internal audit department's expectations are always growing, and it takes the whole team to accomplish the corresponding objectives and add value to the company.

The final core skill is defender, and this relates directly to the helper skill. It is a skill that should be inherent in every audit and will be unbelievably valuable to the entire audit team, especially when operating in the remote audit environment. This skill is linked to the concept of support whether it be with data, business information, or combined effort to complete a task. The audit department always seems to be on the defensive and, to effectively communicate and facilitate change within a business process, internal audit needs to support the team, work product, and the details with a unified approach based on the data obtained during the engagement. Any time an auditor is being challenged in relation to any aspect of the audit, they should remember to support their position with the data. This data being used was provided by the business unit and not created by the audit team. Utilize that approach when you are supporting each other in process discussions or clarifying potential deviation to the business process standard.

Incorporating these eight core skills will assist you in developing a more well-rounded approach in your path through the various levels of your audit department. Also, having a particular title does not create a leader. A leader is someone who effectively executes their own responsibilities while aiding other team members, communicates effectively, and suggests process enhancements both internally to the audit methodology and externally to the business process. In order to effectively plan and track your skills focus and individual development, I would suggest using a personalized development plan. This plan is created with the assistance of your supervisor, as they are in the best position to help you identify skills that require enhancement to ensure your success within the department. An example of the Beyond Audit development plan template follows. Keep in mind that although the development plan can provide a document to detail and track your audit skill development focus, it will not be effective if it is not given the appropriate amount of attention, progress tracking, and follow-up required to improve your audit technical skills.

 BEYOND AUDIT DEVELOPMENT PLAN

Skill/Competency	Required Action	Time Frame	Support/Resource
Effective team communication	Schedule & hold 1x1's	Monthly	Team support

CHAPTER FIVE

The Methodology – Objective Recognition

 IMPROVING THE AUDIT PROCESS

Over the past couple of years, I have been working with internal audit teams around the world to transform their risk-based audit methodology to include a planning phase focused on the business unit's objectives. One of the lessons I have learned over my long tenure in internal audit is that audit departments overcomplicate two of the three phases of an internal audit methodology – the planning and report writing. By making these phases more complex than they have to be, valuable time is wasted in an effort to create the most comprehensive audit plan ever developed and a perfect audit report. Not just experience but common sense would tell you both of those outcomes are not possible. No matter how much time you dedicate in planning or how many revisions you make to an audit report, neither one is going to reach the utopia of audits that some departments are trying to accomplish on every audit. Setting these unrealistic goals for your audit team for the planning and report phases only results in one outcome. After being pushed to achieve unrealistic deliverables, the overworked audit team ultimately realizes that all the time, effort, and dedication did not result in a more detailed, value-driven plan or an audit report that all business partners recognized as the best ever.

Now, the reporting phase will be addressed in Chapter 7, but this chapter will be dedicated to adjusting the internal audit efforts to produce a plan with a more efficient path to get there. Too often, internal audit teams waste time digging through antiquated policies and procedures and diving too deep into the minutia of the assigned business process functions. Why? What do the auditors hope to uncover or reveal by reviewing policies and procedures which are probably not up to date, or examining process details, which in the end, do not really have any impact on the required business deliverables to achieve the corresponding business objectives? More often than not, when questioned as to why there is such a dedicated effort to look so broad and deep into the business process, the response is usually, "This is the way we have always done planning." Now, I know people used to walk to work, but then modes of transportation were developed, and people stopped walking. So, it is time to bring the internal audit planning phase into a more focused, precision approach to increase productivity, value, and business process knowledge.

Just like any other process, task, or assignment, in order to improve it, you must first define not only the purpose of what you are trying to fix and what the current process entails but also why it is not achieving the intended outcome. Remember, everything you do will produce an outcome. The question is, will all the time, effort, and dedicated resources deliver the desired result? Consider the amount of work it takes to plan an audit. Planning, if done correctly, requires a learning curve. Whether the planning activity is for an area that has been previously audited or an area new to audit activity, there is still going to be time dedicated to building baseline business process knowledge and/or updating existing information. In addition, the audit team must understand any and all federal, state, and local rules and regulations that are applicable to the processes under review. And to finalize the audit planning phase, auditors must identify the key process team players along with all the systems utilized within the business unit to execute their day-to-day responsibilities.

BEYOND AUDIT – ORC MODEL

The focus in this chapter will be on the Beyond Audit methodology's objective, risk, and control (ORC) model with a strong emphasis on the objective. Before the discussion begins, there needs to be a clear understanding of how the word *objective* is being utilized in this model. Due to the critical nature of this foundational component, it must be clearly explained and understood in order to follow the directions to finding it within any business process being audited and properly incorporated in the audit planning phase. Too many auditors jump into the planning phase without any real direction. As noted earlier, the planning phase should be the audit phase that requires the majority of the assigned budget time (40–50 percent). This allows for the proper research and business process understanding to identify the associated business objectives.

In the most direct definition, the business objective is the purpose of the business process. Sounds like a lot of technical audit-speak, but it is not. It is very straightforward. The objective of the business process is the *reason* or *purpose* the business unit was established in the first place. To discover and clarify the business objective, ask the simple question of what does the business unit produce on a daily basis and who, as in what department, division, or customer, relies on the information being produced by the business process. The business objective is really trying to document why this business process exists and what it contributes to the company overall. There has to be a specific, documentable reason this business unit exists.

Before the ORC model is explained, it is important to remember that in order to be effective at executing the model, there are required steps to complete that provide the necessary background of the business process. To put it into better context, let us take a step back and remind every internal audit department that the planning phase has three main phases: (1) understanding the business; (2) identifying and documenting business process risks and controls; and (3) developing the audit test approach (program).

Understanding the Business

The first step of understanding the business has three distinct requirements – developing business process knowledge, identifying the rules in the current business operating environment, and documenting the systems utilized in completing the associated business process tasks. While these three steps are all critical, the most important of these has to be developing business process knowledge. Although mentioned previously, it never hurts to stress how important business knowledge can be when you are a member of the internal audit team. Auditors must remember to never stop building their business knowledge if they want to be successful at providing valued input to improving existing business processes. Developing useful business knowledge includes independent research, previous internal audit activity, external exams and reviews, outstanding and closed action items, and walkthrough documentation.

Here are thoughts related to the knowledge building resources. When it comes to independent research, remember to include general internet information pertaining to the operation as well as industry journals, which can provide solid process background (though not specific to how your company executes the process requirements) and basic process terminology. In reviewing previous audit activity, take special notice of the audit objective at the time and what was included in the review. This will provide the auditor planning the current project a perspective on what has been audited in the past in addition to the overall rating on the control environment at the time of the audit. Just like the previous internal audit activity, the review objectives, topics covered, and overall assessment results should be noted to identify any potential trends or topics that might be included in the current audit. In examining the open and closed action items from the internal audit tracking database, pay attention to the length of time from the action item recommendation date to the implementation date. This elapsed time provides an indication of the business unit's commitment to recognizing the value and implementing the internal audit recommendations in a timely manner. Remember, internal audit's recommendations are based on identified and validated business process exceptions which need to be addressed to reduce overall risk to the company. And finally, internal audit will be able to validate the business background information or fill in gaps of the current business process by facilitating walkthroughs. During a remote audit, walkthroughs will be more difficult to accomplish since they cannot be done in person. Successful execution of these requires excellent communication and listening skills to ensure all details of the process are noted from start to finish. During a remote walkthrough, do not think that any question, at any level, is not appropriate. The business partner should expect a significant amount of clarifying questions and recognize the need for same.

Identifying and Documenting Business Process Risks and Controls

The second requirement for understanding the business is identifying the rules that govern the current business operating environment. When discussing business rules, the auditor must realize there are two distinct sources where these rules can originate: internal and external. The internal sources of rules represent policies and procedures along with any management directions. These directions can include supervisory overrides and management discretions. And even though both of these exception-type rules are judgment based, each should include sufficient documentation that explains the reason for the alternative processing method. Conversely, the external sources of rules are regulations and laws that can originate from a local, state, or federal level. The most significant difference between the internal and external rules is that external rules usually have zero opportunity for judgment. Most external rules are compliance based and their requirements cannot be considered optional.

Developing the Audit Test

The final requirement for understanding the business is documenting the systems utilized in completing the associated business process tasks. In this day and age, every business process at some point during their execution relies on an automated system. Some business processes are executed entirely with a software or system tool. Therefore, it goes without exception that all systems and software used in a business process must be identified, documented, and linked to the specific steps in the business process where they are being utilized. To effectively document the key systems incorporated into the business process, an auditor must recognize the specific process points where technology is required. In addition to identifying technology usage, the operating system must also be identified. If this is a business process or operational review, why does there have to be such detail documented with the supporting systems? The operating systems where the business technology resides provide critical information related to the communication of information within the business process. Most nontechnology auditors do not realize that when automated systems used in a business process do not reside on the same operating system, it makes it exceedingly difficult for the two distinct systems to share information. That is not to say that two systems on different operating platforms cannot share information. It is possible, but usually requires "reformatting" of the source data. The main reason the operating systems should be identified is that they provide an early warning system to the audit team to analyze the consistency of the data, from both a number and accuracy perspective, throughout the business process.

Another technology point to consider when documenting key systems in the business process is to note if there is any importing or exporting of data to/from the business unit. Understanding the source of the relied-on data in any business process helps to understand how information is acquired and distributed with this business process. This knowledge of the system closes the loop in building the auditor's business process knowledge, as the planning documentation is fully explained from beginning to end while including the tools, experience, and technology incorporated into the execution of the business tasks.

The completion of the three requirements in understanding the basis provides the internal audit team with a solid foundation to implement the ORC model, which will begin with the development of an understanding of what the word *objective* means in the model when planning a risk-based audit for a traditional or remote audit.

 ## IDENTIFYING THE BUSINESS OBJECTIVE

One quick note of caution when it comes to discussing and identifying the business objectives with the business owner: Always remember the business objective that the auditor is trying to identify is never the business mission statement or a particular business process task. Too many auditors mistake and document the mission statement as the objective when it is presented by the process owners. Be cautious not to accept this; always verify that whatever is given as the business objective links directly to deliverables produced by the business unit. Mission statements tend to be more global in nature and encompass the entire business process rather than the tangible process results. Utilize listening and communication skills to ensure that the business process foundation being built for the planning phase is on target.

It is important to recognize the distinction when defining *objective*. Too often, internal audit departments associate the word *objective* with *unbiased* because auditors, according to audit standards, are supposed to remain without any prejudice or judgment when it comes to evaluating business process control. And while that is correct, auditors must remember that during the planning phase, *objective* is being used as a noun and not an adjective describing auditor behavior. The noun usage of the word becomes the building block for all of the planning information used to create an audit approach and corresponding testing plan. Without identifying the business objectives, the development of the audit objectives and corresponding audit program will ultimately include steps that do not have a significant impact on the achievement of critical business objectives or potentially omit critical testing that should be performed. In order to guarantee your audit methodology is operating and validating the most critical business process steps, ensure your methodology contains the required steps to identify and document the current business process objectives.

To effectively accomplish the goal of identifying the business unit objectives, the internal audit methodology must clearly explain and document how an auditor goes about achieving this mandatory planning phase task. The first step is an internal step in which auditors must be ready and willing to clear their mind of any preconceived notions telling themselves that they already understand the business unit being audited and can document the corresponding business objectives. While I recognize that auditors who have significant audit experience and tenure in their current job believe they have a solid foundational business knowledge of their company's operations, this, unfortunately, is not good enough to complete the documenting of the business unit objectives under review. The reason is that business operations are dynamic and constantly adjusting to both internal and external demands to meet the needs of codependent business units and outside customers and investors. If each business, regardless of location or industry, is constantly changing its process to adapt as needed, how could an internal auditor, even with multiple years of experience and tenure, recognize, understand, and document the current business objectives? The bottom-line answer is, the auditor cannot. This inability to know the current business objectives is not due to a lack of auditor intelligence. Trust me on this point.

Auditors are well educated and are (or at least should be) constantly building their business knowledge. However, it is not possible, and frankly unfair, for business operations personnel to assume auditors are supposed to know everything about every business operation in the company. This may seem like an unrealistic expectation, but it is a fact that auditors face each time they enter into any business unit to conduct an audit. And at the same time business unit personnel are conjuring up this expectation of an auditor's business operational expertise, there is a responsibility on the internal auditors to develop the business knowledge to ensure they can be effective and meet their own objectives of delivering business process validation and value process improvement recommendations.

The most significant challenge to the auditor's objectives is always going to be related to business objective identification because it relies so heavily on an auditor's understanding of the current business process requirements. Unfortunately, there is no stated or mandatory guideline set for auditors to indicate that they have acquired the proper level of business knowledge to be comfortable auditing an area in which they may or may not have any experience reviewing. The key question facing auditors is always going to be, how much business process knowledge do I need to possess to accurately identify the corresponding business objectives? Again, there is no easy answer. The one word of caution is to be careful not to fall back on the drone mentality approach, which was discussed in Chapter 4, when it comes to building your business process and objective knowledge.

A valuable lesson learned is when relying on prior audit work completed for the business knowledge and objective foundation, the auditor must verify and validate the existing audit information being relied on represents the current business objectives and most recent business operating processes to achieve those objectives. With the speed at which the internal and external operating environment changes, assuming audit information from at least 12 months ago is still an accurate representation of business processes is a gamble that no auditor should be willing to take. This is why the planning phase of an audit, especially a remote review, takes the majority of the assigned budget. The good news is that every time the auditor enters into a project, the time dedicated to identifying and building process knowledge will provide the team with a detailed plan for audit testing and continue to foster audit's business relationships.

There is no doubt that the audit team, during a remote audit assignment, will be tempted to trust the previous audit workpapers as the source for developing the current audit approach because it requires the least amount of business interruption, which auditors believe will benefit both the audit and business teams. This is a misconception. Any time the auditor may think they will save by using the drone approach to planning a current project, will quickly evaporate when they realize the process knowledge and documentation from the prior audit does not accurately reflect the current business operations. This assumption mistake will necessitate additional time to validate the testing approach (which was also rolled forward), learn the current process, adjust the test program, and obtain approval for the revised approach. To effectively accomplish these steps will require additional time with the business personnel, which the auditor was trying to avoid by applying the time-saving drone mentality to the business objective identification process in the first place.

Please take my advice on this point and learn from my mistakes. Depending on previous audit work completed as the source for the current business process is never representative of the current business processing environment. While the previous audit work provides an excellent source of business background information, previous audit objective knowledge, and a conclusion of the business control environment at the time of that review, the business process operating details must be updated and validated to ensure the most current business process information is being used to identify the business objectives.

BUSINESS OBJECTIVE IDENTIFICATION CHALLENGE

The question then remains, what is the best approach to obtaining the business objectives regardless of the type of audit? The key to gaining this usually overlooked information does not originate in any documentation or policies and procedures. In order to acquire the business objectives, the auditor must engage with the business process owner. They are the only true source of the business objectives because they are responsible for establishing it and creating the process steps necessary to achieve the objectives on a consistent basis. However, auditors must recognize that even though they know where to obtain the information, getting the business unit partner to discuss and reveal the objectives is a much more difficult task than it may appear. That does not seem to make sense, does it? If an auditor recognizes that the business unit partner knows the objectives, because they developed them, it should just be a matter of asking the question directly and getting a response. That is a funny thing about being a member of the internal audit department. Audit tasks that seem quite simple and direct really never are as easy as they sound. Even when the audit and business partner have a strong relationship, obtaining the business objectives is challenging.

It has to be noted that the business partner is not keeping their business objectives a secret on purpose. Many times, the business partner is struggling to answer the question because they simply do not understand what is being asked or why. To better understand the business partner perspective, consider this: The business partner is being asked to explain their business objectives. Now when the business partner hears this question, they consider the source (internal audit) and immediately wonder why the audit department is asking for this process-level detail and what the auditor is trying to reveal. Does the audit department know something the business owner does not? Why would audit, from the business partner's perspective, be asking me to justify my department's existence in the company? Needless to say, it can be intimidating for the business partner to be asked what their business objectives are, especially from the internal audit department, due to the role each of the teams play. That is why, in Chapter 4, it was noted how critical it is to be able to effectively communicate all phases of the audit methodology. The auditor in this situation must be able to put the business partners at ease and let them know the reasoning behind trying to identify the business process objectives. This is a much more important point in the communication and relationship building process than most auditors recognize. Every auditor has to understand that they are not trying to identify and document the business objectives just because the audit methodology requires it. Auditors must know themselves and be able to explain to their business partner that the mutual agreement and understanding of the business objectives is the foundation on which all subsequent work from the planning phase through the corresponding audit testing is based on the business objectives. If the objectives are not properly identified and validated with the process owner, all testing that follows will not only be a waste of time and effort for the audit team, but also have zero value to the business partner because it does not pertain to any of the significant deliverables in their business process. Then auditors will end up complaining that the business partner does not want us in their business unit and will not provide corrective action for the exceptions noted in the audit report. When auditors are having challenges with their business partners in the reporting phase, remember how the audit team planned the project and it will become apparent the planning phase lacked business objective focus.

BUSINESS OBJECTIVE IDENTIFICATION IN A REMOTE AUDIT

To be successful in identifying the business objectives, especially in a remote project, the auditor has to be not only properly prepared for the planning discussion but also articulate in detailing how the planning phase works. There is a tactical method to obtain the business objectives, and it surrounds the questioning approach used with the proper clarification and support with the purpose behind the specific details being asked. When the auditor and business partner conversation begins, start off with the objective of the planning phase. Clearly and concisely explain that the planning phase, especially initially, is designed to identify the most critical business processes to ensure audit testing precision within the business operations. And while the audit team recognizes that the business unit personnel perform numerous duties, the audit itself will not test every business activity but focus on only the ones that directly impact the achievement of the business objectives. This will provide reassurance to the business partner that audit recognizes the significant effort made by business unit team members in their day-to-day operation. However, the audit activity will be limited to and concentrate on the critical process steps linked to the business objectives as confirmed by audit's business partner.

Remember to emphasize the audit testing is directly derived from the business objectives in an effort to maximize the value to the key business process validation and identification of potential opportunities for business process improvement where the testing results indicate deviations from the process standards. Once the planning background has been explained and the importance of the business objectives identification has been revealed, the auditor can now proceed with obtaining the business objectives. This can only be achieved through direct questioning with the business partner. Business objectives will not be revealed even in the most updated policies and procedures. It takes direct questioning to identify and verify the business objectives. The most effective question I have found is not necessarily the most direct. It is not as simple as asking the business partner, "What are your business objectives?" The unfortunate part is that the direct question approach often leads the business partner to follow up with direct questions of their own. Like, why are asking me that? No one from internal audit has ever asked me that before. What are you searching for? Do you know something that I do not know? It is not uncommon for a business partner to take a defensive posture, which is understandable. It is a situation, from their point of view, in which it appears that the corporate "watchdogs" are asking questions about why the business process exists and what exactly is their value to our company. From that angle, any sane person would have the same thoughts cross their mind. That is why it is paramount for the audit team to explain the questioning approach and recognize early in the audit phase definition that the business partner does not quite understand why these specific questions are being asked. Stress that the internal audit department is a partner to the business units within the company and not a police officer. Our role in internal audit is to work with the business teams to validate their established processes or jointly identify opportunities for improvement.

When the business objectives discussion begins and the auditor starts off with the objective identification question, the business partner tries to develop an answer to validate the importance of his unit in the company, which usually complicates or masks the true business process objectives. Try this alternative approach. The auditor facilitating the meeting must refocus the business partner on the business processes in an effort to identify the business objectives. The auditor needs to always keep in mind that during any business partner meeting, the goal is to alter the meeting environment from an "audit interview" to a discussion about the business with the process expert. This type of switch in tone often results in the business partner dropping the unintentional defensive posture for one about the business processes. Remember, the ultimate goal is to turn every audit and business partner meeting into a conversation about the business process – a process that the partner holds near and dear because it is something they built and/or own, and they will be very protective of that. Every business partner loves to discuss their process and how hard their team works. It makes them proud.

As the conversation takes on a renewed vigor regarding the business process specifics, the auditor can get back to identifying the business objectives. Now, assuming you have reviewed the most recent policies and procedures and understand the process basics, ask the business partner, what are the most critical deliverables that your team produces? If there is any confusion or hesitation on the part of the business partner, consider using the business unit department metrics (if they have an internal business process dashboard), as they often track the most critical business unit deliverables. This shifts the focus from the overall department to the key processes that the business partner oversees. As each key deliverable is revealed, follow up with asking who, inside or outside the company, utilizes the information and/or products being provided by the business process team. After the deliverables and customers have been identified and documented, ask the business partner to rank the deliverables from the most critical to the least. This will provide the auditor with a triage of the key deliverables and assist the audit team in summarizing the business objectives to identify the ones to be included in the audit validation testing. Remember, not every single task performed by the business unit will be under review. The audit team is to remain focused on the highest-profile business objectives that will be included in the audit testing program. After all business tasks have been discussed, documented, and ranked, review them and summarize the business objectives for each one. Be aware that multiple tasks are usually tied to the same objective. Once the objective matching is done, provide the final listing to the business partner for validation. After the validation is received, the audit team can be confident in the planning phase moving forward and identifying what specific testing will need to be done to complete the audit. Even though this step in the audit planning phase takes additional time, the business process details and planning direction will be invaluable and will ultimately save time in the overall audit budget.

As previously mentioned, the planning phase of the audit tends to be over-complicated by many internal audit departments. The reason is that there is too much time wasted on getting into every facet of a business unit when the key is to focus on the most critical process steps. Many audit teams mistakenly focus their planning time on trying to identify risks without understanding the business and its corresponding objectives. Not starting the planning phase of an audit with the documentation of the business objectives makes the planning of an audit so much more complex and confusing than it needs to be. The business objectives provide the indicators to the auditors of where the bulk of their validation efforts during the testing phase should be focused. Additionally, the business objectives also make the risk and control identification process so much easier. Usually when the auditor meets with the business process owner regarding business risks, the business partner is very guarded in the discussion, making the risk identification process so challenging. No business partner wants to discuss the risks in their process because they recognize that each risk will need a corresponding action, also known as additional work for the business team. Now, do not forget in a remote audit, this conversation is being held over the phone or videoconference, which makes it all the more difficult. If the audit team thought getting the process risk detail was challenging in a face-to-face meeting, wait until you experience it in the remote environment. All communications in the remote environment require so much more work and attention to detail. The best technique for addressing this challenging situation is by utilizing the identified business objectives to facilitate the risk discussion.

BUSINESS PROCESS RISKS

At the moment the audit team confirms the business objectives, the natural progression in the ORC model is to move to the business process risk associated with the documented objectives. This is part of the conversation with the business partner, especially on a remote engagement, where they get a little bit distant and their memory seems to be not as sharp as it was in the beginning of the interview. This is due to the fact that no one wants to discuss the risk associated with any of the business processes and the business partner almost always states that process risks are limited and there are no significant delays in their process.

The key to identifying risks is for the auditor never to use the work *risk* itself in any conversation with the business partner. That word strikes uncertainty into the discussion, so leave it out. The most effective audit teams recognize in this phase of planning that identifying process risk is not enough and usually the risks are documented in general terms and not in a detailed perspective linked to the business objectives.

Using general risk terms is not the purpose of the ORC model. In this model, process risks are replaced with *true process risk*. The difference between the two risk types is that process risks are too generic and most often global across the company. When discussing process risks, the auditor begins by asking the business partner what risks their team faces or, the most popular risk inquiry, what keeps you up at night. While these may sound like appropriate questions, they are too broad. Many business partner responses look at these questions from a company perspective and begin listing off global risks like competition, the market, regulations, turnover, etc. One additional common mistake, often made by auditors during any risk identification discussion, is when the auditor asks the business partner about risks to their process and they quickly respond, "losing money." Unfortunately, when the auditor writes that down as a risk, it is wrong. Both the business partner and the auditor are mistakenly labeling "losing money" as a risk when it is not. The business unit losing money is an impact or an outcome, not a risk. Think about it like this: A process risk is realized, and it costs the company money. So, in fact since the risk was realized, it resulted in a loss of money. Losing money is not a risk in itself; losing money is the result of the risk happening in the first place. Even though the other risks noted may be risks to the company, they are not the true process risks needed to effectively utilize the ORC model. True process risks are current business process focused and applied in the identification of the corresponding controls and applicable audit validation testing.

To focus the business partner on the true process risk identification step, tell them that the audit team would like to review the business objectives and discuss how the team completes the corresponding tasks required to achieve their goals. By utilizing the confirmed business objectives to drive the true process risk discussion, the meeting keeps a positive tone and remains concentrated on the business process and detailed tasks. Remember, do *not* use the term *risk*. Instead replace the word *risk* with *barrier, obstacle, hurdle,* or *challenge.* These terms will be combined with the business objective to quickly and directly identify the true process risks that the business faces. Additionally, do not try and combine multiple objectives in one question, because it tends to confuse the business partner and the process details. The way to phase the question is to ask the business partner, one objective at a time, "Let us start with the first objective. Can you describe anything that would prevent your team from completing this objective timely and in the most effective and efficient manner? Tell me any barriers, obstacles, hurdles, or challenges that would impact your team from completing their assigned tasks."

The true process risks are evident in the business unit's key deliverables and what it takes to make them happen in every single transaction that they process every single day. Any distraction or bump in the road in that execution represents a true process risk because it impedes the business unit personnel's ability to complete their job according to the required department guidelines. When an auditor avoids using audit-specific words like *risk* in their discussions with the business partners, the interview turns into a conversation between two people who work at the same company. There is no longer the negative atmosphere of an audit interview or interrogation (as seen sometimes by the business partner), but a productive business operations discussion to jointly identify processing challenges. By making some minor adjustments in the approach to the risk interview, the auditor has earned valuable relationship points from the business partner's perspective through the facilitation of the meeting. And without even realizing it, the business partner has shared critical true process risks that impact their day-to-day operations. This newly discovered risk information can now be incorporated and also used to facilitate the next step in the ORC method, which is the identification and documentation of the current controls in place designed to achieve the stated business objectives.

Recognize this step in the ORC model is to explain how to identify true process risks with the business process and does not detail the risk measurement steps related to likelihood and significance, which must be completed on every audit for all identified and confirmed risks. The one point to stress before moving on to the control part of the model is that while every risk is to be measured and scored for likelihood and significance, these two scores are totally independent of one another. Meaning a score for likelihood has no impact at all on the score for significance. As an example, a risk could have an extremely low likelihood of occurring but, if it did, the significance of the risk being realized could be catastrophic to the business operations. Keep that in mind any time you are involved in a discussion regarding process risk.

 BUSINESS PROCESS CONTROLS

The final step in the ORC model is to accurately document the current control environment in the business process engagement. One critical aspect of the control documentation, performed during the planning phase, is to ensure the accuracy of the identified controls and verify they are the controls that are actually being performed in the business unit and not the controls the auditor would expect to see in a perfectly controlled business operation. There are instances where some internal audit departments include future controls and list control recommendations into the planning documents. Believe it or not, this is a more frequent occurrence than one may think. In order for the ORC model to work effectively, the documentation of controls must accurately represent the current business processing environment because those current controls will be the ones that the audit testing plan will be examining throughout the fieldwork phase of the audit. The accuracy of the current control listing is the foundation that dictates the focus and precision of the controls to be tested. If the control documentation in the planning phase is not current and accurate, the value and actionability of the testing results will be significantly decreased. This will directly impact the strength of the auditor and business partner relationship, as well as the internal audit department's reputation across the company. Remember, the ORC model requires all business process information accurately represents the current processing environment and drives the internal audit testing focus on the key business steps that are driving the business unit objectives.

The most effective method to documenting the current control environment is to utilize the previously identified true process risks to facilitate the control discussion with the business partner. Again, the best technique to keeping the business partner engaged and forthright during this discussion is to avoid using audit-specific technical terms. When speaking about the business process, do not use the word *control*. This is an audit term, and you can rest assured that business process teams are not sitting in a meeting about their own work discussing how to strengthen their processing environment by adding new or enhanced controls. This type of discussion only surfaces when the internal audit department is facilitating the discussion. Business teams remain diligent on the day-to-day job responsibilities and are always trying to discover ways to make their job easier. In this effort, business teams are not looking to add controls, which they see as requiring additional work, but identify process efficiencies, also known as shortcuts, to do their job faster. Auditors must be strategic in the control discussion and keep the process personnel focused on the business objectives. As the ORC method proceeds forward, the auditor will utilize the already identified true process risks to complete the model requirements. In a measured approach, examine each true process risk individually to gain an understanding of the status of the current control environment. Ask the business partner, for a particular barrier, hurdle, obstacle, or challenge in their business process, how they ensure that barrier, etc., does not happen. And continue the conversation by asking, in the rare instance that the barrier is recognized, whether their process notifies them of the deviation from the processing standard in a timely manner. The auditor can then naturally follow that question up with clarification of how the process identifies the deviation as well as what steps are taken to address it and eliminate it from being repeated in the future. It is important to note, with this follow-up question regarding remediation of a recognized control failure, that the auditor will need to press the business partner for the specific steps that adequately address the control breakdown to remediation. Without the detailed remediation steps, it will not be possible for the auditor to effectively test the scenario during the fieldwork phase of the audit and determine the effectiveness and efficiency of the business process. Additionally, all effective business processes must contain complete, accurate, and timely reporting of their corresponding process steps. This reporting should contain all processing details surrounding the activities executed by the business team, including, but not limited to, activity date, processor name, approver name (if required), transaction details, volumes, number of deviations from the processing standard, and the time frames from transaction start to completion. These specific process details assist the auditor in identifying the most critical process transactions and directing the focus of the audit testing to be performed during the fieldwork phase.

During the entire control-focused discussion, at no time did the auditor ask what controls are in place to safeguard the process from true process risks interfering with the achievement of the objectives. Instead, the auditor maintains the discussion of the business process details regarding potential process barriers (risks) and validation that the process delivers the intended outcome on a consistent basis. The simple, but effective, auditor discussion technique regarding risks and controls has proven to be incredibly successful. As the planning phase of the audit moves forward, additional business partner interactions will occur, and it is critical to build an open and trusting relationship with a strong foundation early on in the process. Business partners will view the audit team with a more positive perspective when business personnel observe the auditors focusing on learning the business process and trying to build their business knowledge instead of focusing on identifying exceptions in the business operations before the audit testing even begins.

COMPLETING THE AUDIT PLANNING

As the audit planning process turns the corner with the implementation and execution of the ORC model, the audit planning is still not complete. After completing the ORC requirements, it is time to close the planning loop with two additional steps. These steps are identifying the target areas to be tested and developing the corresponding test program to validate that the business process steps are being executed with established policies and procedures as well as compliance with existing regulations. To identify the target areas, the auditor will review the true process risks identified and select those risks that present the biggest barriers to completing the confirmed business risks. These target areas are usually triaged with consideration that includes, but is not limited to, volumes, dollars, location, process frequency, required rework, exception processing, and transaction complexity. The target areas to be reviewed are focused on the largest risks, which have been obtained from the business process owner, and represent the key transactions supporting the business objectives. Once the target areas have been identified, audit objectives will be developed to explain the purpose of the audit testing to be performed. The last step in the planning process will be to create the detailed audit test steps required to conclude on the accuracy, completeness, and compliance of the business process activity. The audit steps must contain sufficient detail so that the audit team is capable of understanding the requirements for successful execution.

The one concept to remember when developing audit test steps is that almost every audit, remote or otherwise, has internal audit team members participating in the fieldwork phase but had zero exposure to all of the planning activities that took place prior to the testing being executed. Even though all auditors on the engagement should be reviewing the planning documentation, this review of the planning information will not provide the same level of process knowledge and details shared with the auditors who completed the ORC model. The bottom line is to validate that the audit program steps could be given to any auditor and they would be able to understand the test objective and execute the associated steps with little or no clarification.

CHAPTER SIX

Audit Fieldwork

W HEN CONSIDERING THE THREE main phases of an internal audit, the fieldwork phase may not initially appear as critical as the other two, but auditors must remember it is the phase that is created from the audit plan and provides the supporting information for the report. So, while it is between the planning and reporting phases, it is just as critical and requires focus upon execution from understanding the audit tasks presented through the testing to the evaluation of performance. Remember that internal audit is a profession where the workpaper documentation is the lone source of evidence compiled by the audit engagement team to support the conclusions made regarding the business area being reviewed. This audit evidence is created exclusively from the fieldwork testing performed. All audit teams must recognize the importance of their workpapers and be diligent in the creation, completion, review, approval, and adherence to the internal audit methodology requirements and industry standards. No matter how much marketing the audit team performs, audit departments still carry a reputation of rushing to judgment or nitpicking business process tasks, both due to a lack of business process knowledge. Therefore, it is critical for internal audit departments to ensure the audit evidence is obtained through the precision execution of their audit methodology. This precision includes business and audit objective understanding, testing timeline adherence, satisfactory performance of business control recognition, potential control deviation identification, supporting documentation compilation, and workpaper standard compliance. The proper execution and internal audit policy adherence are going to rely on diligent oversight throughout the fieldwork phase. Auditors responsible for workpaper compliance must possess a detailed understanding of not only the internal audit methodology but also the workpaper and industry standards. Additionally, all workpaper reviewers must ensure that the audit workpapers can stand on their own and contain the required workpaper components.

As previously stated, most (if not all) internal audit teams do not have the luxury and staff size to allow each auditor assigned to an engagement to participate in the planning phase of an audit. The most common approach has a lead or in-charge auditor perform the audit planning requirements before the remainder of the audit team comes on board to complete the audit fieldwork phase. While that may seem like the most efficient use of resources, sometimes it is not as effective as internal audit management teams may think. If an audit department does use the lead auditor to plan an audit before bringing on the team to perform testing, the lead auditor must communicate and verify that all auditors participating on the engagement have a clear understanding and knowledge of both the business and corresponding audit objectives. The reason this is so crucial to the success of the audit is that it is not possible to effectively review a business process when the auditors have no knowledge of what it is that the business team is trying to accomplish. How could any business partner or auditor believe the audit results are going to provide a benefit to the business operational process if they do not really understand what the business operation entails or what it is trying to accomplish on a daily basis? When any auditor or audit team is provided the testing program, they need to comprehend the direct correlation between the audit steps to be performed and the specific business objective used as the source to create the audit program. One of the most significant challenges facing auditors, especially on these remote assignments, is the fact that the program is almost unanimously executed with question or direction. Performing audit steps remotely often does not lend itself to a highly communicative environment both within the audit team and especially with the client. So if the audit team is not diligent in reviewing the planning documentation and discussing the testing with the audit team, it is almost certain that the testing, though not tied to any of the current business objectives, will be completed with question. And while additional testing of less significant controls does not hurt the audit team in the end, it does not help contribute to the value of the audit results, since the ancillary controls tested have no real impact on the business objectives. And all auditors can be certain, if the test results have no direct impact on the critical tasks being performed by the operational business team, it will have zero value to the business partner and ultimately impact the strength of the audit and business partner relationship. Whether the audit team is executing remotely or onsite, the communication within the audit team regarding the objectives (business and audit) must be identified and emphasized to everyone on the audit team. Remember, these objectives should have already been discussed and approved by the internal audit management team to ensure the work is linked to the annual and individual audit risk assessments that have already been completed.

Having participated on previous audits, auditors know that it is much easier to complete an audit test when they are aware and understand why the testing is performed and what it is designed to validate. Why the testing is being performed should be articulated and documented in the audit program, specifically stating how and why this testing is going to provide sufficient audit evidence to confirm the business operational personnel are completing their day-to-day assigned responsibilities in accordance with company policy. This detailed audit objective introduces the audit steps listed in the program, provides valuable business unit knowledge background, and is a useful instructional guide, especially during a remote audit. The more information that the audit lead can provide to the rest of the audit engagement team, the more effective and efficient the auditors will be in executing the steps. This is another illustration of the foundational component of having strong internal communications within the audit team, which provides for strong audit engagement performance. Too often in both remote and onsite audits, the audit team becomes so focused (or obsessed) with completing the program steps that it forgets how important understanding the reason (audit objective) for testing ties directly to the business process objective. In development, the audit objective is actually built utilizing the business objective, so it is obvious how valuable this information would be to the audit team. Additionally, it becomes increasingly challenging for the auditor to complete the testing and develop the test workpapers when the audit objective is not clearly evident. As will be discussed later in this chapter, the specific audit objectives are required as part of the critical components in the workpapers. The overall message reinforcing the audit objective understanding will be required in the internal audit methodology, which should state that the audit objective be included and documenting for all parts of an audit program. Having the program spell out the audit objective is wonderful, but an audit program, when executed without business objective understanding, not only takes additional time to complete but also can produce uncertain results due to a lack of business objective knowledge that clearly explains a satisfactory outcome.

The value of the business and audit objectives knowledge is significant, but believe it or not, the creation of a feasible and focused audit objective is even more important. Too often, internal audit departments want to create audit objectives that are very large and encompass multiple layers of business activities without considering the downstream impacts this type of audit objective will have on the team attempting to understand and complete the testing. There is always a feeling of pressure on internal audit departments to try and prove their value to the company, as most business units do not believe or understand the role internal audit plays since they do not generate any revenue like the business processes. While audit departments may not contribute directly to the company's bottom line, audit provides the safeguarding of assets, the validation of business processes, and recommendations for improvements. The audit objectives, testing, and recommendations allow business unit operations to continue to provide revenue to the company. Internal audit should be viewed as a true asset to business unit management. The value that audit provides to their business partners is derived from understanding the business objectives and creating targeted validation testing. Always remember, the business objectives provide process knowledge and direction for the internal audit testing focus and the audit objectives provide an explanation for the program steps required to verify the business process's operational efficiency, effectiveness, accuracy, and compliance.

 FIELDWORK COMMUNICATION

It is important to note that even when the business and audit objectives are communicated and understood, there is another foundational component to precision execution. When remembering and considering that only a few auditors within an engagement team may have participated in the planning phase, it is a requirement to tell the audit program execution team what a satisfactory or acceptable outcome looks like for each test. Many times, the determination of a positive audit test outcome is left up to the individual auditor performing the test. While it is understandable to assume the entire audit team can execute an audit program step, it is unreasonable to assume that the test results will produce an outcome that is consistent with the auditor who created the audit program due to a lack of business process knowledge. Therefore, every time a program is provided to an auditor to complete, the audit lead or in-charge should provide guidance and, where applicable, an example of a satisfactory test outcome. This type of pretesting communication will ensure the audit program step is being executed in accordance with the audit objective and deliver valuable, useful results to the business partner. Just like the previously mentioned concept of every process delivers an outcome that may not be the intended outcome, the audit testing phase is in the exact same predicament. Audit testing, especially during remote audits, not only requires precision execution of the audit program, but also the realization that testing will produce results. And while that statement sounds logical, the tester must ensure the test results are being measured against the expected results and not just a completion of a business process task. Ensure all the auditors on the engagement understand, can identify, and document the expected satisfactory testing outcome. This will reduce audit review comments, rework, and unnecessary wasted budget time.

When considering and creating time budgets, it should be noted that the budget is an estimate of the amount of time required to complete each audit program step. The most underrated component of the assigned budget for an audit test is the fact that the auditor who created the budget time is, hopefully, the same person who performed the planning and created the corresponding test steps for this particular part of the audit. This usually results in a more accurate estimate. However, there are many instances where the person who created the initial budget is not the same individual who will be performing the testing. It is critical to ensure the auditor performing the test review the program, understand the budget, and provide immediate notice as soon as it becomes apparent that the assigned budget is not realistic or feasible to execute the audit program steps as designed. While it is not anyone's fault that the budget is inaccurate, this type of situation is the result of the planner assigning a budget that includes an assumption that each sample item will be identical in process requirements and execution and that all supporting documentation will be readily accessible and provided by the business partner upon audit notification. Now, any auditor who has participated in fieldwork knows that this type of assumption is unreasonable. The most effective way to set a realistic budget is to execute one sample item from each test and determine the level of difficulty associated with the business documentation availability, process step execution, and potential frequency of the need for additional work. With those characteristics in mind, the auditor setting the initial budget can be more accurate. However, no matter what level of planning and preparation occurs during the budget setting process, all internal auditors must recognize the budget is an estimate based on assumption from the business process information obtained and learned at this point in time. The key to maintaining budget accuracy is to communicate internally as a team as the fieldwork phase progresses and understand that a remote engagement is going to require even more scrutiny of the initial budget and the tracking of progress as the audit continues.

FIELDWORK RESPONSIBILITIES

To this point when discussing the precision execution of audit work, the auditors should be focusing on their diligence when preparing for the fieldwork phase of an audit. To reiterate, upon completion of the audit planning phase and the fieldwork phase kickoff, it begins with the assignment of audit program steps. The moment testing has been received, the auditor should read and confirm the understanding of the testing objective and be able to associate it directly to the corresponding business objective. Next, a review of the individual audit program steps is completed and any outstanding or clarifying questions are addressed prior to the start of testing. After that review is completed, the auditor can then request the necessary business documentation and data needed to complete the testing, while also confirming with the audit team what acceptable performance of business compliance will be along with the level of supporting documentation to evidence same. Once those preliminary preparation steps have been completed and the business information received, the testing can proceed. During the testing, there may be a need for additional business documentation, discussion, or explanation, and the auditor must determine the most effective method to obtain that information. With a remote review, the auditor will most likely want to utilize the business contact or audit liaison to present the questions or requests.

As with any follow-up, it is critical that the auditor be organized and have the specific details of what is needed to complete the testing. Also, do not forget to request the delivery date of the information and communicate to the business partner that the audit testing cannot be completed without the delivery of the outstanding information. A target date commitment from the business partner and a diligent follow-up from the audit team help expedite the delivery process. The auditor performing the testing must keep detailed records of what was requested, when it was requested, and the proposed target date. This active tracking of any documentation needed to complete the fieldwork is mandatory to avoid delays in finishing the audit testing.

As the audit testing proceeds, precision execution requires the identification of any deviations from the confirmed business proceed standard. Remember, all potential exceptions must be documented and then presented to the business partner or liaison, if it is a remote audit, for confirmation. To ensure time from the audit or business team is not being wasted, a reasonableness review can be applied to the completed audit testing to determine if the potential exceptions require confirmation. A reasonableness review is simple and requires auditors to take a step back, consider the testing objective and business requirements, and ask themselves, if this information were presented to an individual with zero knowledge of the business processing requirements, would they say the results of the testing look reasonable? Would there be any outstanding questions? Would there be any need for additional information or documentation? Or would the information available be sufficient to draw the same conclusion as the auditor did performing the test? If a reasonable person would not be able to come to the same conclusion without additional information or evidence, then there must be an auditor and business partner discussion to validate the exception details. There is no sense or value to concluding on audit testing without verifying the noted exceptions are not true deviations from the standard. And that exception validation can only come from someone in the business processing unit regardless of the amount of time, experience, or knowledge the auditor performing the testing has within the business area under review or company tenure.

 ## WORKPAPER REQUIREMENTS

It is important to note that there are industry suggestions for best practices when it comes to audit evidence. Those workpaper objectives will be discussed since they should be associated and documented in the internal audit methodology documentation requirements. The methodology workpaper requirements should state that the primary objective of the audit workpapers is to document the planning, fieldwork, and reporting phases of the audit engagement. These workpapers provide written support for all work performed and help to coordinate all phases of an audit in a logical order. The arrangement of these documents assists in the review of completed audit work for an internal quality review for compliance with the methodology and also any external quality assessment that may be performed at the request of management. Additionally, the workpapers constitute a documented record of the audit objectives, scope of the audit, and review results. This logical organization of workpapers also provides direction in developing the audit draft and final report. If the workpapers are completed correctly, they will contain sufficient evidence to support the exceptions noted in the final report as well as the overall rating, if your methodology requires one. For example, the fieldwork workpapers, which include the detailed status memo, contain the exception communication information, which can be directly incorporated, into the draft and final reports. Another added benefit to having formal workpaper standards in the audit methodology is that the audit documentation can provide evidence for external auditors to rely on during their annual company assessment. The diligence and dedication to the audit workpaper standards will ensure external reviews along with reliance work and internal quality exams are able to be completed with no additional work. However, just like any other policy and procedure document, the internal audit documentation requirements must be updated to reflect the most recent audit process requirements. Therefore, if the audit methodology for any one of the three phases changes or if another template is added or removed from the process, the workpaper documentation requirements must be updated.

There is a realization sweeping throughout internal audit departments around the world that audit evidence and the execution of same is going to be scrutinized more closely than ever before. With the implementation of remote audits, the quality, dedication to methodology compliance, documentation, and conclusions are expected to evidence precision execution from start to finish. To ensure your audit workpapers can meet or exceed this increased focused on excellence, verify all of the audit workpapers (planning, fieldwork, and reporting) contain the baseline components to guarantee the expectation of proper and reliable evidence. The Beyond Audit recommended workpaper components are listed in Table 6.1 with a brief explanation of each to follow. It should be noted that these are the recommended baseline (minimum) work-paper components. There will be methodologies that may require additional components in their workpaper requirements.

BEYOND AUDIT – BASELINE WORKPAPER COMPONENTS

Table 6.1 lists the Beyond Audit baseline workpaper components.

TABLE 6.1 Baseline Workpaper Components

Purpose	Signoffs
Source	Tickmark legend
Scope	Exceptions noted
References	Conclusion

Purpose

Purpose represents the foundational information for every single workpaper in your audit database or audit file folder. It represents the objective or reason this workpaper is being included in the file folder. It must explain what the workpaper represents and how it links directly to one of the audit testing objectives. There is a specific reason this particular workpaper was included, and the purpose is the placeholder for this type of information. Without a documented purpose on the workpaper, it will be impossible for another auditor, internal or external, to understand why it is important to the overall engagement or why the review should even be spending time to examine the details of the completed work. Ensure that the purpose stands alone and provides a clear explanation for inclusion. For fieldwork testing, include the specific test step which the workpaper supports in the purpose field. Remember, the purpose statement does not have to be too wordy in length but should effectively communicate what is included and the work that was to be done.

Source

Source is one of the more critical fields on a workpaper. While it may seem literal in its definition, which it is, source represents the foundation for the work that was performed. Throughout a remote audit engagement, the source of the information being obtained from the business partner must always be validated as pure. What *pure* means is that the documentation or data being tested has to represent the best source for information accuracy and completeness. Any time during an audit, remote or otherwise, when a potential deviation is identified, the business partner is going to try and discount or discredit the information. And while the business partner cannot dispute the process (because they themselves described it to you), they will try and argue that the audit team did not have the most up to date or accurate information in their testing. The business partner will refute that the source of the testing information was not pure. So, before any audit work has begun, verify that the testing data is the best source of data available.

The audit team can confirm the source selection by asking, "Is there any other place on the planet in a written or automated format" that would better represent the daily operations for the time period being tested? Once the source confirmation is received, the audit team knows the source is pure and can be documented in the workpaper. The source component of the workpaper provides the details of where the data originated, the specific department and business title of the provider, as well as any automated system names. This not only ensures the source component can stand on its own but also provides guidance for a future review to understand where the information or data was obtained.

Scope

Scope provides the parameters, date ranges, and transaction types of the testing being documented in the workpaper. One of the common mistakes internal audit teams make is that the scope statement is documented in too broad a manner. For example, a scope statement may say "all activity since the last audit." Now, anyone who has ever been in audit knows that this scope statement is unreasonable and is not an effective scope statement.

In the current audit environment, most groups are lucky to get to the highest risk areas on an annual basis, with some high-risk-rated areas not being audited for up to two years. The rest of their audit plan is on a two- to five-year audit cycle. With that said, it is impossible to consider a scope that would include all activity for the previous year or two or even more. Furthermore, it serves no benefit to the business partner to examine all activity in their business process, especially when it has been stated that audit departments want to focus on the most critical process transaction that supports the achievement of the business objectives. That does not include all activity, as there are business tasks that are support transactions but have zero impact on the business objectives. The reason some audit departments document such a broad scope of audit work is that it allows the audit department to examine every single morsel of evidence in the entire business operation – not that any audit team would have the time or resources to accomplish such a lofty goal.

In the end, having a scope that is so broad with no specific true process risk detail does not benefit the audit engagement or business unit management. The scope component should spell out the specific start and end dates of the testing detail, any testing parameter restrictions, and the corresponding transaction types being reviewed. In addition, one of the most overlooked details in the scope component is to detail any exclusions that might apply to the testing parameters. For example, the workpaper scope states the audit team is reviewing the account reconciliation process for the fourth quarter of the previous year. However, if there are any aspects of the account reconciliation that are not going to be tested (i.e., journal entry matchoffs, approvals, or timeliness), the scope statement must detail the testing exclusions so that there is no confusion as to the specific account reconciliation attributes verified during the testing. Do not forget to spell out any attribute that is not included in the testing. No internal audit department wants to portray a business process as adequate or inadequate unless all aspects of the process were examined. The scope component must accurately reflect the detailed testing that was performed.

References

The *references* component of the workpapers is critical because it not only organizes the natural progression of the work but also provides the specific workpaper location of the testing to match the workpaper reference in the program. When done properly, workpaper references provide an easy to follow direction of the work performed and allows links within multiple workpapers to support complex testing to document and portray a complete picture of the required testing to adequately validate the business process being reviewed. The remaining workpaper tip when it comes to referencing is to verify that any time multiple workpapers are utilized to document testing, each workpaper referenced link is done in a circular manner. This will ensure that there are not one-sided workpaper references. For example, there cannot be a workpaper reference on workpaper A-1 stating testing is continued on A-2; then when A-2 is reviewed, there is no reference stating this workpaper is a continuation of the work completed on A-1. A one-sided workpaper reference means the A-2 workpaper is missing an A-1 workpaper reference. Remember to be diligent in all workpaper references, even when it is a reference on the same workpaper.

Signoffs

While the signoff component may seem to be a formality, it represents two distinct audit team members being involved in the development and completion of the workpaper. This involvement in workpaper creation represents accountability and ownership of the work that has been documented. Internal audit department personnel must understand the responsibility of workpaper ownership and the meaning behind it. The signoff from the auditor who developed the workpaper signifies that the work was completed utilizing the best source of available information, in accordance with the current audit methodology requirements, and addressed all required audit program steps to validate the business processing standards. The signoff from the reviewing auditor indicates an independent validation and approval that all required program steps were executed as designed, and the sufficient amount of evidence was received (and included) to support the conclusion. These required signoff components provide an indication of ownership, along with the commitment to quality and diligence in complying with the internal audit department's workpaper standards.

Tickmarks

The more each different workpaper component is revealed and discussed, the more evident the value of each component becomes. This statement could not be more accurate as the next component, the *tickmark* legend, is described. The tickmark legend represents and provides a detailed explanation of every mark utilized on the workpaper for the corresponding testing that was performed. Regardless of the type, complexity, technology, frequency, volume, or dollar amount of the testing being performed, each validation and verification included in the testing must be listed in the tickmark legend. This legend provides a description of the outcome of the attribute tested. Any aspect of the audit test that required confirmation of business process compliance will have a corresponding tickmark to document the outcome. This tickmark legend explains the result of the specific attribute included in the testing. Additionally, any symbol used and documented on the workpaper must be included in the tickmark legend. There cannot be any "ghost" symbols on a workpaper because that will lead to additional, unnecessary questions, not to mention an indication of a lack of auditor attention to detail. A "ghost" symbol means there is no matching symbol in the tickmark legend to explain the symbol evidenced in the workpaper. There can also be a "ghost" symbol that is listed in the tickmark legend but was never utilized in the testing on the workpaper. This is usually the result of a workpaper being rolled forward with no validation of the tickmarks needed and used to complete the current year's audit testing.

Testing Exceptions and Conclusion

The final two baseline workpaper components, *testing exceptions* and *conclusion*, go hand in hand from both a value and importance perspective in internal audit's workpapers. However, it should be noted that while every workpaper will have a conclusion, not every workpaper will have exceptions. Beginning with the exception component, this is the documented condition statement that provides the detailed explanation of a deviation of the business processing standard. The exception component must effectively describe the discrepancy identified during the testing, along with the reference of the supporting documentation. The exception must also be able to stand alone and not be combined with any other noted exceptions, unless it is the exact same situation as the originally noted deviation. One clarification note regarding the exception component is that this component is individual in nature and applies to a specific testing attribute.

The conclusion component documents the results from an overall perspective of all the testing that was completed and documented on the workpaper. In the final assessment of audit testing, the workpaper conclusion will consider the number and nature of any business process standard deviations noted and their corresponding impact to the achievement of the business unit objective in the overall assessment of control effectiveness. Both the exception and conclusion component provide audit validation result details based on the documented evidence in the workpaper. While they both are results-based components, keep in mind that the conclusion represents a summary of all of the testing, whether positive or negative, including a data-based decision on the effectiveness of the current control environment surrounding the business process under review while the exception is singular. Additionally, workpapers may contain multiple exception components, depending on the number of identified deviations, but there will only be one conclusion to summarize all of the work performed.

SUFFICIENT EVIDENCE

One of the most common questions raised when discussing precision execution and documentation is related to how much information is enough. While this is a legitimate question, the unfortunate response is that there is no universal answer. The best way to address the "enough information" question is to apply the reasonable test described earlier. In considering if enough evidence is included in the workpaper, think about whether this workpaper, if removed from all the other completed work, could stand on its own without any additional explanation.

Another qualifying question regarding completeness of the documentation would be, could another internal auditor with no prior business process knowledge not only understand and be able to follow the executed work, but also reach the same documented conclusion? If the answer to that question is yes, then the auditor has a workpaper that is well documented and contains enough evidence to support the conclusion. From a practical standpoint, the review for sufficient supporting documentation should always be based on there being enough documented evidence for any person to be able to pick up the workpaper, understand the testing completed, follow the information, and agree with the conclusion.

For additional assistance with effective documentation to validate precision execution of audit work, there are industry standards that indicate four characteristics of effective documented evidence: sufficient, relevant, reliable, and useful. Even though these are technical audit definitions, they provide clarification to ensure the information being compiled during fieldwork execution can effectively sustain any scrutiny:

1. *The sufficient characteristic relates to the validity of information.* Is it factual? It should provide enough evidence to support the conclusion.
2. *The reliable characteristic is linked to the source of information being used in the testing.* It should be the most current representation of the business data available to validate the business process controls. This is the same concept as ensuring the source of the data used is pure, as previously discussed.
3. *Relevant relates to the documentation compiled and ensuring it directly links to the completed audit work and recommendations.* Recommendations, which will be discussed in Chapter 7, must provide a benefit to the business partner and be relevant to the achievement of the business objectives.
4. *In this scenario,* useful *is a literal definition meaning that the information included in the audit workpaper helps the company achieve its goals/objectives.* If the audit planning was accurate and the fieldwork testing focused on the most critical true process risks, auditors can be confident that the corresponding workpapers are useful to the business partners.

The only other consideration regarding workpaper documentation and completeness to discuss is the request and receipt of the business process documentation and data required to complete the testing. The key to getting this crucial information, especially during a remote audit engagement, is to ensure the auditor has compiled a complete request, listing all data needed for the applicable testing, arranged in a logical order, including any specific report names along with the originating system name. This type of organized request will help to ensure there is no confusion as to what is required and will make any necessary follow-up direct and efficient. Always include a target date for delivery along with a confirmation of receipt and agreement from the business partner. This level of accountability is necessary on remote audits due to the fact that most of the requests are being delivered via email. Remember to be direct in the request and diligent in the follow-up until all requested data is received.

WORKPAPER SELF-REVIEW AND KEYS

As the discussion on precision execution and workpaper documentation ends, there is another critical step regarding workpapers for the auditor responsible for performing the testing and compiling the documentation. The remaining responsibility for the auditor is to perform a self-review of their work to ensure the eight foundational workpaper components are not only evident but also complete. That includes verification that the documented evidence is sufficient to support the conclusion; clear, concise organization of the testing approach and results; and the proper attention to detail with all tickmarks utilized to execute the testing. This self-review is mandatory, and the auditor must be diligent in compliance with this methodology requirement before forwarding the completed audit test workpapers to their supervisor for review and approval.

Before moving on to the next chapter on partnering for results, we are going to touch on the Beyond Audit listing of 10 keys for auditors to help them manage their audit fieldwork followed by a brief explanation of each. These keys will provide useful guidance to any auditor, at any level, in all industries regardless if they are participating on a remote or in-person audit engagement. Keep these keys in mind throughout the fieldwork phase, whether you are the fieldworker yourself or directing auditors on a project.

 BEYOND AUDIT – TOP 10 KEYS TO MANAGING FIELDWORK

Every audit engagement provides an opportunity for the internal audit team to succeed in their efforts to build their business process knowledge, gain a more intimate understanding of the audit methodology, foster an interactive team environment, continue to develop their relationship skills, and provide value to their business partner through targeted recommendations. Table 6.2 provides the top 10 keys to managing fieldwork.

TABLE 6.2   Keys to Managing Fieldwork

1. Know the assignment objectives.	6. Communicate constantly.
2. Know your customer.	7. Obtain required documentation.
3. Set realistic expectations.	8. Manage project risks.
4. Be a leader.	9. Verify deliverables and conclusions.
5. Understand documentation requirements.	10. Evaluate fieldwork execution.

1. Know the Assigned Objectives

At the learning foundation of all of those skills is the word *objective*. As previously discussed, to succeed with any established goal, it is critical that the objective or purpose must be clear. Success for every internal auditor in the fieldwork phase is to provide focused results to their business partner on the most critical business steps. This value is communicated via audit recommendations which have been developed from the audit work performed coupled with a business process representative validating the initial process deviations.

However, no matter how much fieldwork testing is completed or how many business process personnel agree with the results, the business partner will not recognize the value unless it directly impacts them achieving their objectives. The simple translation is that every audit recommendation must assist the business process team to achieve their objectives in a more efficient and effective manner or with less rework. The recommendation must result in process improvements and have a direct link to their specific objectives. Without an increase in process efficiencies, the business partner is not going to make a process change just because it may seem like a good idea. The only guaranteed method that ensures the auditor will provide value in their recommendations is to be certain that when the audit fieldwork begins, the responsible auditor has a crystal-clear understanding of not only the specific business objectives for the test but also the audit objective and how it will provide results that will accomplish either a validation of the business process control environment or an identification of opportunities for the business process team to improve their current operations. Having the business process understand the corresponding business objectives empowers the auditor to be recognized as a valuable asset and resource throughout the audit engagement.

2. Know Your Customer

Developing a relationship is one of the critical components for all internal audit team members. The success of audit activities hinges on the strength of the audit and business partner relationship. Understanding your business partner, their process, objectives, and communication style goes a long way in fostering a positive working environment. Obtaining this level of information takes time and resources. Internal auditors who are looking to cultivate a relationship with their business partners to assist in the execution of audit activities should first turn to the existing audit staff, especially the ones with tenure. Any auditor trying to understand a new business partner should reach out to other team members and ask if they have had any experience with this business team and acquire as much background as possible. Any level of insight into the business unit environment will benefit the current audit team as they try to navigate through the current engagement.

In addition, getting to know your customer includes building business process knowledge. The way to a business partner's heart is to show them that the internal audit department is not just about testing samples but is genuinely interested in understanding the business objectives and the processes implemented to achieve those objectives. The business process focus helps break down relationship barriers and provides the business partner an indication that the internal audit department is trying to provide value by understanding what the business is attempting to accomplish on a daily basis. The only way internal audit can provide such guidance is if they learn and understand the business objectives.

The final point of knowing your customer in managing fieldwork is to quickly recognize the business partner's communication style. If the business partner is someone who does not appreciate small talk and focuses just on what is needed to get the job done, the internal audit team must be adequately prepared and organized for every meeting and remain focused on developing the business knowledge as well as the audit engagement requirements. This focus will communicate to the "business only" partner the same sense of urgency in getting the job done. Conversely, if the business partner appears to want to build a relationship with internal audit through an understanding of the engagement auditor's background, then the communication style and approach will have to be adjusted. The new approach will be a little less regimented and formal and include some small chit-chat about previous work experiences or miscellaneous topics. The key to a successful interaction with a business partner is to try and quickly determine what communication type they are and adjust the internal audit approach accordingly. Communicating in the same styles goes a long way in fostering a positive, productive working environment.

3. Set Realistic Expectations

Too often, internal audit teams set goals that are too aggressive and are based on assumptions from a previously executed audit or the thought that the team can accomplish the engagement in an expedient manner. Although these assumptions can provide a guide for completion of audit tasks or the overall project, expectations must be based on the current project, specific engagement objectives, business partner relationship, and the experience of the audit team. The previous audit cannot be used to set the current project's delivery deadlines unless the exact same work is being executed for a consecutive year. And even if the audit is exactly the same as the prior year, the process, the business owner, and the audit team may be different.

Any deviations, process or player related, will result in changes in the target deadlines. To set attainable expectations, consider the current engagement objectives, scope, and associated tasks that must be accomplished. Then verify the internal auditors assigned have the corresponding skillsets to address the needs of the project. Once this information has been attained, achievable target deliverable dates can be set. However, even with the proper planning and setting of realistic expectations, do not let the delivery dates drive the behavior of the audit team. There are too many examples of when auditors, in their effort to make an established deadline, rush through testing, shrink samples, or skip doing a self-review just to make a deadline. When the expected target dates dictate how audit work is being accomplished, it is time to change the process. Auditors must remain focused on achieving the audit testing objectives in the most effective manner and not adjust their approach just to make a deadline.

4. Be a Leader

During any audit project, remote or otherwise, fieldwork is the one audit phase that can get out of control the fastest. That is because auditors love to expand testing, add sample items, and chase potential exceptions; all of these activities require additional time. Being a leader during this phase means the auditor understands the testing objectives and creates and maintains realistic expectations in performance of the work. And while there may be instances that justify an increase in budget time or sample size, being disciplined and understanding the project requirements should be paramount. Also, the key to being a leader has nothing to do with the auditor's title or role on the engagement but relies on them actively participating on the team and completing their assigned tasks. Audit leaders should be at every level and be focused on their assignments, building business knowledge, and helping audit team members work through any challenges. Leaders on any team always are looking to adapt to the team needs and contribute to discussions and solution suggestions when project risks are recognized. And leaders within a team always accept their role and responsibilities on a project and are never afraid to ask a question regarding assigned project tasks.

5. Understand Documentation Requirements

To be an effective internal audit team member, it is critically important that they possess a solid audit methodology understanding along with a detailed understanding of audit workpaper requirements. Earlier, this chapter described the foundation components of a workpaper, and the precision execution of the audit tasks is going to rely on the auditor's ability to apply those requirements to ensure the documentation adequately supports the audit conclusions. Understanding what each component represents is important, but auditors must be able to organize them to properly explain the documented work. Also, the audit methodology will include details instructing the auditors to provide supplemental notes when required to provide insights and additional explanations when appropriate. These added notes or references are not utilized on every workpaper and that is why the audit team must recognize the opportunity and need for clarification. Understanding the audit documentation requirements and how to apply them helps to reduce the need for review notes, additional work, and client interruption while at the same time producing detailed workpapers that fully explain the testing that was completed.

6. Communicate Constantly

Chapter 10 is solely dedicated to communication being the cornerstone of every internal audit department, regardless of team size, industry, physical location, or experience. And while every audit requires a high level of communication, the remote engagements demand it. There is no way to effectively complete a remote engagement unless communication standards and expectations have been set and the audit engagement team is focused on maintaining the highest level of communications throughout the project. Without any opportunity to engage with a business partner in person, auditors must remain diligent on the detailed level and frequency of communications during the remote engagement. From the moment the audit fieldwork phase begins, upfront and constant communication will feed this audit phase and ensure all information requests, clarifying questions, issue review and validation, and audit testing status is at the forefront – on a daily basis if needed. The keys to success throughout this challenging audit phase are to be an active listener and recognize communication gaps, adhere to a regular status update schedule, and keep the business partner "in the know." Keeping the business partner "in the know" means there should be no instances where the business partner has no idea what the current status of the audit is, and that includes work completed, outstanding requests, potential issues, and target date for fieldwork completion. Too often, audit engagement teams are so focused on completing the fieldwork that the communication requirement, which ensures fieldwork success, does not receive the proper attention. Regardless of the type of the audit being conducted, remember how vital consistent communication is for the business partner.

7. Obtain Required Documentation

Effectively managing fieldwork truly hinges on the request and receipt of information, data, and documentation needed to execute the audit program steps. The key is to review the audit program and physically document the information that needs to be obtained from the business partner. Utilizing a physical list ensures no information will be omitted or forgotten, and it can be provided to the business partner as a formal request. Any time a document can be used in place of a call or voicemail, the chances of receiving the requested information increase significantly. The physical document request also helps to track the status of the request as well as actively follow up on outstanding information. Throughout the fieldwork phase, confirm not only the documentation required to complete the audit testing is received timely, but also any additional documentation needed to support noted exceptions or testing conclusions. The workpaper documentation must be complete for all aspects of fieldwork to help validate that the appropriate level of testing was completed.

8. Manage Project Risks

In number 4 on being a leader, it was stated that fieldwork is the audit phase that can get out of control the fastest if it is not carefully monitored. Understanding the fieldwork objectives, establishing and maintaining a realistic budget, anticipating risks, and reevaluating audit engagement priorities are vital to the success of the project. Ongoing management of project risks, which include known and unknown risks, helps to keep scope expansion to a minimum and foster a proactive handling of risks, if and when they surface. While no auditor can plan for unknown risks, their identification becomes timelier when the audit team remains focused on the testing objectives and maintains a high level of communication throughout the audit testing team. Keep in mind that risks represent any barrier, obstacle, hurdle, or challenge that would prevent the audit team from completing the fieldwork objectives. The most common fieldwork objectives include lack of business process documentation, challenging or unavailable business partner, and difficulty understanding the audit program steps or requirements. Be on the lookout for these fieldwork risks and actively communicate them when they surface.

9. Verify Deliverables and Conclusions

The audit fieldwork phase objectives include accurate and timely completion of the audit program steps and developing conclusions on the adequacy of the established business process controls to achieve the applicable business objectives. In order for the audit team to complete these tasks with precision, adequate supporting documentation and data must be obtained from the business partner and be validated. Without the proper support, completion of the audit program and testing conclusions cannot be substantiated. As discussed, the compiled audit evidence is the sole source of information used to support the conclusion upon completion of the fieldwork phase. Furthermore, this fieldwork information will be utilized to draft the audit report along with the corresponding audit recommendations to improve the business process. Remember to maintain ongoing verification of deviations from the business processing standard and conclusions noted to date in an effort to expedite the reporting phase of the audit. The fieldwork deliverables drive the reporting phase and provide the intelligence for audit reports to be written in a clear, concise, and complete format using the data acquired during the fieldwork phase.

10. Evaluate Fieldwork Execution

While the planning phase drives the focus and direction of the audit testing to be completed and the reporting phase delivers the ultimate internal audit product, it is the fieldwork phase that evaluates the current business process control environment and provides the data and facts to be included in the audit report for remediation. With the level of reliance on the fieldwork phase results, it is recommended that audit teams evaluate the effectiveness of the completed audit testing. This validation includes, but is not limited to, business and audit objective linkage, targeted audit program steps to address confirmed true process risks, adequate execution budgets, ongoing monitoring of testing status, and confirmation for all identified deviations from business processing standards. Once this internal review has been completed, any outstanding information or documentation can be obtained and recommendations to the audit approach and methodology can be made.

Regardless of the type of audit being executed, remote or onsite, executing the audit in accordance with the established internal audit methodology is always going to provide the audit team and business partner with the most effective manner in which to determine that the established business process controls are delivering the intended outcome on a consistent basis with the appropriate level of supporting documentation.

7

The Methodology – Partner Results

COMMUNICATING AUDIT RESULTS

Internal audit is a profession where the information, data, work performed, issues presented, recommendations made, and issued reports are going to be challenged regardless of the size of the department, location, or industry. That has and always will be the nature of being in an internal audit department. In Chapter 3, the discussion was focused on marketing the internal audit department as a partner, but no amount of marketing will ever change the necessity for audit reports to be questioned at a detailed level to ensure the authenticity of the information being presented. With this type of constant scrutiny, it is critically important that the results of any audit along with the documentation and data must be available and validated to support the audit testing conclusions. This will be particularly essential during a remote audit due to the lack of face-to-face time with the business partner. When audit results are being delivered remotely, it is a much more challenging discussion. In this chapter, the focus will be on effective partnering of results and communication of validated issues, which includes root cause identification, action plan development, and linking to the corresponding business objectives.

As previously stated, internal audit teams, regardless of size, location, or business, overcomplicate the reporting phase of an audit. If there is a commitment to transparent communication and a focus on the audit and business partner relationship, the reporting phase of an audit should be nothing more than a summary of all of the work and confirmed issues that have been discussed on multiple occasions prior to the issuance of the draft report. And even though a remote audit, to be effective, demands the highest level of commitment regarding communication, it is easy for this requirement to be overlooked during this type of engagement. Since the remote audit does not provide the auditors with opportunities to interact with the business partner on a regular basis, the communication commitment suffers as the audit team focuses on the completion of the fieldwork to get to the reporting phase. Therefore, the audit team on these engagements must be diligent and remain consistent on the frequency and quality of their business partner communications. The introduction of any potential issues with a business partner will only occur after the audit testing results have been validated by a process authority in the business unit. A process authority is a business team member who performs the tasks, where the discrepancy was noted, and validates the authenticity of the results. After validation, the auditor can then present the issue, error, or exception (whatever term your team uses) to the business partner.

UNDERSTANDING THE AUDIT REPORT PHASE

Before diving into the details regarding the discussion of issues with the business partner, the best format to present issues, and verifying the five components, including root cause, in the report, it is important to recognize the critical nature of the reporting phase of an audit. It is always more effective when an auditor is creating an issues summary or audit report to understand the purpose behind the document to help facilitate the development of same. If an auditor does not know why a document is being created or what purpose it actually serves, then it just becomes another template to complete with no real value inside. Therefore, what is the real reason the internal audit department issues the audit report? Is it because the industry standards say that audit results must be communicated? Is it because that is what has always been done?

In order for the business partner to read and recognize the value in an audit report and the detailed issues, the auditor must realize the important objective of an audit report. The real reason an audit report is issued is to facilitate change. Consider this: Do you believe that a business process area would make changes to their policies and procedures if they were not told by an outside review team that there were weaknesses or opportunities for improvement in their current process? To be honest, most business process teams are looking to find ways to do their own jobs faster and process more transactions with less work. And in order to do that, sometimes current process requirements are not adhered to as strictly as the current policy requires. That is not to say that process workarounds are not acceptable. They are, but the process workaround cannot be an enhanced procedure that bypasses a critical control. Hence, the value of the internal audit work and subsequent report play a critical role in the attempt to drive change to be implemented by the business area management team.

For the internal audit team to be effective in facilitating action from their business partner, internal auditors must recognize themselves as change agents. This is a dramatic shift in how most auditors view themselves because of the existing stereotypes that have been around for decades. As marketing the audit department was discussed in Chapter 3, it becomes paramount for the audit department to put forth a dedicated effort to correct the misconception of what internal audit represents to be changed to the value partner audit has become. To this day, many internal auditors do not admit in public forums, parties, happy hours, or get togethers what they do for a living. And that does not mean that auditors do not talk about their work, it just means that they do not say I am an "internal auditor" because they believe it has a negative connotation and most people in the business environment see internal audit as a necessary evil. Marketing has been discussed previously to try and reflect what internal audit truly provides to a company, but internal auditors themselves need to alter how they portray themselves. The next time anyone approaches you as an auditor in an introductory setting and asks what you do for a living, tell them that you are a "change agent." As a change agent, your role is to utilize information, data, and documentation to identify opportunities for improvement and recommend, through a partnership approach, suggestions for improvement. Let us be honest, *change agent* sounds way better (and cooler) than *internal auditor*.

To be successful in this new change agent role, internal auditors must dedicate themselves to continually learning the business as they build a strong business knowledge foundation. Additionally, auditors must recognize the importance of building and maintaining the internal audit and business partner relationship. This relationship will help foster transparency of information sharing when the two parties meet to discuss any business process or audit activity. While this transformation from internal auditor to recognized change agent will not happen overnight, dedication to transforming the perception of internal auditors as watchdogs to a valued partner will happen over time. But make no mistake about it, this *will* take time and a focused effort from every member of the internal audit department to alter their approach when dealing with their business partners. While this may sound like a simple descriptive word change, it makes a huge difference in how the internal audit department is viewed and how audit reports are more readily accepted.

 ## AUDIT REPORT FOUNDATION

The most effective way to discuss the communication of audit issues and report delivery is to first develop the foundation for the information which will ultimately be documented and distributed in the formal audit report. This foundation must be created in partnership with business unit management through the timely discussion of any and all issues, deviations from the business processing standard, that were noted throughout the audit engagement. Effective communication of issues is the sole responsibility of the internal auditor. The auditor must articulate the validated gap between the testing standard requirements, provided by the business processing team, and the data results of the completed testing. This communication does not require additional assumptions, judgements, or interpretations on the part of the responsible auditor; it is fact and data driven. This data must be measurable and not just be a one-time occurrence. Every process has breakdowns and processor error, but reportable issues are recurring and pose a barrier to achieving the process objectives. And as previously emphasized, no potential deviations are to be discussed with the business partner until the identified errors have been validated with current business process personnel.

To stress the importance of the identified and confirmed issues, a formal communication with a documented summary is held, whether in person or remotely, to properly explain the potential reportable issues along with the corresponding risk to achieving the business objectives. It is important for this communication be executed like any other audit and business partner meeting, with an agenda, communication of the meeting objectives, review of the information details, and wrap-up describing next steps.

Without having a formal meeting, the focus on the significance of the information being discussed can get lost. That is why it is critical that the auditor facilitating this meeting be prepared with supporting documentation for all issues being discussed, actively listen throughout the meeting, and always

TABLE 7.1 Keys for Discussing Issues Effectively

1. Positive tone	5. Honesty
2. Nonconfrontational	6. Confidence
3. Constructive	7. Clarity
4. Timeliness	8. Detail

maintain control using the agenda from introduction to closing. Table 7.1 identifies the Beyond Audit keys to successfully facilitating an issue discussion with a business partner. Although these keys were developed to navigate an issue discussion meeting effectively, they can be applied to any audit meeting. A brief highlight of a few of the selected terms will follow.

 ## BEYOND AUDIT – ISSUE DISCUSSION KEYS

From an audit and business partner meeting perspective, the auditor has control over all of them with the exception of nonconfrontational. The auditor facilitating the meeting must not be confrontational but that does not mean the business partner will take on that same persona. However, the auditor can maintain a noncombative meeting environment by utilizing the other seven keys in each business partner interaction. Even though it may be a tactic of the business partner to be confrontational, to try and get the auditor to question their own results, the auditor must stay the course and focus on the meeting objective at hand, which is to discuss any deviations identified during the fieldwork testing. That should start with the tone of the meeting. Tone is not just how one person speaks to another but also the manner in which they deliver the message. It is important in delivering criticizing or "bad" news that the auditor presents the data, not an opinion, judgment, or subjective view, in a positive, constructive tone. This will set a foundational basis for an even exchange of process-based information to understand the reasoning behind the particular message being delivered. To further assist in fostering a nonconfrontational environment, all issue data must be delivered in a clear and confident manner. This does not mean in a lecturing tone like a parent would to a child or a teacher would to a student, but in a conversational nature, being driven by the data obtained from the business team and reviewed by the audit team. Remember that the goal of every client interaction is to focus on a discussion about the business; it is a conversation between two professionals regarding a process. When the message is clear and supported by the data, it is easier for the auditor to have the business partner focus on the message and not the negative side of the breakdowns in their business process.

The other part of being confident comes from the completed audit work. If the audit team completed the testing in accordance with the current business process requirements, identified potential gaps, and validated the results with business personnel, that will provide the auditor with the confidence to deliver a critical message to the business partner. Do not at any point in this meeting let confidence turn into a condescending tone. That will absolutely turn a conversational type meeting into a confrontational one in an instant. To support the message being delivered, utilize the appropriate amount of detail, if needed, to clarify the message. Always anticipate where the business partner may need or want additional clarification of the testing results. So be prepared with samples selected, sampling methods, specific deviations, targeted testing explanations, and copies of the confirmed deviations identified. You might never have to reference this material in the meeting, but it is always good to be prepared if the need arises.

AUDIT REPORTING THROUGHOUT AN AUDIT

This critical communication of verified issues noted to date, which happens throughout an audit, lays the groundwork for a formal value-based audit report. As the development of an effective audit report is described, keep in mind that the audit status memo discussed in Chapter 4 is one of the most effective supporting documents that an auditor can use when it comes to partnering for results. Keep in mind that the information already contained in the status memo has been discussed, reviewed, and approved by the business unit management, which should make the draft audit report a much more palatable assessment of process performance for the business partner to accept. If the audit team has dedicated the time and effort to effectively utilizing the audit status memo as it has been designed, the issue details can be directly extracted from the template to the formal audit report. However, just like any other goal or objective, it is important to understand what end deliverable the internal audit department is trying to produce to be the most efficient when creating it. To provide some perspective, here is a brief internal audit report discussion.

By definition, a formal audit report is a document providing a detailed explanation for the work completed during the audit engagement. The objective of this document is to communicate the results of the specific audit testing performed by detailing the purpose of the audit, assessing the level of effectiveness of the business controls tested, and the deviations from the processing standards identified. All of this information is compiled to create the foundation for the overall rating assessing the strength of the corresponding business control environment. All internal audit team members having this level of understanding of the audit report purpose will assist them in gathering the appropriate level of supporting data (during the fieldwork and reporting phases) to create a high-impact report which can be understood by any and all recipients. It is critically important to understand the purpose of the ultimate internal audit deliverable to be a world-class audit organization. There are a couple of simple keys to making the internal audit report process successful as well as painless. As previously discussed, when the planning and fieldwork phases are executed with precision and a high level of communication, the reporting phase of any audit (remote or in person) should be nothing more than a formality of all of the validated issues already presented to and approved by the business partner.

The first key is to ensure that all team members on the audit engagement have been clear and direct in all communications with the business partner regarding the audit process and any issues identified, confirmed, and noted in the status memos. And the second key, and probably the biggest, is every internal audit department should have a report template that accurately captures the audit process and corresponding results. While industry standards state all audit results must be communicated to the business partner, there are no specific standards when it comes to the information and depth of topics which should be included in an internal audit report. In order for any internal audit report to be effective, it must convey the audit topics covered along with the results for each. Additionally, all issues identified during the audit engagement must be included with the proper level of detail to support, not defend, the audit conclusions on the effectiveness and efficiency of the business operations that were reviewed.

EFFECTIVE INTERNAL AUDIT REPORT COMPONENTS

There are numerous versions of internal audit reports available, but at the end of the day, the most effective report is the one that accurately communicates the work performed along with the results and ultimately persuades the business processing management team to implement the agreed-on, documented changes evidenced in the report. In order to facilitate change in the business unit, the internal audit report should, at a minimum, contain the following components:

- Overall opinion or rating
- Audit objectives and corresponding ratings
- Exception issues built with the five components
- Business process background summary

When properly documented, these components provide the basis for accurately and clearly conveying the results of the completed audit testing. Each one plays a vital role in communicating the corresponding audit activity to any reader who may or may not have been involved in the testing or even in the business unit being examined. An effective internal audit report delivers a supported conclusion on the business operations reviewed and recommendations with actions to address any opportunities for improvement in the achievement of the business objectives.

Overall Opinion

The report should state an overall opinion. Even though this component is not required in any communication industry standards, it is the most practical way to benchmark a business process's performance and can be utilized by audit in future engagements and company performance summary metrics. Remember that the overall opinion represents a summary statement evaluating the effectiveness of the tested controls throughout the audit. This opinion is probably the report component focused on the most and even garners the most attention during the report development process. It is paramount to utilize the audit test results in the development of the opinion.

While the component may contain the word *opinion*, there is nothing subjective about it. This component is created from the data-supported audit testing results, which do not and never should contain subjective opinion. The overall report opinion should always be fact based and have the proper level of supporting evidence. This opinion is derived from a clearly defined set of ratings that consider the overall risk to the business unit achieving its objectives.

Consistently applying these ratings in selecting the overall audit opinion is a significant challenge for the internal audit team, but doing so keeps auditors focused and honest when determining the overall opinion so that judgment does not become a factor in the opinion selection process. Judgment or personal perspectives have no place in the audit report process, as the focus must remain on the data and documentation examined throughout the audit. Auditors must dedicate their report generation efforts to creating a meaningful report to facilitate change instead of wasting time discussing differences in perspective or judgment. Auditors must remember to utilize the data when it comes to determining the effectiveness of a business control environment. Internal auditors should know their limitations; good ones do. Because every auditor knows if a discussion focuses on business process judgment, it is going to be nearly impossible for the auditor to convince the business partner to see the auditor's interpretation. This is due to the simple fact that the auditor does not, and will never, have the same business processing experience as the business partner. It is a losing battle that is not worth the fight. The overall opinion should tie directly to the current control environment and how effective it is at achieving the corresponding business objectives. This is the exact discussion topic the auditor wants to facilitate with the business partner to properly explain and support the overall rating listing in the audit report.

Table 7.2 provides the overall opinions incorporated in the Beyond Audit internal audit report template. These opinions have been developed from 30-plus years of internal audit experience and have been the most effective

TABLE 7.2 Beyond Audit – Overall Audit Report Opinions

Color	Opinion
Red	An overall unsatisfactory or unacceptable state of control. The red opinion indicates significant business risk in the achievement of the business objectives and exposure to the company that requires immediate remediation. The overall control environment does not provide reasonable assurance regarding the safeguarding of assets, reliability of financial records, and compliance with company policies and government regulations.
Yellow	An overall improvement required state of control. The yellow opinion indicates the current business controls need improvement to ensure consistent achievement of the business objectives. Failure to address the control deficiencies could result in an overall unsatisfactory or unacceptable control environment.
Green	An overall satisfactory or acceptable state of control. The current business risk is being managed effectively. The current overall control environment provides a satisfactory level of assurance regarding the safeguarding of assets, reliability of financial records, and compliance with company policies and government regulations.

at conveying a clear message on control environment effectiveness. There is something to be said for being direct and simple when it comes to overall opinions in this type of report. There are many examples of reports with five or more opinions, but it should be noted that the more opinion options that are available, the more confusing the message becomes. Experience and results have shown these three opinions to be the most successful at facilitating the critical message of control effectiveness as well as business action implementation.

The one nuance to these audit opinions is that they used colors instead of words. There is a very specific reason for this: Business partners spend a significant amount of time disputing wording, especially related to the audit opinion. For example, it is monumentally challenging to get a business partner to agree that their process "needs improvement." The dispute from the business perspective is that the opinion "needs improvement" sounds like the business personnel do nothing right, rather than merely that there are parts of the business process that require enhancements to ensure the business objectives are achieved on a consistent basis. Well, that is not how the business partner interprets that rating. Ultimately, what will occur is a lengthy discussion about the rating definition and no time dedicated to the issues. One would think that the business partner would want to focus the discussion on what were the breakdowns in the business process that facilitated the needs-improvement opinion instead of debating the opinion itself. The unfortunate part is that time is wasted on wording instead of focusing on the real business process points that require attention. Previous success has shown that using colors to communicate the overall audit opinion eliminates unnecessary discussions and endless wording changes to convince the business partner to accept the final opinion.

During the report-generation process of the audit report phase, remember that the objective of the audit report is to obtain agreement on the depiction of the current business process environment along with the overall opinion in order to obtain impactful business action plans to improve the current control environment. Utilizing color ratings instead of words allows auditors to direct the conversation to the issues noted and focus the business partner on developing corrective action plans. At the end of all the work, discussions, and endless wordsmithing, it does not matter if the internal audit report template your department utilizes contains words or colors, as long as the audit methodology rating system is consistently applied and linked to the risks identified during the audit testing. The overall opinion must be supported by the business provided data tested and specifically support the testing results. The key to an effective opinion is to verify that any independent reader will not have to interpret the opinion to determine the severity of the risk or the level of urgency needed in the corresponding action.

Audit Objectives and Corresponding Ratings

The audit objectives provide an explanation of why (purpose) an audit was performed and specify the particular areas of focus that were determined jointly with the business partner during the planning phase of the audit. Keep in mind that all audit objectives are created from the business objective to ensure that there is value and line of sight that aligns the audit testing with the achievement of the critical business objectives. The key for auditors to remember when creating the audit objectives is that understanding the business objectives is mandatory in the creation of the specific audit objectives to be tested during the fieldwork phase. Too often, auditors make assumptions regarding their level of knowledge pertaining to the business objectives and it just results in the development of nonsense audit objectives and nonvaluable test results and recommendations. It is necessary to dedicate the proper amount of time to understand the business objectives and properly create strategically targeted audit objectives focused on the critical control supporting the operational business process.

To provide perspective and a complete picture of the controls tested during an audit, the audit team can strengthen the message by including a corresponding rating for each completed audit objective listed in the audit report. This level of detail assists the reader in understanding not only how each business control environment performed, but also the overall opinion determination. The individual audit objective ratings are scored in the same manner and with the same rating options as the overall opinion to ensure the consistency of the message. Table 7.3 details the audit objective and corresponding ratings incorporated in the Beyond Audit internal audit report template. It is strategically arranged to provide one of the most effective ways to

TABLE 7.3 Beyond Audit – Audit Objectives Rating Table

Audit Objective	Objective Rating		
	Green	Yellow	Red
Objective 1			X
Objective 2		X	
Objective 3	X		

document the objectives, along with the corresponding risk rating given to each objective. Every audit objective tested during the engagement will be documented in the table, with each receiving their respective performance rating. Remember to inform the business partner that this table represents how well the business unit personnel succeeded in achieving the listed objective. An "X" will be placed under the corresponding rating for each audit objective listed. For example, in Table 7.3, audit objectives 1 and 2 received a red and yellow rating, respectively, and will thus require a corresponding business action plan to address the weakness. This table also helps to prioritize business unit management efforts to develop and implement specific action for any yellow or red ratings. The use of color ratings in lieu of words creates an additional sense of urgency for both the business partner and the independent readers.

Exception Issues Built with the Five Components

By the time an internal audit report reader gets to the issue or exception detail in the report, they already have been exposed to the issue topic and its severity, given the corresponding color rating from the objectives table. This background information provides perspective to the detailed data that will be shared in the five components of the issue. The five-component approach to documenting issue details provides the auditor a framework to stay clear and concise in the explanation. Remember, the objective of the issue detail is to communicate a clear message to all independent readers so they can comprehend and agree that this issue should be included in the report and needs the business partner's attention to address the risk.

Contrary to popular belief, more words in any issue do not translate into a stronger message. Often, they instead cloud or confuse the real message. The real key is to stay diligent with the five-component approach and drive the message with data. Wordiness can cause a reader to miss the true issue detail and force them to interpret what they are reading, which is the biggest enemy of internal audit reports, no matter what type. At no time do you want to require a reader to have to interpret information – especially details pertaining to the overall rating, issue severity, or issue data – because the true message will not be delivered and the corresponding actions coming out as a result of the audit report will not be effective.

To ensure all internal audit reports are impactful (resulting in positive change), use the five-component approach to construct the issues identified during testing. This approach will ensure the development and communication of a complete message requiring no interpretation. The five components are listed below and will be explained in a brief summary to follow. Each component serves a specific purpose in explaining the results of the audit. When developed correctly, the five components naturally provide the appropriate level of detail and clear explanation as to why a particular issue is included in an audit report.

1. Condition
2. Criteria
3. Cause
4. Effect
5. Recommendation/Action

Condition

The condition is the most straightforward component of the five, but it too often poses a challenge to auditors when they go to create it. It cannot be stressed enough to not complicate the report-generation process. Let the five components work for you and follow the development advice. In the simplest form, the condition is a pure factual statement detailing exactly what was identified as a result of the testing. The condition is a captured moment in time regarding the sample selected along with the completed testing. Before drafting the condition, ask yourself, "How did the testing turn out? What was identified?" The answers to those questions are the true condition statement.

If the testing revealed that 13 of the 25 invoices tested did not contain an approval signature, then that is the condition statement. No more, no less. Bottom line – the condition statement is a pure statement of fact, and it details exactly what the auditor identified during the execution of testing. Remember that the condition is the data results of the testing and should stay focused on the data, not opinion. There should never be a need to interpret the condition because it is a fact and is irrefutable. Too many times auditors try to utilize the condition to justify the reasoning for including this issue in the report. That is a mistake. The condition is not a component used to convince a reader of anything. The condition is just providing the results to set the stage for the remainder of the five component details.

Criteria

While the condition component may be the most straightforward of them, the criteria is the easiest to document. The criteria represent the standard or process requirement established by the business partner indicating the business process requirements to be performed. The criteria are the easiest to document because it is the exact process standard which was obtained and verified during the planning phase of the audit and included in the audit test program for validation. The process standard remains consistent all the way through the audit from planning to reporting. Auditors can obtain the criteria specifics by examining the audit program and extracting the test program requirements. As previously discussed, the processing standard or criteria can only be established internally, from policies and procedures or management decisions, or externally, from government regulations. Documenting the criteria will always come from existing documentation already established in the internal audit workpapers. Remain diligent with the details and ensure the testing criteria used in the fieldwork matches the issue criteria details. It is important to stay consistent in the wording and level of documentation.

Cause

Cause is the component that explains why the condition component exists. In order to effectively document the issue cause, the auditor has to determine why the condition occurred. And while this may seem like a simple question and answer to present and obtain from the business partner, it is much more difficult than it appears. The cause component is, and probably always will be, the most challenging component to identify accurately. Regardless if the audit is a remote or in-person engagement, each person involved in this component discussion has a different perspective on why the condition exists. It is the auditor's responsibility to take the testing results data and facilitate a discussion with the business partner to accurately identify the true cause. However, just to make it a little more complicated and difficult, finding cause is not going to be enough. The key to facilitating real change in a business process requires the auditor to identify root cause. There is no argument that identifying why a condition exists is important, but the explanation has to go further and deeper to determine why it occurred.

Unfortunately, *root cause* is a term used almost universally by audit departments, yet it still remains one of the most frequently misunderstood terms in the audit environment. This situation is the result of each audit department having just a little bit different definition, if any, of what root cause represents. Every audit department should not only require root cause to be identified for every issue noted during the testing phase, but also have a clear and communicated definition of what root cause is and how to find it. The other key concept to recognize about root cause analysis is that it is a reactive method of solving an issue that has been identified during the audit testing. If a root cause analysis is being used, it is because an identified and confirmed problem has been documented. Understanding that the root cause identification process is detective in nature focuses the research on the forensic review of the sample tested and the confirmed exceptions noted in the business process. This approach helps provide the auditors with valuable results and provides the business unit personnel with suggestions to strengthen their current control environment.

There is good news and bad news when it comes to identifying root cause. The good news is, root cause does exist for every issue and can be identified. The bad news is there is no confirmed "best method" to guaranteeing the identification of root cause. Here are some baseline facts when it comes to identifying root cause. The process requires effort, resources, and time on the part of the auditor to get to the bottom of the root cause barrel. These requirements also include the business partner in the root cause identification process. This identification process is a significant challenge because the data may point in one direction of cause and then the business partner is indicating something different. There are so many differing opinions as to the best method to incorporate to find root cause, but ultimately it comes down to the discussion facilitation with the process owner to identify the simple "why" that resulted in the current situation.

One of the most popular approaches to finding root cause is the *five-whys* methodology, which is literal in definition requiring asking *why* five times to identify cause. It may seem like a good idea, but more often than not, asking *why* five times does not always result in the identification of root cause. Make no mistake about it, this approach takes time, discipline, effort, process knowledge, facilitation skills, and a willing business partner. But if the auditor genuinely wants to find root cause, think of it in a more practical approach.

The Beyond Audit approach to identifying root cause is called *finding the first domino*. Consider the process that was tested in the fieldwork phase as a line of dominos. As the audit testing is completed, the auditor notes a fallen domino. The fallen domino is documented, and the search begins for the reason it has fallen (or in process terms, failed). To identify the root cause of the process failure, the auditor, along with the business partner, will have to work together and identify the first domino that caused this particular one to fail. This first-domino approach takes discipline and dedication to the business process details to work backward to identify the initial breakdown. Finding a reason for a fallen domino in the process is simple, but finding the first domino that resulted in the process failure takes research and time.

The investment in time and effort in truly identifying root cause using the first-domino approach is absolutely worth it. This effort is rewarded with targeted actions, stronger business partner relationships, and an increase in auditor business process knowledge. Think of all those instances where the audit team has identified repeat findings or when a business action plan does not result in real change. The reason that failed action plans and repeat findings occur is due to a lack of root cause identification. Do not fall into the trap of settling for a symptom fix instead of a root cause fix, because in the end it will only result in more work and an increase in the associated business process risk. Remember that root cause analysis is a combination of business process knowledge and professional skepticism to facilitate the business process questioning approach and must be done in a collaborative approach with the business partner.

To complete the root cause discussion, here are a few tips to remember. The biggest one for auditors is to realize that no matter how intelligent, experienced, or tenured they may be, it is impossible to identify root cause on their own (see Table 7.4). Even smart auditors do not possess the business knowledge depth to understand the fallen dominos and the supporting reasoning behind that. In that effort, auditors must rely on and leverage existing business partnerships to help in the root cause identification discussion process. Like it or not, the true reality is the auditor needs the business process information that the business partner possesses. And one final tip would be for the auditor to adequately prepare for the root cause discussion meeting, master the data acquired during the

TABLE 7.4 Root Cause Identification Keys

The primary objective of identifying the root cause is to document the source of an issue and create a tangible, effective action to address it.

This identification process requires additional auditor time, dedication, and effort to perform the research and collaborate with the business partner to find the answer.

Recognize that there is a root cause responsible for every identified issue.

Understand the difference between a symptom of the confirmed issue and the actual root cause.

Resist the temptation to accept the first response when asking the business partner what they believe is the root cause of the issue being discussed.

Confirm the root cause identification by posing the question, "If an action is created for this root cause, will the condition be effectively addressed?"

Remember to keep asking "why" until there are no more "whys" left to ask.

Leverage strong communication and relationship skills in every root cause analysis discussion.

fieldwork testing phase, and actively work with the business partner to identify and document the first domino.

Effect

The effect component is a hinge or stage gate component. What that means is the effect statement is the determining factor of whether an issue makes it into the audit report or becomes a discussion item with the business partner. If the effect is the impact of the existence of the condition, then it must be evident and pose a significant risk to the achievement of the business objective for the issue to make it into the audit report. If there is no identifiable impact, there is no reason for the issue to be reportable.

Look at the impact statement like this. Each time a condition statement is communicated to the business partner, their immediate response is "So what?" The business partner is asking the auditor point blank, Why should I care about this deviation from the business processing standard? Auditors must be prepared with a response, supported by the testing detail and data, to adequately explain the corresponding risk and exposure to the achievement of the business objective(s). The effect component is not based on the auditor's judgment or opinion, but the specific testing data that has already been discussed and verified with the business process personnel. Auditors must remember to use the data, and not opinions, to drive the discussion. Business partners can effectively challenge auditors when it comes to process opinions but are unable to dispute validated business data. Auditors must maintain focus during these discussions and remember to rely on the confirmed business data to support, not defend, the issue being discussed.

The cause component drives home the impact of the existence of the condition and details the potential exposure to the business unit and ultimately the company. The impact or effect of the exposure could relate to timing, accuracy, reporting, or client exposure. When documenting the effect component, the key is to be specific and, when possible, quantify the exposure. Keep in mind that not all effect statements have to be quantified in dollars. A significant effect can be related to performance accuracy or timing that has no direct dollar impact but could cause a delay in communication or another department of critical information or delivery of a product to a client or consumer.

The remaining point before moving on is that there will be times when the business partner, upon discussing and acknowledging the confirmed condition, cause, and impact, decides not to do anything about the validated impact and to live with the associated risk. As this is within the business partner's authority, the auditor must recognize and realize that the business partner is not only choosing to accept the exposure identified during testing but is also setting the risk appetite for the overall business process.

This type of information assists the auditor in understanding the business partner's willingness to accept a higher level of process risk even after being told of the potential impacts. In this situation, the auditor must communicate to the business partner that the issue will be detailed in the report along with the business partner's response of risk acceptance at the current level. The business partner's risk appetite or acceptance of a known potential impact does not alleviate the auditor from documenting the issue with all five components to ensure there is adequate awareness of the auditor's results and corresponding business response.

When considering the five-component approach, even though the cause will require the most effort, the effect is often the component that is most contested by the business partner in order to downplay the significance of the errors noted. To address any challenges, ensure there is a clear correlation between the condition and the cause components that are driving the specific exposure detailed in the effect. After all the information has been identified, confirmed, and discussed, auditors must remember that if there is not an identifiable impact on the business achieving their objectives, the effect does not warrant being included in the audit report.

Recommendation (Action)

The recommendation is the final component of the five-component approach and specifically documents the action necessary to address the identified cause (root cause). Many internal audit departments mistakenly develop an action that addresses the condition and not the cause. That is a critical mistake because that recommendation will result in a symptom fix and the root cause will continue to pose a risk to the business achieving its objectives. The other clarification that must be noted is that the recommendation in this approach is specifically defined using the word *address* when it comes to the associated risk. The objective of the recommendation is not to eliminate risk but to address it. Meaning, bring the risk into an acceptable level of performance so that the business process can achieve its objectives in the most effective and efficient manner. Unfortunately, there is no way to eliminate all risk, it is just not possible or feasible. However, some auditors try to create a complex recommendation to eliminate the identified risks, but in the end this effort will fail. Auditors must work with the business process partner (experts) to develop reasonable, achievable actions to reign in the identified risks and improve the business process. Always remember, a recommendation does not have to be complex to be effective, it just has to address the risks.

There are so many factors that come into play when audit teams are trying to clarify partnering for results. Auditing, especially in the remote environment, requires a strong communications foundation (to be discussed in Chapter 10) to be effective in every phase of an audit as well as the business partner relationship responsibilities. If you look back at Chapter 4, there was a discussion of the various skills a successful internal auditor needs to possess to perform their job effectively. And while those skills are critical and represent the characteristics audit executives want in every member of their team, audit is always going to be judged on the ultimate deliverable – the final audit report. To help better prepare for the audit report delivery challenges, the most common internal audit report challenges are listed after the background summary. Identifying, understanding, recognizing, and addressing them in the most effective manner should assist every audit team in the audit report generation process.

Business Process Background Summary

The business background should be the smallest section (two to four sentences) as it provides an overview of the process area being audited. This section should focus on the main objectives of the business process and include, when available, any current data related to business process volumes and dollar amounts. The key to this section is to be brief and detail information specific to the business process and information and/or products produced, which can be for internal or external partners. Remember that this section does not require the audit team to document all activities performed in the business area. Only pertinent data should be included to clarify the most critical business processes.

 AUDIT REPORT CHALLENGES

- *No standard format.* Without a standard audit report format, there will be a lack of a consistent deliverable being generated from the internal audit department. Many times, the lack of consistency results in different styles and products being produced, which ultimately impacts the reliability of the internal audit department itself.
- *Inconsistent application of audit opinion.* Even if the internal audit department has a standard audit report template, there must be a process in place to

ensure the overall opinions are applied consistently, regardless of the type of audit (remote, in person, compliance, financial, operational, etc.).

- *Untimely issuance.* The target delivery of a final audit report should be within 30 days of the completion of fieldwork. The longer the delivery time goes, the less impact the report and corresponding recommendations will have.
- *Incomplete five-component detail.* Without a dedicated effort to complete the five components, there will be missing information needed to effectively convey the errors noted along with their corresponding risks.
- *Striving for perfection.* Too many internal audit teams attempt to create a perfect audit report. Do not bother, because it does not exist. Adequately document the report template and stick to the data in the communication of the results of the audit.
- *Reviewing for style, not content.* All internal audit report reviews should be examined to ensure they contain an adequate level of detail, proper support, and a constructive tone. PERIOD.
- *Reporting black hole.* The black hole represents the part of the internal audit report generation process in which a report draft is delivered but does not receive the proper attention. Each part of the report generation process should have a standard 24-hour turn around requirement.

CHAPTER EIGHT

Internal Audit Value

I NTERNAL AUDIT DEPARTMENTS HAVE long been challenged to justify their existence. As was discussed in Chapter 3 regarding marketing the internal audit department, auditors have long been viewed as outsiders or the enemy. In reality, audit departments serve an unbelievably valuable role and provide an internal system of checks and balances to their business partners. For an exceptionally long time, internal audit departments have been trying to identify the most effective method to measure the quality or value of their product. How should audit measure quality? Should the quality metric be determined by the number of issues noted during an audit engagement? Or in the strength of the audit and business partner relationship? How about measuring quality based on the number of recommendations made or created business partner actions? There have even been suggestions that internal audit department measure the quality delivered based on an audit client survey. Hence, the higher the survey score, the better the level of quality delivered. This type of quality metric discussion has been going on for decades. The discussion around delivering quality and tracking that performance is still in development. In Chapter 9, the internal audit dashboard will be discussed along with specific metric suggestions and their corresponding performance criteria. But for this discussion, the focus will be on action plans, from the development, to the implementation, and ultimately through to adoption of same. Additionally, the critical process of reporting surrounding action plans will be examined.

DEFINING REAL ACTION

As discussed in the previous chapter, the audit report is the ultimate deliverable and it also happens to contain the issues noted during the audit engagement along with the corresponding proposed management actions. While that might sound all well and good, noting deviations from the business processing standard and supporting them with data does not equate to the business partner taking the management action from the report and implementing it in a timely manner to address the verified process risk. Internal audit departments (for the most part) diligently track and follow up on the implementation of business management action plans and, in certain cases (depending on the risk level), will request documentation to evidence the action plan implementation before closing the particular action item in the internal audit action item tracking database. On the surface, this sounds like a foolproof plan to validate that all management actions detailed in the audit report were implemented effectively and in a timely manner (by the agreed-upon target date).

As we dive deeper into the concept of developing a business partner action plan (from this point on referred to as *action plan*) with the business partner, the concept of "real action" must be considered. There is a monumental difference between an action plan and a real action plan, and it is not just the addition of an adjective. An action plan is a suggested solution from the business partner to address a gap identified during the audit testing. What auditors and business partners sometimes miss is that the initial suggested action plan is just the beginning of the formulation of a real action plan. A real action plan has three distinct characteristics:

1. It specifically and adequately addresses root cause and the corresponding risks.
2. It has an action item owner that possesses two distinct attributes – the ability and authority to take the action item from concept to reality.
3. It has a realistic and attainable target date.

When examining the first characteristic of adequately addressing the root cause, it is important that the auditor review and approve the proposed action plan and consider if the exceptions identified in the audit fieldwork phase would be prevented or identified with the enhanced action plan suggestion. The auditor should also brainstorm with their team members if all potential business processing scenarios are being considered while keeping in mind the enhanced control cannot address every possible scenario but should be able to address the most frequently processed.

Once the review and approval has been completed by the auditor, the next step would be to discuss the details with the business process owner who drafted the initial action plan. That discussion should include a review of the action plan, its direct linkage to the achievement of the business objectives, as well as any potential aspects that could be added to strengthen the proposed action plan. It cannot be stressed enough how important it is for the responsible auditor to work with the business partner to develop an action plan that adequately addresses the root cause. In that effort, the auditor should feel comfortable challenging the business partner when it appears that the proposed action plan will not effectively or adequately address the confirmed root cause. Upon finalizing the agreed-upon action plan, the auditor should reconfirm the business partner's confidence and conviction regarding the action plan by asking, "If this plan is implemented as described, will it address the root cause and bring the corresponding process risk down to an acceptable level?" If the business owner replies with anything other than yes, the proposed action plan is not complete, nor does it contain the sufficient level of details to address true process risk.

After the proposed action plan has been reviewed and approved by the auditor, and then validated with the business owner, there should be discussion of which business team member should be assigned the specific responsibility of incorporating the control enhancement into the current policies and procedures. When identifying who on the business unit team should own this action, remember that the second characteristic of a real action plan is selecting an owner who has the ability and the authority to make the action plan a reality. Too often, action item owners are assigned just because they work in the same business area but, unfortunately, do not understand the details of the identified issue or the corresponding suggested action. Here are some key considerations:

- *The action plan owner must understand the process.* How can an action item owner implement a business process enhancement without understanding the details surrounding the recommended change? The answer is, they cannot, but appointed owners will often try their best to implement the change given their limited knowledge on the topic.
- *The owner must have the ability to make the action plan work.* The owner must clearly understand what was identified in the audit testing, the verified results, the corresponding business process impact, and the parameters of the proposed action plan.

- *The owner must have the authority to implement the action plan.* When it comes to explaining the authority attribute of a real action item owner, it is simple. When an action implementation plan requires coordination of business unit team members or external business partners, it is critical that the real action item owner is recognized as the business team representative who will be responsible for directing the action plan through the implementation phase. Without a formal assignment, communication, and acknowledgment of the action item owner, it is difficult for that owner to direct efforts and instruct other team members. The bottom line relating to the authority attribute of a real action item owner is that all participants involved on the action plan implementation team are notified of the true action item owner. This official assignment of duties makes coordination efforts a lot easier for the action item owner.

The final characteristic of a real action plan is to verify the proposed action plan has a realistic and attainable target date. It seems simple enough, as every action plan has a corresponding implementation target date. However, what makes a target date realistic or attainable? Who has the responsibility for making that determination? Think about it for a moment, that this determination is a judgment or an opinion; as with any judgment or opinion, it is subjective. In order to remove the subjective factor from the target date creation step, suggested parameters can be established based on the corresponding risk of the issue details identified during the audit testing.

The Beyond Audit methodology framework establishes standard target date requirements for action plans based on the potential exposure to the achievement of the business objectives. If the identified and validated process risk of the audit issue is rated a red or high risk, then the proposed management action must be implemented within 90 days of the final report issuance date. And if the corresponding risk of the audit issue is rated yellow or medium risk, then the proposed management action plan must be implemented within 120 days of the final report issuance. It must be stressed and specifically noted to the business owner that the clock for these action plan implementation requirements begins as soon as the final report is issued and distributed. This clarification has to be communicated to the process owner, as the 90- or 120-day clock is not tracked from the documented target date in the report but the date the report was issued. This clarification must be made because even if the initial target date, which was documented and distributed in the final audit report, is changed or updated by the business partner after the report issuance, the implementation clock requirements do not adjust with the revised target date.

There have been many times where business partners would adjust the target date so that their target dates would never be identified on the delinquent action plan report. And while that may work from a reporting standpoint, it does not address the outstanding and growing risk associated with the initial audit testing results. For the action plan implementation to be effective, the implementation time frame requirements must start with the final report issuance date and track all outstanding action plans through to implementation.

It should be noted that there is an exception to the action plan implementation time frame requirements: Where the action plan includes a technology solution, it is very unlikely and unrealistic to assume that a technology-based action plan could be effectively implemented in 90–120 days. And while the implementation target date is not without boundaries, auditors must recognize the need for an extended implementation deadline for the associated technology plan to be completed accurately and under the appropriate supervision. All of that being said, there is another requirement. If the proposed action plan includes a technology aspect or a technological sole solution, then the technology portion of the action plan can be extended but the additional requirement will be that the business owner must create an interim action plan that includes an enhanced control environment to identify and track any transactions that are potential exceptions while waiting for the technology solution implementation. This ensures that the business maintains sufficient control over its process until the technology update has been completed.

 ## STEPS IN CREATING AN ACTION PLAN

In order to effectively discuss action plans and their implementation, it is important to lay down a foundation regarding action plan development. Consider how an action plan is created. There are four steps when initiating change in the business unit via an audit action plan: development, implementation, adoption, and reporting.

In the most direct approach, internal audit identifies an issue, validates the deviation, presents it to business unit management, and documents an action plan to address it. Simple; one, two, three, and the issue is fixed, right? If action plan development and implementation were that easy, everyone would want to become an internal auditor. Unfortunately, internal auditors know that the process of obtaining an action plan is an uphill battle, let alone having the business team implement and adopt an enhanced process requirement. So let's look at the four steps in more detail.

Action Plan Development

Where does the action plan development process begin? To understand the initial phase of action plan *development*, the auditor must begin with the root cause. Root cause is the first domino that resulted in the business process issue being identified. For any action plan to be effective, it must be developed to address the root cause. Keep in mind that the action plan should be created with the specific objective of "addressing" the root cause and not eliminating it. Too often, internal audit teams try and work with their business partner to create an action to "eliminate" the root cause when in fact there is not an action big enough to accomplish that task. As previously discussed, the objective of the action plan is to reduce the associated risk of any business process failure to an acceptable level since it is impossible to eliminate 100 percent of the risk. There will always be exceptions in a business process, but those exceptions will be limited in number and significance of impact if an effective set of controls is implemented to guide the business process.

The one aspect of the action plan development process that is the responsibility of the internal audit is to challenge the business partner when proposed action plans are suggested. The auditor must constantly and consistently ask the business partner if the proposed action plan, when implemented, will completely and effectively address the identified root cause. Most of the time, the business partner will say, "for the most part," or "it is a good start." And while those represent an adequate start to the action plan development discussion, the auditor must follow up by asking, "How can we strengthen that action plan to be more comprehensive?" For auditors to be successful in this challenge, they have to keep the focus on the discussion of the business process objectives and how to strengthen the current supporting process to achieve results on a more consistent basis with minimal rework. The business partner will recognize the discussion focus and, hopefully, continue to build on their action plan suggestion. While the auditor will use the root cause component to drive the action plan development step, it is important that all throughout this step the auditors keep feasibility in mind with any and all business partner action plan suggestions. Part of challenging the business partner in regard to action plan development is to ask if the action plan being suggested is feasible. For example, the action plan suggestion could be too complex, too complicated, or too costly to implement or even to afford. Once again, the auditor's role includes a significant focus on listening in every single meeting. If for a moment, the auditor misses the opportunity to question the business partner about action plan feasibility, an action could be presented that looks amazing on paper and in concept but is not possible to implement. Auditors must remain diligent regarding their listening skills during the action plan development conversation and even more so if it is during a remote engagement. Feasibility should always be on the auditor's mind during action plan development with considerations regarding staff size, process knowledge, staff tenure, implementation timing and oversight, and cost just to name a few.

Action Plan Implementation

The next step in the action plan process is implementation. This step is completed in two stages: examination and verification. The first stage of examination of the proposed action plan is to validate the action has actually been put into place within the business unit completely, accurately, and timely. Just for clarification, *completely* means all pieces of the action have been done with zero left outstanding; *accurately* means the action plan was incorporated into the current business process exactly as described in the internal audit report action item detail; and *timely* means within the target implementation documented date.

The examination step of the action plan includes an inspection of the supporting documentation detailing the implementation process, which includes the rollout of the business process change, the communication plan to announce the change, and updated policies and procedures evidencing the change specifics. Once that documentation has been reviewed, the auditor can proceed to the second step, which is verification.

The verification step requires the auditor to actually observe the business process enhancement or revised documentation in the current business process. It is important to note that to accomplish this step effectively, the auditor must allow adequate time for the newly implemented process to be incorporated into the business unit. It is suggested that internal auditors allow thirty days for their business partners to introduce any business process change or update, which will allow the business unit personnel to clearly understand the change and be able to effectively incorporate it into their daily responsibilities. Experience has shown that trying to perform the verification step of the implementation process does not work if the auditor is attempting to obtain confirmation of the process enhancement on the day or even the first week of implementation.

Auditors must give the business unit team adequate time to adapt to the revised process and associated responsibilities. This will also help to build the auditor and business partner relationship, as the auditor is not only showing patience in the responsibilities but also allowing the business team to become comfortable with its own process.

Action Plan Adoption

The next step in initiating change within the business unit is adoption. This particular step is one of the audit methodology steps that is unique to the Beyond Audit methodology and too often overlooked or omitted by internal audit departments around the world. The majority of audit departments believe, as evidenced in their documented audit methodology, that once the implementation step is completed there is no need for additional work to be done on an action that the business partner has said was completed and the auditor validated the supporting documentation to evidence same. And while those two activities did occur, neither ensures the process change detailed in the audit report was successfully incorporated into the business process. It is understandable for you to assume that the business partner did it and audit validated it to be true, so, therefore, audit has no more responsibility regarding this closed action plan. But consider this: Has internal audit ever gone back to perform an audit in a subsequent year and noted a repeat finding that is practically, if not actually, identical to the last audit engagement in that area? What is strange is that there was a significant discussion around this same issue, which resulted in a comprehensive action plan to address the identified risk. Even stranger is the fact that internal audit reviewed and approved the development and implementation of the action plan details. But something must have happened between the implementation of the new business process requirements and the current audit testing, because it does not appear from the current testing results that the change worked. And there is documented audit testing evidence to support the failure of both the business process and the supposed revised business process. The reason why the "new or enhanced" process failed was because it was never truly adopted by the business processing personnel. This is where internal audit teams must recognize there is a concrete difference between an action plan being implemented versus adopted.

The most effective way to understand this difference is with an analogy. Consider New Year's Eve; it is an exciting time for everyone and almost all people make at least one New Year's resolution, usually pertaining to self-improvement – losing weight, being more dedicated to exercise, spending more time with friends or less time on social media. This happens every single year. When we make these resolutions, we truly mean it. We *want* to get healthy, spend our time better. The most important point to recognize here is that we are committed and excited about the change. The new year begins, and focusing on health or priority changes is part of the daily routine for about a month. But it becomes less important as time goes on. Even with the best intentions in mind, this particular New Year's resolution does not become a reality on a long-term or sustainable basis. And whether the excuses are related to celebration events, hectic work schedules, or new job responsibilities, there seem to always be reasons or barriers standing in the way of maintaining the commitment. In the end, it just does not happen.

Now look at the same exact logic when it comes to a business partner committing to developing and implementing change within their own business process to improve the strength of their control environment. They understood the process risk and were truly focused on creating business process enhancements to address the identified gaps. After discussions with the audit and business processing teams, the enhanced process controls were developed and incorporated into the audit report action plan. All parties agreed to both the action plan details and the implementation target date. The business team was excited about the process enhancements and immediately began to use them. And then one day, the business processing team either forgot why the new process requirements were implemented, got tired of the extra work, realized there was no oversight of the revised process, or just decided the new process requirements did not really impact the final product. So, the original habit of processing and documenting daily activity crept back in.

Now, keep in mind, the revised process was in full operational swing when the internal audit team went back to the business unit to validate implementation. Auditors examined the new policies and procedures, supporting documentation, and evidenced the activity during a walkthrough of the revised process. Upon review, it all looks good. The action plan was implemented as required and documented in the audit report action plan. The reason the action plan ultimately failed was because there was no audit verification of adoption. The revised business process was implemented but never truly adopted. Just like a promise to go back to the gym, the intention was there, but the reality of the situation is that it is too easy to revert to what you have been doing for the past few years. And the business processing team feels the exact same way.

Action Plan Reporting

Action plan reporting represents a formal process to track all internal audit identified actions along with their current status. This report is utilized internally for the responsible auditors to maintain an active follow-up on outstanding actions and remind action item owners of deliverables and approaching deadlines. In addition, the reporting can proactively identify action plan delinquency to signal the need for any action that needs to be escalated to receive the proper attention to address the confirmed risk. These reports are also used externally, as they are distributed to every action item owner and their management team to ensure there is consistent and regular communication regarding the status of all action plans. This type of reporting ensures communication channels evidence the commitment that the internal audit department has made to being transparent with all business process audit activities. The Beyond Audit methodology also produces action plan status reports and includes them in the quarterly Audit Committee reports to notify the committee of the internal audit department's efforts to address business process risk by actively monitoring and following up on outstanding action plans.

 ACTION PLAN ADOPTION PROCESS

As we noted, the audit department can follow all four steps and then discover that the action plan was not adopted by the business unit. What internal audit departments are going to need to do is draft, develop, and incorporate a formal examination process to confirm that a business partner's action plan has truly been adopted. Without verification that the business action plan has been incorporated into the daily operations, it will be impossible to ensure identified true process risks remain well controlled within the business process. This additional internal audit validation process will also be documented and included in the existing internal audit methodology, along with the action plan adoption detailed steps and templates, if required.

The Beyond Audit methodology incorporates a continuous audit (CA) process, developed internally, which not only validates the implementation of a business action but also provides business generated data to confirm the adoption of same. This customized CA testing approach is proven to deliver accurate and timely results, which can be used as part of a risk-based audit or specifically for confirmation of business action plan adoption. Without a formal process, there will be no way to determine that an implemented business action plan was truly adopted into the daily operations of a business process. And that is what truly causes future business process breakdowns and ultimately repeat audit findings. To properly address the critical need for action plan adoption, the Beyond Audit CA methodology is outlined below. This methodology can be seamlessly incorporated into any audit methodology and deployed as needed.

To effectively utilize a CA methodology, whether it be for audit testing or action plan adoption, it is mandatory that the audit team understand how to define the CA approach. The CA methodology continues to be the most misunderstood and underutilized testing approach used by internal audit departments. To help audit teams understand the CA approach, the definition will be explained first with a formal audit "book" definition and then with a simple definition, which effectively explains the CA approach to the business partner. The audit definition is direct and remarkably similar to the risk-based audit explanation. CA is one of the many tools used with the internal audit profession to provide reasonable assurance that the control environment surrounding an operational process is suitably designed, established, and operating as intended. That definition sounds great. So official and filled with audit-type words like *reasonable assurance, design, established,* and *operating as intended.* Although these words are used constantly by internal auditors, they are literal in their definition. Remember that internal audit is providing a reasonable assurance of the control environment because it is not possible for internal audit to guarantee any process is 100 percent effective due to the fact that internal audit cannot test every possible scenario. Internal audit's validation is on the most critical controls being tested on a representative sample basis. And this reasonable assurance concept is one that is applicable in all internal audit offerings. That is where the *reasonable assurance* wording is coming from in the CA definition.

When looking at the *design, established,* and *operating as intended* description of the CA process, do not get overwhelmed by the terminology. The design characteristic is focusing on the documentation available, which accurately describes the business process requirements to ensure that when the steps are executed in accordance with the policy, the desired outcome will be achieved. The validation point for most auditors when it comes to the design concept is, can the policy be given to a reasonable person without knowledge of the business process to execute the tasks as required? If so, then the process has been suitably designed. The next part of the CA definition surrounding the control environment is to verify the operational process is established. The *established* term, in this definition, is directly linked to the suitably designed concept. To ensure the process is established, the internal auditor will confirm that the process documented in the policies and procedures is the actual process the business process team is currently executing. Too often the documented policies and procedures do not match the work being executed by the business team. Auditors will find it increasing difficult to conclude on the control effectiveness of any process if they cannot determine what the baseline process standard is supposed to look like. Policies and procedures, especially in action plan adoption verification, must be updated and reflect the most current business process requirements. If not, change will never be incorporated successfully or be effective. And the final part of the CA definition regarding the control environment is operating as intended. This is most effectively explained by just looking at the literal definition. Is the process control operating as intended or, in other words, is the control or action plan doing exactly what it was supposed to do and delivering the expected outcome? If it is, then the action plan is operating as intended. It is important that internal auditors do not overthink these characteristics and create testing to adequately determine compliance. A properly drafted and executed CA testing will validate business action plan adoption. Before the CA process overview is described, remember that the CA methodology validates the strength of the newly implemented business action plan to determine whether the control produces repeatable, reliable results. Just validating the control effectiveness upon its initial implementation will not provide any assurance that the action plan was properly designed, truly addresses root cause, and has been accepted and incorporated by the business team. The CA action plan adoption testing provides the most effective method to review the implementation process and confirm adoption.

CA METHODOLOGY OVERVIEW

The CA methodology is simple, direct, and broken down into three phases: the foundation, approach, and execution.

Foundation

The foundation consists of four steps:

1. Create the target area.
2. Create the testing objective.
3. Set the testing frequency.
4. Select a testing technique to verify the action plan execution and results.

First, the target area is used to document the specifics of the action plan to be tested. When considering specifics for the testing, the auditor must consider what the new control is supposed to do (its objective), what a satisfactory outcome looks like from a documentation standpoint, and if there is any need for a technology requirement in the testing. These facts will assist the auditor in understanding the target area or, in this case, action plan detail to be verified.

The second step is for the auditor to create the testing objective. The testing objective should be straightforward and easy to comprehend. Too often, auditors make it too complex instead of just documenting the purpose of the new control and how to effectively test it. The testing objective, drafted from the action plan objective, details the reason the new control is being examined and verifies that the control is generating the intended outcome. It is critically important that the testing objective be documented and communicated to the responsible auditor who will execute the steps. Understanding the testing objective is more critical than the testing itself. A clear understanding of why the testing is being performed provides the responsible auditor with the proper perspective when executing the corresponding steps to determine adoption.

The third step in the foundation is the one that sets the CA testing approach apart for all of the other internal audit methodologies, and it is the testing frequency. Frequency of testing is the most significant difference among audit testing approaches and truly distinguishes CA from all the others. When it comes to verifying adoption of a new business action plan using CA, the recommended frequency as detailed in the Beyond Audit methodology is called "6-9-12." This is the recommend testing frequency for any new business action plan that generates results multiple times per day in its operations.

Before explaining the 6-9-12 frequency, it must be noted that this testing does not begin until the business unit has had 90 days after internal audit has validated implementation. This 90-day grace period provides the business process team members with the appropriate amount of time to become familiar with the new business action plan.

At the conclusion of the 90-day implementation window, the 6-9-12 CA testing approach can be implemented to determine action plan adoption. Here is how it works. This testing approach is executed monthly and to start, requires six consecutive months to be sampled, selected, tested, and reported. After six consecutive months of testing, the next testing period is at the end of month nine, and then the final testing period is at the end of month twelve. For month nine and twelve, the testing sample is done across the previous three months.

For simplicity of explanation, this example will assume that the CA action plan validation testing would begin in January. So, the six consecutive months of testing would start in January and continue monthly with testing in February, March, April, May, and June. Then testing would not occur again until September and that testing would include samples from July, August, and September. The CA testing methodology would conclude with the final round of testing in December, which would include samples from October, November, and December. The "6-9-12" testing frequency is simple in concept and execution but provides valued information regarding the newly implemented business action plan. This valued information comes in the form of recurring results which will indicate whether the new action plan has been adopted in totality or whether there are aspects of the new process which need enhancements to the details or just reinforcement of the critical nature of the control improvement. These conclusions will not be based on speculation or opinion but on data acquired from recurring testing executed as required by the CA methodology foundation.

The final step of the foundation phase of the CA methodology is the testing technique. The requirement here is to ensure that the most effective testing technique is selected to verify the action plan execution and results. Of course, the testing technique will be determined by the business process requirements, but most often, the testing technique used to verify action plan adoption is transaction testing. Transaction testing requires the responsible auditor to select a sample and test the outcome to determine if the newly implemented action plan is delivering the intended outcome. Reperforming the steps required by the action plan is the most effective way to determine compliance and also provides the internal auditor with the opportunity to continue to build on their business process knowledge by getting exposure to transaction-level details in the business process.

Approach

The next phase of the CA methodology is the approach. The approach consists of three steps: sampling, criteria selection, and technology. The sampling to be used in the action plan adoption testing is based on the 6-9-12 testing frequency. The most common question that arises when discussing sampling is, how many should be selected? While there is no right or wrong answer to this question, the Beyond Audit methodology recommends a sample size of 15 per testing period. The reasoning behind 15 is that after many discussions with sampling experts, statistics scholars, auditors (both internal and external), and regulators, the conclusion was that the overall sample size needed to be representative of the transaction selected. All that means is, did the auditor review a sufficient amount of evidence to draw a conclusion that the new action plan has been successfully incorporated (adopted) into the corresponding business process? The sample size of 15 was chosen because it was divisible by three (when the auditor is completing the last two cycles of testing and incorporating testing for a three-month period), and it provides a significant total number of sample items tested. After the 6-9-12 frequency testing has been completed, the auditors will have reviewed 120 action plan transactions to ensure they are being properly executed under the new process requirements. Every auditor will agree that 120 transactions is more than appropriate to draw a conclusion regarding a new business action plan. Some auditors may even consider it to be too many transactions. But given the scrutiny and associated risk, the new control action plan should receive the appropriate level of focus by internal audit to ensure the control is effective and the risk has been mitigated.

The second step in the approach phase is the development of the criteria and attributes to be used in the action plan testing. The criteria and attributes steps are critical to ensuring the corresponding validation testing is accurate and reflects the specific steps needed to determine the action plan being examined is delivering acceptable performance. These steps must be detailed and be able to be understood and executed by an auditor who may not have been involved in the original audit that identified the need for this control enhancement or is familiar with the current business process under review. Like an audit report, these review steps must be clear, understandable, and able to stand on their own and be executed as designed.

The final step in the approach phase is technology. In the CA methodology, technology must be examined to determine if there is going to be a need for an understanding of the technology portion of the new action plan testing or if the auditor completing the validation testing is going to need access to a specific automated system to complete testing. While the technology step in the approach phase is not a significant barrier, the responsible auditor must recognize the technology requirement early (before testing is to begin) to ensure they have the proper knowledge and access to complete the testing in a timely manner.

Execution

The final phase of the CA methodology is the execution. The execution consists of three steps: performance, reporting, and closure. Performance, although simple in its definition, must be stated so that all internal auditors attempting to incorporate a CA methodology into their audit activities have to be told and recognize that for CA to be effective as a testing tool, the CA methodology has to be performed in accordance with the specifics of the methodology. That means, if the frequency of testing is set to utilize the 6-9-12 approach, all associated testing must be performed, no matter what initial results may indicate. There are times when auditors completed the first three months of testing without any questions or exceptions and then artificially concluded that the new business action plan has been properly adopted. That simply is not true. To ensure the accuracy of the adoption of an action plan, the full cycle of testing must be performed. There are no exceptions or shortcuts when it comes to the CA methodology. That is why under the execution phase, the first step to be understood, discussed, and stressed is performance. Outside of the reporting of results, performance is the most critical step in the execution phase. Remember to remain diligent to the methodology requirement and execute the plan as designed.

The next step in the execution phase is reporting. The reporting in the CA methodology is the same as the reporting requirements that apply to any other internal audit activity. That includes a standard report template (the Beyond Audit methodology uses the same report template for all audit activity) detailing the objective of the testing, testing performed, data-driven results, and applicable recommendations and actions if necessary. Do not forget the role of the communication of internal work performed in an effort to add value to the business processes. This CA report is one more opportunity for the internal audit department to show that they are truly a partner to the business management team and are constantly striving to not just improve the products they deliver but also add value to the business teams. The one difference between a CA report and the other internal audit reports is that the scope and the testing is very targeted and directed at the specific control(s) related to the corresponding action plan being verified. The advantage of the action plan CA report is that it is short and direct and being generated on a repeat basis documenting the results of the completed control testing. Also, any identified breakdowns can be quickly identified, addressed, corrected, and verified in the subsequent testing months.

The final step in the execution phase is the notes for action plan closure. Keep in mind during the audit engagement that part of the reporting process is to enter the identified business action plans into the action item database and then track and report on their implementation. Once the action plan has been completed and implementation is verified by internal audit, the open action plan is marked closed, pending adoption (according to the Beyond Audit methodology). As part of the CA testing process to confirm action plan adoption, the CA results are tracked in the action plan database as required in the execution phase, referred to as the action plan closure status notes. Each month, at the completion of the CA testing, the results are entered into the action plan database so that there is documented evidence of the adoption testing performed, as well as any additional changes that may have been required to strengthen the original action plan to ensure a smooth adoption. This documentation step plays a key role in providing specific business data to deliver to the business partner and management the real-time status of action plan adoption and the audit and business partnership working to strengthen the control environment.

 ## ACTION PLAN TRACKING

In an effort to remain dedicated to real action plan adoption and the facilitation of change within the business process, the internal audit department is going to have to take the responsibility of implementing an effective and efficient action plan tracking system. This system will record, track, and follow up on all action items that are identified in the audit reports. And the active maintenance with regard to action plan tracking does not end there. Internal audit departments must document and communicate the status of open action plans on a monthly basis and distribute these implementation statistics to the business management team as well as the individual action plan owners. To ensure the action plan tracking reports contain the most up-to-date information and intelligence from the business unit as well as the action plan owners, the responsible auditor (the auditor who identified the issue during the audit engagement) will contact the action plan owner every month until implementation.

While this may seem like a tedious task for the audit staff, it does not take a significant amount of time to document the status of an open action item and confirm that the business unit is still on track to meet the agreed-upon target date. This monthly check-in not only ensures the internal audit action plan tracking report is accurate upon distribution, but also provides that the auditors actively build and foster their relationship with their business partners.

The Beyond Audit action plan tracking report template contains every open action item broken down in four distinct sections; action by risk level (higher, moderate, lower); action by status (on target or delinquent); action by selected risk (higher greater than three months and moderate greater than six months); and an action item summary indicating monthly activity of actions opened, completed, and remaining. Each one of the action item tracking sections is summarized by responsible division. This type of summary allows the internal audit to actively track their outstanding action items while holding the business partner accountable for the corresponding implementation. In addition, the action item status report is not only distributed to the action item owners and the divisions in which the issue was originally identified but also gets sent to the entire business management team so that there is transparency among the executive team to understand where the most significant actions are being forged. There are internal audit departments that do not develop and distribute action plan status reports. These audit departments work closely with their business partners, identify issues, communicate the audit results, recommend action, and then leave the responsibility for implementation and on-time delivery up to the business unit.

Upon the following audit engagement, internal audit will verify that the issues and actions identified in the last report have been properly addressed by the business. While this may work for some internal audit teams, it is not the most effective manner in which to facilitate change. Having no formal follow-up on outstanding action items creates an environment that allows critical action items to be delayed, neglected, or ignored because there was no accountability assigned during a formal follow-up plan. And just for the record, sending a reminder email to the action item owner telling them that there is still an audit identified action plan outstanding in the business area does not count as diligent follow-up.

Every single day, people get hundreds of emails. Many of them do not get the right amount of attention, if any. And it should be clarified, this lack of focus on the outstanding action item by the responsible business area is not due to some malintent or dislike for audit. Remember that business personnel have ten other fires burning, and the audit plan recommendation and action can get lost in noise or triaged out of the important work or tasks that need to be completed daily. Also do not assume that the delinquency of an action plan is due to ignorance on the part of the business partner. It is not. The lack of proper attention to the open action plan is due to a lack of follow-up on the part of the *internal audit department,* which forces accountability onto the business partner, along with the corresponding sense of urgency based on the documented risk to the business objective achievement.

The most important characteristic of the internal audit action plan tracking reports is to validate every action plan listed with the most up-to-date status. The last thing an internal audit department wants is to have a business owner reply to the entire action plan status report distribution stating that it is inaccurate and contains outdated information. At no time can an audit department afford to have the accuracy of their reporting questioned. The lesson learned here is to verify and validate all corresponding information with the appropriate action item owner before any finalization and subsequent distribution of the action plan status report.

Remember from Chapter 7 that it is helpful to call the internal audit team *change agents.* The key to bringing the concept of being a change agent into reality is to work to facilitate "real change." Real change in any process makes a positive difference. If the internal audit team can remember that facilitating real change focuses on the development, implementation, adoption, and reporting of the joint effort between the audit and business teams, then both teams will benefit from change, which allows the internal audit department to continue to grow in experience and business knowledge and the business team to grow in becoming a more efficient and effective service within the company. The development requires the target action plan to be created in a partnership; the implementation is the result of the business team outlining the new steps and communicating them with their team while the audit department validates those efforts; the adoption is the business team adjusting to the new process requirements with internal audit confirming adherence to the new process steps; and reporting is data-driven, evidencing their adoption testing work and providing detailed reports of their real change process enhancements to their business unit partners. This work and documented reporting continues to drive the message of the benefits an effective audit and business partner relationship can deliver when both sides are driving to the same objective of facilitating real change.

CHAPTER NINE

Internal Audit Dashboards

F
OR ANY INTERNAL AUDIT department to be successful, there has
to be a system of checks and balances to determine performance accuracy and integrity. The most effective way to record and track internal
audit performance is by incorporating a dashboard that captures key metrics
that are representative and reflective of the current internal audit methodology.
This chapter will define and explain a dashboard, as it is much more difficult to
develop and implement a concept without really knowing what it is. In addition,
the benefits of the dashboard along with the corresponding components and
metric suggestions will be identified as well as how to interpret specific metrics
and develop a corresponding action plan to address the gap.

As with any addition to an internal audit department's workload, it is critical to understand why the internal audit department wants a dashboard and
how they intend to use it throughout the department. The first question that
must be answered is, "Why do I want this?" The internal audit department
management team must have a clear answer as to the purpose of how the dashboard is to be incorporated and used within their own group. Considerations
include, but are not limited to, whether this is the best method to track audit
methodology compliance; the most accurate process to track audit plan performance; the most effective way to measure our value to the company; or the
most efficient way to validate that our audit methodology does not contain
any gaps.

After examining the motivation behind implementing a dashboard and
making the decision to move forward, the common consideration to follow is

how an internal audit dashboard is created and what is the most effective way to go from concept to reality without wasting countless hours. In order to build the dashboard, or anything, it has to be defined so that the team members involved in the development understand what the end product should look like and how it should operate.

 ## DASHBOARD DEFINED

So, here is the easiest way to define and understand an internal audit dashboard. A dashboard is a listing of measures of key internal audit department processes or outputs. All of the measures included in the dashboard must link directly to the internal audit objectives. Any measure being recorded and tracked that does not have an impact on the achievement of the department objectives provides zero value to the management team in their efforts to gauge department operations. The selected measures also should include tasks that are linked to both internal (department) and external (client) objectives. The mixture of these two types of objectives ensures the key deliverables throughout the internal audit methodology are being effectively tracked and managed. Additionally, the one key when defining and trying to comprehend the dashboard process is to recognize that these selected measures must originate from the current internal audit methodology.

If an internal audit department does not have a documented and communicated audit methodology, it is impossible to create and implement an internal dashboard. Consider how challenging it would be to try and create key measures surrounding any process if the process itself has no rules, guidelines, or requirements. If that were the case, all of the selected measures would be based on subjective process requirements and probably differ in performance completion depending on the person who processed it. It is not possible to create a dashboard without current policies and procedures or, in this instance, an internal audit methodology. Assuming the department has fully documented and communicated methodology, the determination of how many measures should be tracked must be made. The Beyond Audit methodology recommends that an internal audit dashboard, especially upon initial implementation, should consist of 7 to 12 individual measures. Now, this number could vary starting at a low of 5 and a high of 15, depending on the level of detail in the audit methodology. There is no absolute answer stating that the number of measures to be tracked in an effective internal audit dashboard is a definitive number.

The total number of measures to be included depends on the number of key processes or outputs that have been selected as the most critical to the success of the achievement of the internal audit department's objectives on a consistent basis. If the department has identified the key deliverables, then that becomes the correct number of measures to track. The internal audit dashboard should provide a snapshot of the key deliverables in the audit methodology, along with their performance for the specific time period being tracked. The components of the dashboard will be discussed in detail later in the chapter. It is important to remember that the performance dashboard concept originated from the automobile dashboard. In theory, either dashboard is supposed to provide you with an up-to-date status of performance; in a car, it is speed, oil pressure, gas, etc. And in a business dashboard, it provides a status of the key deliverables of the specific process. Either one is supposed to give a view of the performance being tracked and the concept works very effectively when it is designed based on the supporting process requirements.

So, to effectively develop an internal audit dashboard, let us review the required steps necessary to build a dashboard that will accurately track and report on the effectiveness of key internal audit deliverables. As previously stated, it is not possible to develop a working dashboard unless the audit department has an established audit methodology. The audit methodology is going to be used as the foundational document to construct the internal audit dashboard. Before we go into the methodology review, it should be noted that there is usually a team assigned to the development of the dashboard. This team is made up of auditors across the department at varying levels to ensure there is an active discussion of the methodology requirements as well as a confirmation on the understanding of the methodology requirements. Like any project, there has to be a planning phase to understand and agree on what the final deliverable will be. This planning phase includes the obtaining of the current audit methodology, identification of any established process workarounds, recognition of key process deliverables, and documentation and communication of any chief audit executive expectations. No matter what the team or chief audit expectations may be, the internal audit dashboard will be a data-based reflection of performance measures which will originate from the internal audit methodology. Just like for audit clients, the data and documentation will drive the results in order to ensure that the information being captured and communicated to the audit team is based on actual, irrefutable data and not the opinion of any audit team member.

BEYOND AUDIT – DDIO METHODOLOGY

Using the current internal audit methodology is going to provide the foundation for the dashboard, but this project, more than most internal ones, is going to need a formal development structure in order to ensure its success. The Beyond Audit methodology has created one of the most effective dashboard development approaches, and it is called the DDIO method. Like all the other audit terms, DDIO is an acronym that stands for Define, Develop, Implement, and Operate. While the method is not that complicated, it creates a discipline and accountability as the dashboard goes from a concept into reality with formal checkpoints along the way.

DDIO – Define Phase

The dashboard development process begins with the Define step, which first and foremost requires that a dashboard sponsor be appointed and the development team members be selected. The sponsor is usually the chief audit executive, but it can also be a senior audit team member who has a detailed understanding of not only the audit methodology, but also the overall objectives of the internal audit department. The sponsor is someone who can be relied on in the event there is a development challenge that requires an independent perspective. The main deliverable during this initial phase is to create a formal project charter to drive the development process, as well as to provide a guide to keep the development team on track and focused on the project at hand.

As with any formal project charter, the project objective (purpose) must be clearly defined and stated. Formally documenting the project objective and communicating it to the entire development team ensures that a common goal has been established and that all team members involved recognize the outcome upon completion. This also tends to maintain project focus and efforts during the development process. After the objective is formally documented, the specific deliverables will be discussed and documented. During the project charter development, there should be a discussion regarding what internal audit wants the final dashboard to look like and what critical components it needs to contain. A concept picture must be established at this point so that the specific details can be created in the Develop and Implement steps of the DDIO method.

After establishing the objectives and identifying the deliverables, all project charters require consideration as to what potential risks and likely benefits could arise and be recognized in this development process. Obviously, there are numerous benefits to an internal audit performance dashboard. The first and most critical is the ability to verify consistent compliance with the established internal audit methodology. Unfortunately, even when internal audit departments have well documented and communicated methodologies, there is almost always a lack of consistent compliance with that methodology. This inconsistency is mostly due to the fact that auditors create new ways to complete tasks and bring personal or previous audit experience into their current job. And while neither of these things are bad, it does make for an audit department compiling an inconsistent product or audit documentation. A fully integrated dashboard assists in the identification of methodology inconsistencies and helps drive the focus back to the objectives of the formal, established internal audit methodology. Other benefits include things like audit phase delivery compliance, effective template usage, action item tracking, and even audit staff development and tenure. On the flipside of this requirement are the challenges that a dashboard development team faces, also known as the risks. Now, the risk specifics will vary, depending on the development team. However, the important concept to note here is when documenting the potential risks, have a discussion to address the question of what could stand in the way or prevent the development team from achieving the project objectives. This type of discussion is free form to solicit any thoughts or suggestions of events, information, data, technology, or management support that could hinder the development. This is truly one of those times where there is never a bad suggestion to put out there to be discussed as a potential barrier. It is a confirmed fact that when risks (barriers) are identified, discussed, and documented, development teams are more aware of them and more quickly recognize the impact of risks being realized. The last component of the project charter to complete is the timeline and corresponding target dates. The timeline must clearly indicate the delivery of the initial completed dashboard as well as the interim target dates with their specific deliverables. The formal documentation of these deliverables and dates helps the development team maintain focus and keep the team on track to deliver the completed dashboard on time. The other advantage to having target dates and deliverables is so that delays in the delivery can be proactively identified and communicated to the team and project sponsor.

DDIO – Develop Phase

The next step in the DDIO method is Develop. Develop is the step in which the current internal audit methodology is obtained and reviewed since it serves as the source document from which all of the dashboard measures to be selected will originate. The different techniques for analyzing the audit methodology will be discussed but it is important to understand that the identification of the key process steps which produce audit products, internally and externally, will be required in this step of the DDIO methodology. The selection of critical audit process steps will provide the detailed measures that will be tracked and measured on a recurring basis. This review and identification of audit deliverables should be discussed in detail to identify the most critical steps and deliverables within the audit process. Remember, not every step in the process can be selected as a dashboard measure. The objective of a dashboard is not to get too granular in the analysis but to identify the most valuable steps that contribute to the overall audit product. The detailed discussion of the development step requirement will include a review of the three most popular methods utilized in breaking down the audit process into the key phases and deliverables: flowchart, narrative, and SIPOC (utilized in the Six Sigma process). It will be up to the individual dashboard development teams to select the technique they are most comfortable with in reviewing their audit methodology.

This step in the dashboard development process of breaking the audit methodology (or approach) into the three main phases and the corresponding responsibilities in each one will ultimately determine the specific measures to be tracked on a recurring basis. The breakdown and documentation of this process can be accomplished using a few different techniques. It is important to note that even though the auditors assigned to the dashboard development project are (or at least should be) intimately familiar with the internal audit methodology, it is still a required step in the dashboard development process to formally document the internal audit methodology process just like an auditor would document the specific steps in a business process being audited. This formal documentation step provides the dashboard development team with the illustrative information to view the audit process along with the specific required deliverables included in each phase of an audit.

Process documentation in audits or any other project always seems to rely on the preference of the creator. The following is an overview of the three options to assist you in selecting a favorite technique.

Flowcharts

Starting with the *flowchart*, the advantage of this techniques is that it creates a visual representation of the process and it becomes much easier to visualize the flow of information from start to finish. Also, gaps or breakdowns in the process are more easily identified in a flowchart than any other technique.

While there are no glaring negatives to the flowchart process, some believe the development of the flowchart takes too long. That may have been true in the older days of flowchart development, but the creation of process documentation software makes the flowchart process much simpler and quicker.

Narrative

Another technique used in the audit document process is the *narrative*. The biggest advantage to developing a narrative is the fact that any team member could do it, as it is just a written prose of the process details. The narrative, in its most basic form, is a story describing the process from start to finish. That task seems pretty direct and simple. However, this may be the biggest disadvantage when it comes to the narrative. The reason behind that is the written story must contain the proper level of details as well as the identification and documentation of the most critical parts of the process.

Further complicating the story could be that the person documenting the process details does not have the most intimate knowledge of the audit process, which leads to potential gaps in the formal audit procedures. Additionally, identifying the most critical control or delivery points in a process may be more difficult to document when being described in a narrative as compared to a flowchart. The pictorial depiction in a flowchart makes critical process hand-offs and deliveries much more evident than when it is written in paragraph format. So be cautious in selecting what appears to be the easier documentation type. At the end of it all, it might be more time consuming to complete the fully described narrative than the flowchart.

Six Sigma – SIPOC

The final type of internal audit methodology documentation suggestion is called the SIPOC – Suppliers, Inputs, Process, Outputs, and Clients (Table 9.1). The SIPOC is a documentation technique that forces, for lack of a better term,

TABLE 9.1 SIPOC Template

Suppliers	Inputs	Process	Outputs	Clients
Source of the input	Information required to complete the process step	Required steps to execute the process	Product generated by the process step	Recipient and user of the process product

the developer to utilize the specific deliverables in the process to facilitate the creation of the SIPOC while at the same time capturing critical information regarding each individual step. Here is how it works.

The most efficient way to complete the SIPOC template is to do it in a very deliberate order that helps to facilitate the flow of information. The SIPOC template completion documentation will begin with the Process column first, then the Outputs, then the Clients, then the Inputs, and finally the Suppliers. While it might seem counterproductive to start in the middle of the template, it is the most effective and efficient way to document the process being examined.

The Process column, which initiates the SIPOC process, compiles and documents the individual process steps from start to finish. The Process section represents the execution of the process, or in this case, the audit from planning to report generation. Whatever steps are required to complete an audit from beginning to end will be recorded in the Process column. The good news is that completing this column of the SIPOC template is most difficult, as the corresponding information has to be obtained from the internal audit methodology documentation, while the remainder of the columns in this particular template are derived from the information documented in the Process column.

After documenting the Process information, the next step is to complete the Outputs column. The output information is identified by considering every single step detailed in the Process column and asking, "Does this particular step, on its own, generate an outcome?" If the Process step does generate an output (or outcome), then it is captured in the Outputs column, which evidences the direct linkage between the two. If the process step does not create an output, then no information needs to be recorded in the Outputs column. This question is repeated for every step in the Process column until all of the corresponding outputs are captured. Next, the Clients column is filled in utilizing the same approach as the one used to complete the Outputs column. For every single output documented, the Clients column is completed by asking, "Who uses this specific output to complete their own task or make a decision?" If it helps to better understand this column, the Beyond Audit methodology calls the individuals or groups, detailed in the Clients column, users, or recipients. Because whatever information is placed in the Clients column indicates that they need the process generated information to complete their own tasks, thus the name, *users*. After the Clients column has been completed, the next step in the SIPOC template is to move to the Inputs column and follow the same thought process using the information already documented in the Process column to identify the corresponding inputs. For each recorded process step, ask, "What input is needed to complete this individual process step?" The input can be financial, as in a cost per unit or amount processed, or nonfinancial, such as an invoice, approval, date, item number, batch total, or authorization code.

Whatever input is needed to complete the associated step must be documented as an input. Also, the Inputs column has the same requirement as the Outputs column in that it captures any and all information that could be used to complete the corresponding steps recorded in the Process column. The final required step to complete in the SIPOC template is the Suppliers column. To document this column, the information identified in the Inputs column is used as the driver in determining where the specific input information was generated. Ask, "Where did this particular input come from?" The easiest way to look at the Suppliers column is to think of this information as the source. The inputs identified had to come from somewhere, like another internal department or an outside vendor, or possibly from a report, invoice, or system. No matter what the source, the input had to be generated from somewhere or someone, and that is what is to be recorded in the Suppliers column.

Once all of the columns have been completed, a more complete view of the process emerges, along with the flow of information that is required to complete the particular steps of the process and the intended outcome of each step that was documented in the Process column. The main reason behind the SIPOC inclusion in the Beyond Audit methodology is that this particular template changes the auditor's perspective on process documentation from one of capturing the individual steps from start to finish to asking detailed follow-up questions to become more intimate with what type of information is required to complete the process and who else inside or outside the company is relying on the process. That type of detailed process information provides auditors with enormously powerful insight and makes them more effective audit team members. In this instance, it provides auditors with a more insightful view of the internal audit methodology requirements.

Beyond Audit SIPOC Example

One of the most important keys to ensuring the SIPOC is completed accurately is to verify that the source documentation (in this instance, the documented internal audit methodology) is the most up-to-date version and contains all of the current corresponding templates, which are required in each phase of the audit.

Always remember that the source documentation is what drives each column of information inside of the SIPOC, which will ultimately be used to

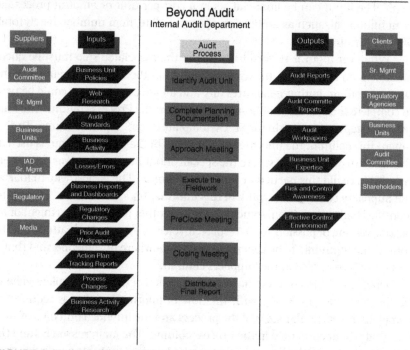

FIGURE 9.1 SIPOC internal audit.

identify and build the specific measures inside of the internal audit dashboard. Figure 9.1 is a high-level example of a completed internal audit SIPOC.

This SIPOC example is just for informational purposes to illustrate the organization of information which would be included in a completed template. Obviously, the process column would have a much more detailed description of the audit steps necessary to execute an audit from start to finish. For example, the process step listed in Figure 9.1 that states Complete Planning Documentation would include all the necessary steps required in the planning of an audit, including, but not limited to, review of prior-year workpapers (if available), identify and document the business objectives, facilitate an entrance meeting, complete business process flowcharts, develop a risk and controls matrix, create an audit program.

The level of detail included in the Process column does not have to be at the individual task level but should capture the main activities of the audit from start to finish. The Beyond Audit methodology suggests that when developing an internal audit dashboard, three SIPOCs should be created for clarity of details, one for each phase of the audit (planning, fieldwork, and reporting). This segregation of main phases of an audit also ensures that the SIPOC does not get too large and difficult to follow.

DDIO – Implement Phase

The next step in the DDIO method is Implement. This step not only includes the dashboard design, presentation, but also details the data collection, scoring, and communication process. Believe it or not, presentation of the dashboard measures plays a critical role. The most effective dashboards are the ones that provide a clear picture upon review and do not require much, if any, interpretation. Too often, internal audit teams attempt to overload the dashboard with information in an effort to strengthen the message, but the information abundance technique often fails. As discussed in Chapter 7 in reference to the audit report, too many words or information does not help with the message delivery but usually confuses the reader.

The same is true when it comes to the dashboard. Think about the dashboard in your car. When a driver glances down to see the speed limit or the gas gauge, there is no additional information or explanation needed. The measure itself delivers the intended message. That is the objective of the internal audit dashboard. The measure itself and how it performed against the corresponding criteria will immediately indicate success or failure without any other explanation needed. That is how the development team will know the measure has been properly selected and depicted on the dashboard. Do not underestimate the value of the dashboard presentation. This step is not just a formality but a critical part of the implementation step of the development methodology. The other critical part of the implement step is the identification of how the corresponding data will be collected and development of the criteria against which the data collected will be measured. A formal plan must be developed that will detail how the data retrieval process will work, including the method, timing, and source from where the data will be pulled. Keep in mind, once the parameters of the data retrieval process are set, they remain consistent. The data collection process does not change each time the dashboard information is retrieved. This consistency is mandatory if the dashboard information is to be of any value when comparing performance on an ongoing basis.

Once the data collection process has been formalized, the next requirement of the implementation step is to set the measurement criteria. These criteria, or scoring system, will establish the specific parameters with in which the data will be evaluated. The type of scoring system to be used will again be up to the individual dashboard development teams. Typically, the scoring system consists of three levels to indicate that the measure is on track, needs focus, or is failing to meet the requirements. The three different scores can be portrayed with numbers, words, or colors. Most dashboards use colors (green, yellow, and red) to indicate performance, as it provides immediate focus on the failing measures (red). However, at the end of the day, it does not matter if you use words, numbers, or colors, as long as the measures that are failing to meet the audit methodology requirements get the proper level of attention needed to address the performance gap.

The most important component of the measurement criteria is not how it is scored but the individual parameters that separate the three different scores. These criteria parameters must be established and represent an absolute value when being applied. What that means is that there is no exception when scoring the retrieved data. There is no interpretation of the data, consideration of workload, or extenuating circumstances, team, or client challenges. The data represents the current performance, and is placed into the corresponding criteria scoring that matches the specific parameters. The interpretation or reasoning behind the score or failure will be explained after the dashboard results have been presented. The key in this step is to maintain the consistency and integrity of the reporting and allow the dashboard to accurately represent true audit performance. With that in mind, the dashboard reporting is the final requirement in the implementation step and has its own standards of communication delivery.

While the dashboard communication process is standard, it relies on the other pieces of the implementation step to be successful. To implement an effective dashboard process, strict communication guidelines should be known throughout the entire audit department. That begins with the understanding that all dashboard information is compiled at the end of the last business day of the month. So as an auditor, everyone understands that for information to be included in the dashboard, all pertinent audit documents and requirements must be completed by the last business day of the month or it will not be included in the current dashboard data retrieved. If the information is not completed by the end of the month, it will appear in the dashboard data as if it was never done. While that might seem harsh or too aggressive for some audit departments, it is the only way to let internal audit teams recognize the critical role of the dashboard. If you want to implement a successful dashboard process, make zero exceptions when it comes to this rule. With the stringent rules surrounding dashboard development and communication, there is no time allotted for exceptions (excuses) and constant updating of the dashboard report.

Once the data is pulled and compiled, the dashboard is communicated to the internal audit team leads by the fifth of the following month. This provides the audit team leads with 10 days to review and research the dashboard information as they prepare for the monthly team meeting, which is scheduled for the fifteenth of the month. It is in that meeting where the dashboard details will be discussed and explained.

DDIO – Operate Phase

The final step in the DDIO is Operate. The operate step consists of the announcement communication of the dashboard process to the entire internal audit department, which includes a clear message to the team, so everyone understands their role and impact on the dashboard. Too many times, individual audit team members believe that the dashboard is a "management" tool and that auditors have no impact or influence on the process. Nothing could be further from the truth. It is critical for the internal audit management team to stress that the dashboard is a measurement tool of team performance.

Regardless of an auditor's title or role, every person in the audit department has an impact on the monthly reporting. An additional message that must be strictly conveyed is that the dashboard in no way, shape, or form is designed as an individual evaluation or performance tool. This is not about how well an auditor performed on a particular assignment. The dashboard has been designed and implemented to ensure the audit methodology has been designed and implemented effectively while delivering a consistent and quality product to the business partners.

After the dashboard objectives have been clearly stated and understood, the dashboard initiation date will be established, and the first set of data points will be collected and reported. At this moment, the initial dashboard report will be examined and the detailed metrics reviewed to ensure the dashboard project charter requirements have been achieved and are delivering the expected performance measures that facilitate the audit process. Remember, the selected measures and corresponding criteria must be kept up to date and reflect the most current internal audit methodology requirements. As the dashboard process evolves, there will be instances where the performance criteria will have to be adjusted as the audit process becomes more effective and efficient. The measurement criteria should be challenging and attainable. Establishing unrealistic or unreasonable dashboard criteria does not work and ends up not only frustrating the team but also creating more work than is required during a normal audit.

There is one final note of caution: While dashboards provide a valuable insight into the audit methodology compliance and performance of an audit team, there is one huge negative impact that dashboards sometimes create within an audit department. The biggest risk a chief audit executive or audit management team takes when implementing an internal audit dashboard is that the established and communicated dashboard requirements start to drive auditor behavior on an engagement. What that means is that many auditors, while participating on an audit, will do whatever it takes to make the corresponding dashboard measurement criteria so that their audit is not listed as an exception on the dashboard. Trust me when I say that this happens more often than not. Auditors do not want to be seen as the reason for failure, either during an audit or as a contributing factor as to why an audit is listed as an outlier on the dashboard report. That is why it is so critically important that the audit management team stresses that the dashboard is designed to focus on opportunities to identify audit process weaknesses and strengthen the audit methodology. The only way that process improvements can be made is if weaknesses in the methodology are exposed and solutions are considered. Do not, under any circumstances, let your internal audit dashboard drive the behavior of anyone on your audit team. That is not a productive environment that any auditor would want to be included.

AUDIT DASHBOARD FUNCTIONS

Now that the review and selection of the most critical points in the audit methodology have been identified via the SIPOC, it is time to discuss the overall dashboard and explain the corresponding components necessary to provide an adequate level of detail to communicate the results. The dashboard itself consists of two sections, the metrics (measurement) page and the corresponding criteria page. Figure 9.2 shows the detailed dive into the specific fields that should be included in the metrics page. Upon an initial glance, it looks

Dashboard Metrics

Critical Measures	Benchmark/Target	Monthly Performance	Status ▫ ▫ ■	Prior Mth Trend	Comments
Report Timeliness - Risk Based Audits	6 Weeks	8 Weeks	▫	⟷	Includes three reports issued
Professional Staff Productivity	80%	64% Average	■	⬇	Prior month was 73%

FIGURE 9.2 Beyond Audit dashboard terms explained.

like an overwhelming amount of data, but in reality it is a listing of a specific performance measure with an identified target goal and then data showing the actual performance. So do not let the initial appearance of the dashboard prevent you from examining the enclosed information. For ease of updating, formatting, and potential trend analysis, most internal audit dashboards are reported using Excel. It does not matter what software you use to capture and report your dashboard as long as it is accurate and properly reflects the source data when rating the performance of each metric.

The first column in Figure 9.2 in the Beyond Audit dashboard template is the critical measure that identifies each measure on the dashboard. This is followed by the benchmark/target for the measure. This states the requirement needed for the measure itself to be considered satisfactory (or in our template – green). The next column states the captured data (actual performance) for the associated time period (usually a month). The next two columns provide perspective on the data – first on the performance for the month and then a trend arrow indicating the current month's rating compared to the previous time period. This performance arrow indicates whether the particular audit measure has been consistent, deficient, or improving in performance. The completed dashboard consists of these five columns and conveys a very impactful message when built correctly that can identify opportunities for improvement and drive positive change in the internal audit department. One additional point to be noted: Some internal audit groups include a sixth column in their dashboard for comments. This comment field can be used to explain an anomaly in the data or specific details/challenges surrounding the collection of the data. While not required in the dashboard itself, the comment column is a solid addition to the dashboard format in the event that any clarification relating to a dashboard measure is required.

The second section of the dashboard is the criteria detail page (Figure 9.3). This is also a five-column template and is structured exactly like the metrics page beginning with the measurement name and the corresponding benchmark/target in the first two columns. The following three columns detail the

Dashboard Metric Criteria

Critical Measures	Benchmark/ Target	Criteria ▭	Criteria ▭	Criteria ▭	Comments
Report Timeliness - Risk Based Audits	6 Weeks	6 Weeks	7 - 8 Weeks	9+ Weeks	Elapsed time from fieldwork to final report issuance
Professional Staff Productivity	80%	80%	75% - 79%	< 75%	For staff auditors with no management responsibilities

FIGURE 9.3 Beyond Audit dashboard criteria detail page.

specific performance requirements associated with each potential rating of green, yellow, or red. There is no ambiguity related to these rating parameters as they are detailed and specific and require zero interpretation. They are specific to ensure it is simple to assign a rating with the actual performance for the time period to eliminate any potential dispute or disagreement with the conclusion. Remember, the dashboard is based on the actual performance data and is not impacted by any subjective scoring or auditor interpretation. As was indicated with the metrics page, a sixth column for comments can be added to the criteria page if desired. Again, not a requirement for the dashboard itself, but it does provide a space for any clarification commentary.

While deciding on the format of the dashboard is important, there is a more critical decision to be made, and that is selecting an audit team member who will be the metrics leader. The metrics leader is the individual who is responsible for all aspects of the administration of the dashboard. This person will own the dashboard, which means they will be responsible for the compilation of the data from various sources, development of the monthly metrics and corresponding performance scores, distribution of the completed metric reports to the audit management team, facilitation of the audit dashboard meeting, and receipt and tracking of any required action plans.

Given this list of critical roles, the auditor chosen to be the metrics leader must possess a certain set of skills that can be directly applied to this demanding assignment. First and foremost, this individual must be disciplined and organized, as this role requires someone who can multitask at a high level and focus on the results being driven by the compiled data. Multitasking requires a strong discipline because this auditor has audit responsibilities as well as having the additional task of dashboard creation, maintenance, and reporting. Just because this person is responsible for the dashboard does not alleviate any of the day-to-day audit deliverables. The dashboard job is an add-on. Keep that in mind when determining which member of your team can handle this challenging assignment. This person also must possess an intimate knowledge of the current audit methodology and its requirements because the dashboard itself is based on the audit methodology deliverables. In addition, this team member has to be comfortable with being challenged on the dashboard results. If auditors thought it was difficult to field questions about data and results from a business partner, just wait until those types of questions are being posed from the audit leadership team. It can be quite daunting and intimidating for the metrics leader. However, like any other audit position, if the metrics leader has tone from the top support (chief audit executive) coupled with the data integrity to support (not defend) the audit performance dashboard, there should be no problem with addressing questions from the audit leadership team. Remember, the metrics leader will facilitate the monthly metrics meeting to discuss the internal audit department's performance, and the selected participants (usually the internal audit management team) will explain any of their metrics that received a yellow or red rating. Additionally, the metrics leader, when applicable, will be responsible for obtaining and tracking any action plans from the meeting that are required to address any deficient measures.

As discussed, when dashboard metrics are not meeting their benchmark or target, that same metric will receive a yellow or red rating. In that instance, the management team will decide the best technique to address the failing measure. The Beyond Audit methodology recommends two different techniques to problem solving. One is a brainstorming approach, which is recommended for smaller and less complex issues. The other is a formal project methodology when the problem itself is more complicated or potentially is a department-wide issue. For the less-complex identified issues, the brainstorming problem approach is called ICONS, Identify Creative Options for New Solutions. This can be accomplished by selecting a few audit team members to discuss the measure and its performance over the last several months to try and identify the root cause and develop multiple suggestions to address the problem. These suggestions will then be presented and discussed with the internal audit management team to decide, as a team, what the most effective course of action would be to address the deficiency. This decision and corresponding action will be implemented and tracked to conclude on the action plan effectiveness. Ultimately, the implemented action plan will be measured by the dashboard results in the coming months to decide the appropriateness of the steps taken and if additional enhancements or changes are required. When a dashboard measure indicates a significant deviation from the methodology, a complex issue, or potentially a department-wide concern, then a formal project methodology should be applied as the brainstorming session will not be sufficient to fully understand the issue and identify root cause to determine a solution without a formal approach.

The recommended formal project methodology is called a DMAIC, which stands for Define, Measure, Analyze, Improve, and Control. The reason this project method is the most effective for use with dashboard identified gaps is that the DMAIC comes from the Six Sigma process and focuses on the data. Combining the DMAIC methodology with the dashboard process creates a natural flow of information, since both are created with data to drive the most accurate results. The DMAIC requires formal documentation (project charter) and analysis in evaluating the problem, comparing data results, utilizing root cause to develop an action plan, and monitoring the results to determine if the proposed action plan addressed the problem. Remember to select the appropriate problem-solving technique for opportunities identified in your internal audit dashboard.

An effectively designed dashboard created from the current internal audit methodology can be a valuable tool for the audit management team to utilize in running the internal audit department. The dashboard has numerous benefits when implemented effectively. The biggest benefit of the dashboard is that it facilitates trending and other analysis. The critical deliverables in an audit methodology are being formally captured on a recurring basis and then displayed effectively for a period-to-period comparison. Keep in mind that this comparison is being done on an ongoing basis so that audit department management teams are receiving current data to proactively identify trends, both positive and negative. Another benefit is that, whether the audit team wants it or not, a specific outcome of the dashboard is that it creates discussion.

As previously mentioned, communication should be the foundation of all internal audit departments, but sadly, not all departments communicate effectively internally on a consistent basis. The dashboard facilitates a more communicative environment because the data collection is always objective, universal across the department, and creates a common reference point for all team members. This "team" approach, which the dashboard creates, ensures there is discussion among the team as the successes and challenges are identified on a consistent basis. This consistency of evaluation focuses internal audit teams to strive for department excellence while establishing a standard measurement process throughout the department.

One last benefit to consider is that the dashboard speeds improvement. The dashboard information, when communicated and addressed in a timely fashion, facilitates the initiation of improvement activities with targeted action plans. The dashboard also provides a proactive tool that more easily identifies performance gaps because it focuses on the audit methodology deliverables across the department. Too many times, the focus of audit teams is to complete audits, and that focus could result in some of the technical methodology requirement omissions or gaps going undetected. These potential omissions or gaps will be identified in the dashboard if it was created using the internal audit methodology as the source. These identified and validated benefits can be used in the internal audit department's discussions when determining how the department could benefit from a dashboard.

A thought-out, well-designed dashboard focused on the key deliverables of an internal audit department will assist the management team in fostering a positive learning environment. In order to accomplish this, it is important that during the development, creation, implementation, and monitoring of the dashboard, remember that the dashboard itself is a developing concept. As with any new concept or tool, it is paramount that there is a clear understanding of the objective. Always keep in mind the real objective that the dashboard has been implemented in the first place. To accompany the objective, the internal audit team must recognize that while the dashboard has many uses, it does have limitations. The biggest limitation is that it will not capture every aspect of an audit methodology. There are instances where audit departments implement a dashboard and believe that will provide effective monitoring over all audit activities and ensure 100 percent audit methodology compliance. The dashboard will do no such thing. The dashboard tracks critical components of the audit methodology, but proper oversight and governance can never be replaced.

The other consideration for dashboard success is to ensure that however the audit department structures the dashboard, the audit management team and the metrics leader must remain consistent in all aspects of the process and provide the proper support for the initiative. This can be accomplished through constant team support and effective dashboard documentation of the approach and the results. Also, always remember that any changes to the current internal audit methodology must be reviewed against the current dashboard measures to ensure no adjustments are required to the specific metrics or criteria to reflect the audit methodology changes.

To help in the development of the internal audit dashboard, detailed below are eight bulleted items which have been compiled over the past 20 years that identify recommendations to discuss within your team as you move forward in your dashboard process.

 AUDIT DASHBOARD – LESSONS LEARNED

It is critically important that every internal audit department recognizes that developing and implementing a functioning dashboard, even when they have a fully documented established methodology, still requires time and effort. These are some advantages and challenges to using a dashboard:

- It takes time to implement.
- It requires audit methodology and planning.

- Achievable metrics must be developed.
- Realistic metric criteria must be created.
- Communicate dashboard objectives and expectations to the audit team.
- You must still identify and select a strong metrics leader.
- Utilize techniques to identify root cause based on dashboard data.
- It assists the team in facilitating needed change with proper action.

The final advice to remember is that the dashboard is a performance tool to assist departments in the proactive identification of compliance with their own methodology and opportunities for improvement. But these goals can only be achieved if reasonable metrics and corresponding criteria are properly established, root cause techniques are applied, actionable plans are implemented, and real change is tracked and verified. If these tips are utilized, any internal audit department can improve on its current operations.

CHAPTER TEN

Communication Focus

S THE REQUIREMENTS, DEMANDS, and dynamics of executing an internal audit change, the internal audit department must adjust to the new environment in which audit engagements are being completed. As the audit operations move from in person to a remote requirement, the reliance on effective communication will continue to grow and become more demanding. Throughout the book to this point, communication and its impact on the audit process has been referenced and stressed as a contributing factor for success. This chapter will analyze the communication model, skills, profile, and key deliverables needed in each phase of an audit to ensure success as internal audit teams try to navigate the new audit engagement environment successfully.

Communication is a critical skill that all auditors must possess if they want to succeed in the audit operating environment and this skill will be scrutinized to a much deeper degree during a remote audit engagement. Consider how much more reliance will be placed on an auditor's words and message when all requests will be facilitated over the phone or via videoconference call. As with any audit skill, the objective of the skill must be understood in order to recognize the effort needed to accomplish the corresponding objective. Communication as a foundational skill is no different. The first step to developing a strong communication foundation is to recognize the importance of the communication model. Too many internal audit departments believe communication success comes from building their relationship skills with business partners. Unfortunately, this is an incorrect assumption. It is not possible to create strong business partner relationships without recognizing the mandatory role that the communication model plays in ensuring relationship success. The communication model provides the foundation for which all exchanges of information occur, regardless if it is face to face, on the phone, or on a video-conference.

The communication model consists of three parts: a sender, a receiver, and the medium in which the message is being delivered. This chapter will provide both direction on verbal communication techniques as well as suggestions for clear and consistent written communications to provide to your business partner in each phase of the audit as evidence that internal audit understands the value of the message during an audit engagement (remote or otherwise).

UNDERSTANDING THE COMMUNICATION MODEL

When examining the communication model, the sender and receiver roles are clear cut. The sender is the individual delivering the message while the receiver is the individual accepting the message. The challenge in the communication model is always going to be the delivery medium. The medium is the method in which the message is conveyed from the sender to the receiver. The message can be delivered face to face, via videoconference or meeting, over the phone, or in a written format such as an email, text, or instant message. From the beginning of the list of potential message medium delivery options, the types go from strongest to weakest. There is no substitution for delivering a message in person. Do not underestimate the power of meeting in person, as it provides the individuals sharing the message the opportunity to formally meet and obtain a recognition of the intentions of the person delivering the message. Also, it allows the person sending the message to more quickly identify the receiver's lack of understanding or comfort with the message being delivered, both of which can be quickly addressed with qualifying details explaining the message or how the message itself was determined.

If the situation presents itself, even during a remote audit engagement, to deliver a message in person, take it. The value getting introduced and being able to communicate the objectives of the internal audit department cannot be measured. That is why it is critical for all internal audit team members to be prepared for every single meeting. That does not mean internal audit does not have the opportunity to speak to the business partner directly like in a video-conference, meeting, or on the phone, but nothing takes the place of a one-on-one, in-person, message delivery.

After considering the direct contact message delivery, the focus can shift to the nondirect mediums that include email, text messaging, or instant messaging. While all of these mediums are successful in message communication, none will ever be as effective as one of the direct message types just discussed. The biggest challenge with a nondirect message delivery medium is that the message itself has a much larger possibility of being misunderstood, unclear, unsupported, or just ignored. Consider how many messages (of all types) a person receives on any given day. There are way too many to count, and often a large percentage of those messages go unread. When internal auditors are dealing with a critical request, question, or message, pertaining to a remote engagement, receiving a response timely has critical implications not only to the message itself, but also to the overall review. That is the primary reason internal auditors must be aware that in all business partner communications, auditors must deliver the right message, to the right person, at the right time. Let us take a quick look at each one of the internal audit (mandatory) message characteristics.

Right Message

When it comes to the *right message*, there can be no doubt that the message being delivered is clear, concise, and contains the proper information to support it. The biggest barrier to the message recipient not receiving the intended message, which is often the situation, is when the message itself is not clear and requires interpretation when heard or read. Be aware of one absolute fact – interpretation is the number-one enemy of any message. Too often, the message being delivered makes perfect sense when it is being spoken or when it is being read. But the unfortunate truth is that the message only makes sense to the sender and will not be clearly understood by the receiver. Of course, the sender believes the message is crystal clear, because they wrote it or are speaking it and have the benefit of all the background knowledge which leads them to develop the message in the first place. However, in actuality, the message is missing some critical component (data, background, risk, etc.) that is making it unclear to the recipient. When delivering any message in person or otherwise, be certain to step back and verify the message is complete in content, contains no ambiguity, and requires zero interpretation. This can be accomplished by completing a cold review of the message before an in-person meeting or the sending of an email. As you review the message, put yourself in the place of the message receiver and determine if there is a clear, concise, fact-based message. This will reduce the amount of time spent trying to explain or justify the original message in the meeting or in an email session.

Right Person

The next characteristic is to ensure that once the right message has been scripted, it is delivered to the *right person*. When determining who needs to receive the message, the internal auditor must understand the specific objective(s) of the message and not think about the list of recipients, yet. The message details will provide the auditor with the information required to guarantee that all impacted parties are getting the same direct, clear message. Too often, internal audit teams provide the message (questions, clarifications, preliminary testing results, or issues) to the business partner contact who may or may not know what to do with the associated message. The message information itself should direct the internal auditor to recognize the business team member for whom the message is intended and that they understand how to handle the information. There are numerous instances where the internal auditor spends time drafting the appropriate message only to have the message go unaddressed because the correct recipient never received it. To ensure the audit message is conveyed correctly, identify the business partner who is in the best position to hear, answer, and provide explanation to the specific message when needed.

Right Time

The final characteristic of the right message being delivered to the right person is to ensure that the right message is delivered *in a timely manner*. For any instance where an internal audit team uses the word *timely*, there should always be a specific day or date range associated with the statement. However, when it comes to delivering the right message, timely does not have a date or range. *Timely* in message delivery means the message will be delivered after the data and corresponding information have been reviewed (internally by the audit team) and verified (externally with the business partner) and the message has been scripted to include the information and supporting data necessary for a clear, concise delivery to the appropriate business partners and requires no interpretation. This type of focus and dedication to the message details and creation eliminates debates over message validity and wording choices that will result in wasted time doing unnecessary rework. Remember to understand the message objective, verify the details, understand the recipient's perspective, and take the necessary time to craft a complete message to keep all parties "in the know" during the engagement and maintain a high level of transparency in the internal audit and business partner communications.

 ## MESSAGE DELIVERY

No matter how internal audit is viewed within your company, communications are always going to be challenged by the message recipient just because of the source delivering it. In order to be certain that the intended message is being received, there are some suggested skills when it comes to the delivery. Communication associated with any internal audit engagement is going to be challenging because the role of internal audit is to examine business processes to verify that the corresponding control environment is producing the intended results. And in any case where the control environment is not performing as designed, the internal audit team will record the details, verify their validity, and present those results to the business partner. That presentation of results, in any form of communication, is likely to be received with skepticism and resistance.

Take that confirmed fact of the internal audit role and compound the difficulty of message delivery with the new environment of remote auditing. This new environment presents an even more challenging situation for the auditors because the message details must be crystal clear and be able to stand on their own (as all messages should), since there are no in-person opportunities to meet and explain the details or address ongoing validation which may be required from the business partner. One of the aspects of remote auditing that exacerbates the message delivery challenges is that in this day and age, too much reliance is placed on the email medium in communicating information. Email is already depended on too much during a "normal" audit and ultimately becomes the primary communication medium in remote engagements. Email should not be the primary medium of communication, no matter what type of audit activity is being performed. Email is sufficient for the physical delivery of the information, but it is always recommended that you follow up with a phone call to confirm delivery and to communicate expectations along with a time frame for response, if required. To ensure the delivery of the internal audit message is clear, consider these few tips. Keep in mind that these communication suggestions can be applied to every type of communication medium but are particularly valuable during remote engagements.

Don't Get Emotional

In any communication, it is important to remove emotion from the delivery. An emotionally charged environment is likely during audit engagements, and when a critical or constructive message has to be communicated, the level of emotion becomes even more relevant. The important thing to remember is that the message being delivered is not an opinion-based message: it is a message based on business partner–produced data and facts. During these communications, all subjectivity needs to be removed and there must be a focus on data, which, at the end of the day, should be irrefutable (if it has been properly verified with the business partner in advance).

The key to keeping emotion of out of the message delivery process, or at least in check, is to respond to any questions and not to react. It's one thing to simply say *don't get emotional*, but in reality, it is exceedingly difficult not to get caught up in the emotion of a heated discussion and react to direct challenges and criticism with the same level of defense and aggressiveness. With practice and patience, it is possible for an internal auditor to maintain meeting control and not react when presented with a challenging situation. But make no mistake about it, maintaining control and not getting excited during an emotional discussion is much easier said than done.

Whenever this type of discussion arises, remember that the internal audit message is a presentation of confirmed facts, not opinion, and respond, instead of reacting, with confidence. It is a learned skill, but it provides a solid foundation for the message content and presents a positive, well-prepared approach to message delivery.

Reduce the Noise

The next tip to consider is to filter out any noise that might be distorting, covering, or confusing the intended message. Believe it or not, too much information, data, or clarification wording can complicate the message trying to be delivered. Too often, internal auditors "crowd" a message with unnecessary wording in an effort to strengthen the message, when in reality the additional wording only makes the message more confusing. I know it is not popular but stick to the message specifics and deliver the information in a very direct, not condescending, manner and tone.

Removing the filters in written or spoken words provides a more direct and easily understood message. The key point to remember with this tip is that many times what is being said or written is not what is actually being heard by the intended recipients. Put yourself in the position of the recipient and ensure that the message being delivered, via any medium, is clear, concise, heard, and understood.

Having supporting data and anticipated questions ready for any potential challenges also helps. At the end of the conversation, always confirm the understanding of the message and corresponding objective before moving on in the discussion.

Make the Call

Another tip for message delivery is to pick up the phone. As previously mentioned, there is an existing dependence on email because it is simple and does not require the uncomfortableness that an in-person meeting can present. Utilizing the phone provides direct access to the message recipient and allows the internal auditor to be able to speak the message rather than write it.

While it may be easier to speak the message rather than script it in an email or text, the message sender must still adequately prepare to ensure the message content is complete and the delivery is confident and fact based. However, don't memorize your message because it will sound too rehearsed, robotic, and insincere. Memorization will come off disingenuous, which is usually accompanied by a lack of confidence in the message trying to be delivered. If the sender adequately prepares, though, meaning they understand the message objective and the need to communicate the information, the contents and delivery will be on point and much more compelling. So, in delivering your message, be confident but not condescending, use data and confirmed facts, not opinions, and when possible, use the phone rather than email.

Listen with Purpose

The final tip for communicating a message is to listen with a purpose. It is so easy in any conversation to drift off and lose focus. Many times, people find themselves in a meeting or on a call and realize that they have not been paying attention for the last five minutes and are not even sure what the status is of the current discussion. It happens to everyone, but the real key to is maintain an active listening style, as meeting participants never know when they will be called on to offer their perspective. If, and when that does occur, you want to be prepared.

Listening is the key foundational skill when it comes to being successful at communicating. The most important advice to remember when it comes to listening is to focus with the intention to gather information and build a detailed understanding of the topic being discussed. The crucial mistake that meeting participants make when they are in a meeting or on a call is that they are thinking about what they will say next rather than paying attention to comprehend what is being said. Believe it or not, there is a huge difference in those listening objectives, and it creates a disconnect for the participants in any meeting if they are just there to listen with the intention of responding.

The perfect analogy is when someone participates in a webinar. Everyone has been in at least one webinar, and for the majority, if not every person, participants are listening to the webinar but not giving it the proper attention in order to effectively learn. What most participants are doing is waiting for the survey question so that they can answer and receive credit for attending the webinar. That is the easiest way to illustrate listening with the intention to respond and not with the intention to understand. When you are in any meeting, actively listen and provide input with facts and/or data to support the critical point being discussed.

THE VALUE OF LISTENING

There is always going to be a debate regarding whether an individual is a good listener. Due to the critical nature of listening in regard to communication, here are some clarifying points when it comes to effective listening. Remember, if you strive to be an excellent communicator (written or spoken word), listening is going to be at the core of achieving success. No meeting participants, in person or otherwise, will care or pay attention to anything being communicated unless it is something that impacts them personally or helps them do their job more effectively or efficiently. And it will be impossible to know what matters to a message receiver unless you have been listening effectively throughout the entire audit engagement. To become a listener focused on active participation and learning, you have to truly listen. That means that when you are not actively speaking in a meeting, you maintain a keen focus on the flow and details of the conversation and do not allow yourself to drift off or try to mentally move forward in the meeting, anticipating the next time you may speak. The conversation, if effectively facilitated, will move naturally through the agenda, and all pertinent topics will be covered. But remember that nothing takes the place of or provides valued insight to the business partner and their concerns like active listening.

The other characteristic of an active listener is this type of person is constantly documenting the critical points, components, or conversation details being discussed in the meeting. The written record of details provides the active listener with a history of points that may or may not need to be followed up on later in the discussion for clarification. With the speed at which meetings are moving and the variety of topics being covered, do not rely on memory if additional clarification must be obtained relating to any information presented earlier in the meeting. Also, documented notations convey to all meeting participants that the internal audit is focused and participating in the meeting, trying to facilitate positive change. Additionally, this documentation is the most effective way for any communicator to validate critical process or issues information based on what was specifically discussed throughout the meeting. Topic validation is a critical component of listening and facilitation of the discussion to agreement and ultimate closure of a topic. Remember to be active in your listening and diligent in the documentation.

 ## BEYOND AUDIT ADVISOR APPROACH

In an effort to provide guidance in the successful facilitation of meetings (especially during a remote audit engagement), the Beyond Audit methodology provides a technique called the advisor approach. The eight steps of the advisor approach are listed in Table 10.1. An explanation of each step will follow.

Meeting Preparation

The advisor approach is simple, and it begins with communicating the internal audit process surrounding the delivery of messages in any audit scenario. Knowledge is shared throughout the internal audit team via the communication model, ensuring that every team member understands the critical impact that the medium has on both the sender and receiver. Additionally, each internal audit team member must recognize and understand their role not only in the communication model but in the facilitation of every meeting from start to finish.

TABLE 10.1 Beyond Audit Meeting Advisor Approach

1. Define the communication process.	5. Facilitate the discussion.
2. Understand your role.	6. Obtain validation and agreement.
3. Prepare adequately.	7. Close the meeting.
4. Explain the meeting objectives.	8. Maintain transparency.

A common misconception is that if auditors are going to attend a meeting, they must provide their two cents' worth on each topic. Successful participation in an internal audit and business partner meeting does not always include a speaking role, however. Know your role in the meeting: Oftentimes, successful business partner meetings do not require all participants to speak. Every meeting is a singular event and there is no rulebook for exactly how each meeting will go. Follow the meeting agenda to effectively facilitate the discussion. If there is a point discussed requiring clarification for which you can supply supporting data or validation, then this is the moment where participation is most valuable. However, if the meeting is being executed according to plan and the business partner is receiving it well, just remain focused on listening and building on your audit and business process knowledge.

Even though it has been stated multiple times previously, there is no substitution for effectively preparing for a meeting. Remember, it is not about memorizing your information or role in the meeting, it is about becoming intimate with the data supporting all of the information that is scheduled to be discussed (as detailed in the agenda). The level of preparation provides process and business knowledge to provide value in the meeting. Do not let anyone tell you that you do not have to prepare for the meeting if you completed the work to be discussed. In reality, the opposite is true. When you have completed the fieldwork regarding testing, which is going to be discussed in the meeting, you should review the details and clearly understand all aspects of the completed testing because you can be sure the details of that testing will be called into question.

The testing aspects include, but may not be limited to, the explanation as to why the testing was performed in the first place; how the sample was selected; what was the source of the sample selection; what attributes of the process were tested and why; initial testing results; who validated the testing results; and why the testing results need to be discussed. That type of depth and interpretation of completed audit work is not information that an auditor is going to be comfortable discussing without proper preparation.

Even the most seasoned internal audit teams should strive to adequately prepare going into any audit partner meeting. Let us be honest – there are not many internal auditors who can confidently say that they adequately prepare for every meeting. With the demands of the internal audit job, projected budgets and time frames, and clients, internal auditors must make a dedicated effort to prepare for meetings, as they play such a huge role in the internal audit industry.

Meeting Facilitation

As the meeting preparation is completed, the audit team is ready to facilitate the meeting. The next four steps relate directly to the successful facilitation of the internal audit and business partner meeting. That successful facilitation starts with the explanation of the specific meeting objectives that are going to be covered. This explanation formally announces the topics to be covered in this meeting and should match exactly to the meeting agenda which was distributed in advance. This type of meeting information helps the internal audit facilitator keep the meeting on track and ensure that the most critical messages are covered and adequately communicated with the proper level of supporting documentation. While this step might seem insignificant in the overall communication process, it does provide a strong foundation for the meeting details and the stated expected outcomes upon completion. The next step in the meeting process is the actual facilitation of the meeting.

Although it is not specifically stated in the eight steps in the Beyond Audit Advisor Approach, no meeting should begin without introductions. The reason it is not specifically spelled out in the advisor approach is that there is a misconception that all meetings begin in the exact same manner, and that meeting kickoff supposedly included participant introductions. But just like any other assumption, hundreds and hundreds of meetings take place without any formal or informal introductions. This is especially true in the remote audit environment. With so many conference calls, videoconferences, or online meetings, participant introductions have become a thing of the past. It is time for introductions to be brought back into the formal meeting methodologies, as there are too many risks that exist when internal audit meetings are being facilitated with strangers.

Communication specialists always say that knowing your audience makes you a better communicator, yet meetings happen on a daily basis with an unknown number of strangers in almost every meeting. Incorporate a bullet item on your meeting agenda for introductions. Be certain that you know the business partner representatives and internal auditors who are attending the meeting that you are facilitating.

Once the introductions have been completed, then the facilitator can begin the meeting, which starts with solicitation for any questions or additions that any participant may have for the agenda. Notice the wording of that statement. There is no solicitation for changes to the meeting agenda, only questions or additions. Changes are not permitted because the agenda contains the specific topics that must be covered in the meeting. So, asking for changes to an established audit agenda is not appropriate. The participants may have clarification questions regarding the agenda items or potentially want to add another topic but changes (deletions or alterations) to established agenda points are not allowed. Also, another quick note is to recognize that while business partner suggested additions are welcomed, they are ultimately placed at the bottom of the agenda with the communicated expectation that the newly added agenda item will be addressed if meeting time permits. In the event the meeting ends without addressing the added agenda item, internal audit can either address it offline directly with the business partner or set up a follow-up meeting. Either way, it is critically important that internal auditors recognize the need to adequately cover the original agenda items as drafted and not be distracted with the request for changes or newly added topics. Once the agenda has been reviewed, discussed, and confirmed, the meeting can begin and item by item each will be explained with any questions being addressed along the way. Each time an agenda point is discussed, there should be a review and confirmation verifying the business partner's agreement with the corresponding item. Agenda items should not be considered complete (meaning discussed, agreed to, and ready to move forward) until the business partner verification has been obtained. After each agenda item has been discussed and validated, the next phase of the advisor approach can be addressed – to formally close the meeting. The closure of the meeting is the part in which each agenda item is reviewed and any outstanding elements are stated and recorded. There is also a formal communication to obtain a delivery date commitment for all outstanding documentation or data that came about as a result of the meeting discussion. In addition, all information agreed to regarding outstanding information and the delivery of same will be documented in the formal meeting minutes, which are created by internal audit and distributed to all meeting participants. The meeting minutes creation and distribution is a formal communication requirement of the Beyond Audit methodology, designed not only to instill a discipline in the internal audit department for documentation and accountability but also to ensure that communication of agreed-upon issues and outstanding documentation and data are formally shared with all participants, along with the corresponding delivery dates.

The overall key to successful communication, especially in meetings, is to ensure throughout all internal audit and business partner interactions that there is transparency. Transparency is critical to establishing and maintaining the reputation of the internal audit department as a partner and an asset to the business units within a company. Utilizing the advisor approach and maintaining transparency throughout the audit department also helps to increase the value of the audit work products being offered. Consider all of the barriers that exist in the current internal audit and business partner relationship and then compound that with executing audits remotely, and it is easy to understand how critically important it is for internal audit to be transparent in every communication and interaction with their business partners. Internal audit's overall goal is not just to be seen as a necessary nuisance in a company but to build strong partnerships with business unit management in an effort to increase the value and business relationships as both parties must recognize they are striving to reach and exceed the same objectives and goals. In that effort, relationships remain at the foundation of working in unison to achieve the same goals.

 ## INTERNAL AUDIT RELATIONSHIPS

In discussing relationships, internal auditors must recognize the success factor in that audit departments who champion relationship building with their business partners have a greater rate of success with audit engagements. Whether audit departments like it or not, their success is dependent on the effectiveness of their business partner relationships to provide audit with the critical data, documentation, information, and intelligence to execute the audit engagement requirements. It is up to internal audit to build and maintain the business partner relationship throughout every audit and beyond to foster the partnership environment which is based on performance and trust. To create that environment, every internal auditor must recognize the role and accept the responsibility of developing business partner relationship on a constant basis. The other aspect to this commitment is the acknowledgment that this is true for the entire audit department. It is not the responsibility of the leadership team or the chief audit executive, but a mandatory requirement for all members of the audit department with each member realizing their actions are reflective of the whole audit team. This type of team effort needs a strong foundation of communication from the chief audit executive on down to illustrate their commitment to providing value to their business partners on every audit engagement, which can only be accomplished through a committed relationship development approach. To accomplish this communication-focused relationship building process, every internal audit department should consider implementing the Beyond Audit three pillars of relationship building methodology. The three pillars are identify, build, and maintain.

Beyond Audit – Identify Pillar

With regard to the identify pillar, it will be the responsibility of each individual auditor to consider each business partner as a relationship target. The business partners most receptive to the internal auditor and business partner relationship are the ones who are looking for external validation of their existing business processes and recognize internal audit as being able to deliver value. It is important for the internal auditor to be able to explain the relationship objectives as well as the benefits that a successful internal audit and business partner relationship would provide. These benefits would include, but not be limited to, more effective audit execution, better internal audit business knowledge, more efficient audit planning, more transparent recognition of the business process perspective, and access to an independent resource to assist in new control considerations, system implementations, or process enhancements. The identify pillar also requires both the internal audit team and the business partner to acknowledge and accept the demands that a sharing relationship requires on both sides.

While the internal audit department will drive the relationship development process, it is important for the business partner to accept the responsibility of timely response to audit requests in an effort to complete audit assignments. As in any relationship, there is always going to be one party that will work a little bit harder or bend a little bit more to ensure the relationship is successful. The internal audit and business partner relationship is no different. In this instance, the internal audit department will ultimately own and be the more giving half of the relationship due to the simple fact that the internal audit department wants, and frankly needs, the relationship more than the business partner.

Consider this: Could the business unit complete its daily job responsibilities if the internal audit department suddenly did not exist any longer? And the answer to that question is overwhelmingly, yes. As a matter of fact, if you asked the business partner that same question, *yes* would not only be the answer but they would probably say that an operating environment without internal audit could possibly be more productive because there would not be so many interruptions.

The unfortunate reality, too, is that internal audit could not complete their daily job responsibilities without the business partner. Being a lifelong internal auditor, it is difficult to admit, but deep down, it is true. Not to say that internal audit could not perform audits if it had no help from the business partners. Audits *could* be completed, but the end results of those audits would be worthless to improving the business process since the audit was executed based on general business process knowledge instead of the business specific requirements established by the business unit management in each area of the company. Any recommendations made would be irrelevant, given the unknown process requirements that internal audit was trying to improve. Internal audit does and will always need the business partner to provide detailed process requirements for internal audit to do their job effectively and provide process improvements to their business partners. Hence, internal audit wants and needs the relationship with their business partners.

Beyond Audit – Build Pillar

The identify pillar is followed by the build pillar. This pillar requires the actual development of the relationship with the business partner and it should begin with marketing. Believe it or not, there are numerous individuals within the business process environment that do not truly understand what internal audit represents, what audit actually does, or even why audit was created. Some business personnel still see audit as a necessary evil within a company and sometimes even view it as a major disruption to the daily business process. An effective marketing plan is the only way to dispel these false assumptions, but internal audit marketing will only work if there is a clear and consistent understanding of how internal audit is defined. Remember, it is so much simpler to complete a task when there is a clear expectation of definition of the objective being communicated. The critical question which must be addressed is, does everyone in the audit department understand what audit represents and can they clearly articulate that to the business partners? If not, no amount of marketing will help the internal audit team overcome these myths and misconceptions about what audit does and why they do it.

So, start the internal audit marketing process by explaining that internal audit is an independent, objective assurance activity designed to improve an organization's operational effectiveness and efficiency. Internal audit is designed to assist the organization in accomplishing its objectives with a formal methodology to evaluate and improve the control environment. Now that sounds great for a book definition by using a bunch of audit specific words, but it will not be effective at explaining the internal audit process to a business owner. The key for internal audit is to provide a clear definition of the group and remove the audit terminology for ease of understanding.

The Beyond Audit recommendation for marketing the internal audit department is to communicate to the business partner that internal audit is a team that is in place to help the business unit in the achievement of their objectives by providing an independent assessment of their operations. And it is key to include in the definition that the independent assessment of business operations can only be accomplished in partnership with the business unit personnel. The objective of effectively marketing the audit department is to clarify that internal audit is a partner to the business unit. In no way, shape, or form was internal audit created to be a policing arm of the business to identify problems.

Internal audit is most effective when, in partnership with the business team, audit is providing validation that the design, implementation, execution, reporting, and governance of business operations is delivering the intended outcome. The Beyond Audit methodology labels these critical business components *the foundational five*, and internal audit's primary responsibility is to be able to conclude on the sufficiency and effectiveness of the foundational five based on data provided by their business partners. Utilizing this type of language and information in the marketing of the audit department will provide the foundation to clearly explaining the true objectives of the audit function. After the objectives and intentions of the audit department have been defined, do not forget to document and include the services provided by internal audit that are available to the business partners. Again, another misconception regarding internal audit is that they only provide testing to find things which are broken or incorrect in the business operations. That could not be further from the truth. Although internal audit is always going to be responsible for assisting business operations with validating their control environment (effectiveness of their foundational five), there are other services provided by internal audit which include, but are not limited to, project participation, system implementation, new process reviews, and continuous, culture, operational, and performance audits. It is critical that the internal audit marketing includes all of the services currently provided by the department in its efforts to partner with the business team to help them achieve their stated objectives.

Marketing the audit department is just the start of the build pillar responsibilities. Remember that all types of relationships, inside and outside of work, are based on trust. It is internal audit's job to create a foundation of trust with the business partner in order to foster the development of an effective working relationship. This trust component of the build pillar can only be established if the internal audit team clearly states the audit objectives, listens to the business partner's concerns, and executes the audit as it was described in the entrance meeting. Building the trust with a business partner is based on ensuring there are no surprises throughout each phase of the audit being executed. Trust is earned and built over time with each interaction with the business partner playing a critical role. At the end of the day, the business partner wants a fair assessment of their foundational five with consideration of their perspective being included in the evaluation. If internal audit executes all services with this same approach and attitude, it will quickly establish the trust foundation of the relationship because without trust, an effective working relationship can never be established. The clearly defined audit services, effective audit marketing, and trust component of the build pillar are all created from upfront and honest communications with the business partner. As detailed in this chapter, communication is going to be the key not only to effective execution of audit services but also in developing strong internal audit and business partner relationships in an effort to provide valued services and facilitate real change within the business operations.

Beyond Audit – Maintain Pillar

The third and final pillar of relationship building is the maintain pillar. This pillar represents and reinforces the concept that internal audit wants and needs the relationship to work in order to execute audit services with precision. There are too many business process details that need to be learned by internal audit to complete their engagements and the business partner possesses these critical process details which can only be accessed through strong relationships. The maintain pillar also is a reminder for internal audit personnel to provide the same level of consistency and high customer service to all business partners, whether or not there is an existing working relationship established or if the business partner represents a new client. In either instance and in every situation, the business partner will receive the same high level of quality and commitment to excellence in every audit engagement. The maintenance of these relationships is based on the continual value delivery of audit products that are developed in a team approach with the respective business partners.

The focus on the three pillars of relationship development will result in a realization of value from the gathering of process-level data in the planning of an audit engagement, to the status memo discussions of potential deviations from the business processing standard during fieldwork, to the partnering to find root cause and action plan development in the reporting process. Effective relationship development will pay dividends to the internal audit team throughout the audit and beyond as the business partner recognizes internal audit as a valued partner who can be relied on to deliver useful results. Recall Table 3.1 from Chapter 3 the internal audit myths regarding the department, along with the reality of what internal audit provides. These concepts can be incorporated into your internal audit methodology to ensure the department is being viewed correctly for the work, dedication, and services which you provide.

BEYOND AUDIT – INTERNAL AUDIT MARKETING

Myth	Reality
▪ Police officer	▪ Partner
▪ Crusader	▪ Change agent
▪ Enforcer	▪ Efficiency expert
▪ Assassin	▪ Advocate
▪ Stressor	▪ Solver
▪ Rebel	▪ Risk expert
▪ Problem	▪ Provider
▪ Disrupter	▪ Driver
▪ Criticizer	▪ Coach
▪ Watchdog	▪ Winner

Strong communication and business partner relationships provide audit with the necessary tools to drive audit quality and value through the execution of all three main audit phases. It allows audit teams to plan engagements with precision and purpose utilizing the detailed process information shared as a result of strong relationship. Strong communication throughout the critical audit phase has shown a reduction in time wasted during the creation of the audit planning approach and the corresponding documentation. This detailed plan creates a fieldwork phase that can be executed with precision as a result of the shared process details that have been incorporated into the audit program details. These process details guide the audit team to focus on the most critical elements of the business unit's foundational five and result in focused recommendations linked to the achievement of the business unit objectives. And while the business partner relationship provides critical data for focused planning and precise execution of fieldwork, there is no bigger impact that the internal audit and business partner relationship has than on the reporting phase of an audit from the draft report to issuance of the final product. Instead of the reporting phase being a battle of words and wills between internal audit and the business partner, the existing relationship within these two groups allows the reporting phase to be focused on addressing any confirmed deviations from the established business processing standard with detailed, root-cause based actions to improve the business partner's efforts to consistently meet their objectives. Remember to utilize the established audit phase templates detailed in the audit methodology to help facilitate a high level of communication throughout the audit engagement. Never underestimate the power of audit methodology adherence and a strong working relationship to allow internal audit to be recognized as a valued partner throughout the organization. And remember that the maintenance of the internal audit and business partner relationship is ongoing and does not end at the completion of an audit engagement.

Before moving on from the communication topic, there is one more tip from the Beyond Audit methodology that assists in the internal audit goal of transparent communication in every interaction with the business partner. There are times when existing audit relationships have been destroyed as a result of a bad meeting. And while meeting facilitation has been discussed in this chapter, below is a quick reminder chart to help prepare internal auditors for effective facilitation of business partner meetings. Consider these components each time internal audit is going to facilitate a business partner meeting.

 ## BEYOND AUDIT – MEETING FACILITATION KEYS

Component	Explanation
■ Set objective(s).	■ Remind all participants why the meeting is being held and what is to be accomplished by the end.
■ Properly plan.	■ Prepare for the meeting and anticipate challenge points.
■ Create agenda.	■ Detail the specific steps and topics to be covered in the meeting.
■ Execute effectively.	■ Use the agenda to facilitate the meeting and maintain control.
■ Document results.	■ Develop and distribute meeting minutes to communicate meeting decisions and next steps.

CHAPTER ELEVEN

Analyzing Internal Audit

W HILE THE BOOK TO this point has focused on the execution of audit engagements with consideration of process changes required to be successful in the remote audit environment, this chapter discusses the need to perform an advanced evaluation of internal audit operations and will introduce a new proprietary tool that allows internal audit departments to examine their department operations to proactively identify strengths and opportunities for improvement. The days of relying on the (hopefully) updated dashboard results to inform internal audit senior management that the audit department is successfully executing audit engagements timely, with precision, and with the corresponding audit phase templates are fading fast.

Let us be honest with each other and admit that internal audit is not as critical of themselves when judging execution performance and compliance as compared to the judgment and scrutiny that internal audit places on business partner during an audit engagement. Plus, the internal audit dashboard process (detailed in Chapter 9) comes with some process risks. For one, the dashboard must be actively monitored to ensure all metrics reflect the current audit methodology and a compliance requirement for the use of corresponding audit phase templates. The template usage is not a guide and must be held as a requirement for audit execution consistency.

Another risk that impacts the dashboard is the establishment of realistic corresponding performance criteria to effectively record and score performance. Too often, internal audit dashboard metrics do not have strict criteria to successfully challenge the audit team to focus on performance. To verify that the internal audit department is ready for the strict requirements and demands of a remote audit engagement, there needs to be a documentation and process-level evaluation of the internal audit operations and supporting audit methodologies. The review and evaluation of the current audit process needs to include a review tool for each component of the audit department to provide a comprehensive method to validate the effectiveness of the audit department and provide confidence in the audit methodology application.

BEYOND AUDIT – ARB METHODOLOGY

To provide internal audit departments with a data-driven evaluation tool to measure their operation, the Beyond Audit methodology has created an innovative self-assessment tool known as the Audit Risk Barometer (ARB). The ARB, much like the internal audit dashboard, has the requirement for the internal audit department to independently and objectively review their audit methodology and corresponding operations through six different and distinct categories with the objective of validating their audit methodology can deliver actionable plans to address noted opportunities for improvement. Internal audit departments are never as critical of their own operational performance as they are when evaluating a business unit operation during an audit. This is coming from a 30-plus-year veteran in internal audit. In working with teams around the world, internal audit knows they are so much more demanding of their business partners than they are of themselves. The ARB is a process that will allow audit departments to take a fresh view of their department as they address specific categories of focus. Too often internal audit departments get caught in the "drone army" mentality, previously mentioned, and focus on completing assignments to move the audit coverage needle rather than working diligently to understand true business process risk and evaluate and conclude on the corresponding control environments. The ARB will take an in-depth examination of your current audit department operations from the existing foundational audit methodology to the value product delivered on each audit engagement and four other detailed categories in between to complete the evaluation of the audit operation. The other four categories will include the audit team, execution precision, data utilization, and services provided.

Upon completion of the ARB process, the audit department is provided an overall risk score as well as a blueprint to address any opportunities for improvement identified and the recommended corresponding training to effectively close the performance gap. With the rise in demand for remote audit engagements, there is more pressure than ever on internal audit teams to effectively execute the audit requirements without the benefit of being able to interact directly with their business partners. In no other time in history has the reliance on the established audit methodology, use of data, and team performance been relied on so independently to ensure the audit execution and the validity of results are accurate, supported by business data, and contain validated report issues with complete corresponding action plans to address the exceptions. In this dependent remote audit environment, internal audit departments must have confidence in their detailed audit methodology and teams to execute with precision. This level of confidence can only be obtained through an honest examination of the internal audit operations utilizing the ARB to facilitate this targeted internal review. As in the case of the internal audit dashboard process, the ARB results are dependent on an honest assessment and admission of actual performance in all six categories as they apply to the current audit methodology.

In this day and age with all of the scrutiny on internal audit activity and results coupled with the requirement to execute reviews remotely, the pressure on the internal audit has been intensified as well as the critical need for a detailed structure and formal methodology to support all audit activities. And while almost every internal audit department has documented audit methodologies for the audit services they provide, most audit teams cannot be certain that their audit methodologies are adequately built (from risk structure), have the appropriate level of audit templates to support the objectives, and are actively monitored to ensure compliance. There is no better time than the present to perform an internal review to validate that the internal audit activities are properly executed, documented, and supported. The only way to achieve that goal effectively is to complete the ARB to determine what level of risk and exposure your audit department currently faces and what part, if any, of the audit operations requires action(s) to address confirmed performance issues.

The ARB process is structured with six individual categories with each one containing a stated, detailed objective. Then, there are a series of statements pertaining to the corresponding objective statement which must be answered. The number of statements utilized to determine the overall risk score per category ranges from five to seven unique statements. Depending on the answer, a corresponding score is assigned and then the individual scores for each statement are totaled to provide a grand total score for that category. Once the scoring has been completed for all six categories, they are combined to create the overall risk score. There are three possible outcomes to the overall risk score to indicate what level of risk your internal audit department is potentially exposed to relating to its operations. The three possible risk levels are low, moderate, and severe. These risk levels are self-explanatory, with low being the target goal for audit departments and then depending on the severity and number of opportunities for improvement, internal audit departments that require enhancements will receive a moderate or severe score. While the ARB will not be detailed in its entirety in this chapter, the six categories will be identified and a couple of supporting statement examples from each category will be reviewed and explained.

ARB Category One – Foundation

As previously stated, ARB begins with the most critical aspect of the internal audit department operations, which is the audit methodology, and that is why it represents the first category in the ARB. The audit methodology in every department provides the backbone and structure to support all audit activity, along with the corresponding guidelines and requirements for each audit phase. The audit methodology in the ARB is known as the foundation as it provides the baseline requirements for all audit activities that can be offered and executed by the internal audit department. The foundation objective states, "The methodology documents provide the guide to execute the audit services with quality and completeness of documentation to support the conclusions." This foundation objective is all encompassing of the three main phases of an audit, including all necessary evidence needed to be obtained and verified to support any recommendations and conclusions.

One of the statements supporting the foundation objective in the ARB states, "The internal audit department has documented methodologies for every available audit service." This supporting statement, as is the case with all six of the ARB objective detailed statements, must be clearly understood and communicated to all participants completing the ARB assessment in order to effectively comprehend and link the supporting statements to the category objective. Without that baseline understanding of the category objective, the ARB results will not be accurate and could present a false conclusion when it comes to the effectiveness and/or efficiency of the audit operations pertaining to one of the ARB categories.

When discussing the foundation (audit methodology), it must be clarified that the category objective is stating that for any audit-related services performed, there is a documented methodology that provides specific details for each phase of the audit, which would allow any internal audit team member to participate and contribute on the audit engagement without any prior experience. The supporting methodology should provide adequate detail to communicate the work that must be completed to execute the audit assignment. The detailed statements that support this category will provide depth and clarification for the audit methodologies being referenced. One example statement that would appear under the foundation heading in the ARB is, "The planning phase of a risk-based audit should receive the largest percentage of budget time." As discussed in Chapter 5, the planning phase requires knowledge building, focus, and dedication of resources to fully identify, comprehend, and document the business process objectives along with the corresponding true process risks and controls. The time spent gathering this information provides the business understanding to create the targeted testing plan. With this type of planning approach, the fieldwork phase, as discussed in Chapter 6, becomes a focused executable linked directly to the necessary activities to achieve the business objectives. And this focused testing phase, along with regular business partner status updates, allows the internal audit team to efficiently discuss and document any potential deviations from the business standards and complete the report phase requirements in a timely manner. When the proper allocation of budget and resources is executed in this manner, there will be plenty of time to dedicate to planning (about 40–50 percent) and allow for the audit engagement to be completed in accordance with the corresponding methodology.

Another example of a statement supporting the foundation objective in the ARB states, "All internal audit methodologies contain the mandatory templates for each audit phase." Throughout the previous chapters there are various references to templates and their completion requirements. This supporting statement is asking every auditor to verify that for all the internal audit offerings, there is a corresponding documented audit methodology not only detailing the required audit phase steps, but also including the mandatory templates that must be completed to effectively document the work performed and provide the necessary evidence to support the associated work. The completion of these required templates also provides evidence to the audit workpaper reviewer that the appropriate work was completed in a particular phase of an audit engagement, which allows the team to proceed, with confidence, to the next phase of the assignment. Keep in mind that the templates documented in a specific audit methodology are not included as a suggestion to assist auditors to arrange their work, but as a mandatory methodology requirement which must be completed and complied with on every audit.

ARB Category Two – Team

The second category in the ARB assessment is team, which represents the current internal audit team, not a projection of what the optimal team makeup would be in a perfect working environment. The corresponding objective states, "The internal audit team contains the right mix of experience and focuses on knowledge and skill development through consistent communication." One of the statements supporting the team objective in the ARB says, "Communication is the cornerstone of the internal audit department." As discussed in Chapter 10, communication is the key to successful internal audit departments, as it represents the vehicle in which all business information knowledge, data, and documentation are acquired to execute an audit assignment. Make no mistake about it, the degree, or degrees you have earned in college or university will not matter when it comes to obtaining the necessary information from a business partner. The ability of internal auditors to be successful at their job is not based on what degrees they earned but on their ability to communicate effectively with all levels of business management. Communication skills will drive the information-gathering phase of any project, which will in turn drive the auditor's ability to complete the audit engagement.

Adding more pressure to this transfer of knowledge and information is the fact that all of the requesting is going to be done in a remote environment. Although that makes the task more daunting, there is still that baseline requirement of being able to communicate effectively, no matter what the situation demands. As previously discussed, communication must be the cornerstone of the internal audit department to ensure that there is a constant flow of information within the audit team, as well as with the business partner. Although there will always be a critical focus on the workpapers compiled to support the audit conclusions, the only way to obtain the data and documentation detailed in the audit workpapers is through effective communication. Keep in mind that the need for the internal audit and business partner relationship to drive the audit process will only be developed and maintained with communication.

This communication focus to support the team objective is not just about the business partner relationship; it is also for the critical development of the internal audit team. The more often an internal audit team communicates with each other, the more effective the team becomes. Internal communication within an audit department can also include monthly one-on-one meetings, which are held with direct reports to keep team members on track with regard to individual performance as well as audit workload concerns. The sharing of internal audit experiences and knowledge, business process knowledge, and even business partner knowledge creates a more well-rounded team ready to address any potential challenges in the execution of an audit assignment. Additionally, in these highly communicative audit teams, the staff is more comfortable discussing current challenges with team members and most often becomes proactive in the identification and solution development of audit challenges. Never underestimate the power of internal team communication as it fosters a learning environment regarding both internal audit skills and business process knowledge development.

Another example of a supporting statement for the team category of the ARB states, "Each internal audit team member has a custom development plan focused on their learning objectives." There is no doubt about it that internal audit's success is based on their ability to be able to continually develop business process knowledge. It really does not matter how long someone has been in internal audit because audit experience does not directly translate to understanding the business objectives and corresponding supporting processes. In order to effectively develop audit skills, there has to be a dedicated effort and commitment on the part of the auditor to reflect, recognize, and document the specific development opportunities they have identified and want to focus on improving. The most successful method to accomplish specific skill development is for the individual auditor to obtain the learning map, which details the expected results and core competencies required for their specific position (staff, senior, manager, etc.) and determine what skills the auditor should focus on first. Usually after examining the corresponding learning map and comparing their current skillset and position requirements, the auditor will document the outstanding skills needed in their personal development plan. It is important for all internal auditors to recognize when they set unrealistic expectations on their development plan, as that only leads to frustration and failure to accomplish their goals. The development plan should include the most critical skills needed to be successful at their job responsibilities and the ones that require the most effort. Internal auditors can also work with their teammates or supervisor to help focus the development plan and ensure it does not become a burden or barrier to their learning. Keep in mind that an individual, customized development plan provides each auditor with a specific roadmap of the skills required to meet and exceed the needs of their specific job.

ARB Category Three – Precision

The third category in the ARB assessment is precision that represents the effectiveness and efficiency of the internal audit operations when completing audit engagements. This precision is in reference to the execution, timing, and level of supporting documentation compiled to support the audit's conclusions. There is so much reliance placed on proper execution of the audit program to produce review results and supporting documentation, which is why the existence of a documented audit methodology from category one in ARB is so important to guide the internal audit staff to the precision execution of the audit engagement requirements. The precision objective states, "Each phase of an internal audit engagement is executed in accordance with the audit methodology requirements, including the associated template requirements." The audit methodology itself will provide the detailed conditions that must be completed for each audit phase before moving to the subsequent phase. Although work can begin in different audit phases simultaneously, the internal auditors must remain disciplined to complete all required work in each phase before determining all associated work has been completed. It should be noted that this multiphase work comment is in reference to the reporting phase having activity throughout the audit as the report draft can be worked on beginning in the planning phase. The one word of caution related to phase completion is to ensure the finalization of all planning phase requirements before moving on to fieldwork, as the fieldwork phase direction and focus are solely reliant on the information obtained during the planning of the engagement. Deciding to begin the fieldwork testing prior to finalization of the planning phase could result in unnecessary work being completed and wasting budget time. Stay focused and follow the audit methodology requirements to ensure audit execution efficiency.

One of the statements supporting the precision objective in the ARB says, "The source of all planning activity should originate directly from the business objective." One of the most, if not *the* most, critical aspect when it comes to precision execution of an audit engagement is the focus of the work performed and the corresponding results. This focus must link to the business process objectives to ensure that the work performed during the audit is related to the essential business process activities that are responsible for generating the process outcomes. While there are numerous activities and controls that can be examined during an audit, the focus must be on the activities that have been identified to have the most significant true process risks associated with the achievement of the business objectives. The only way to validate that the audit focus is correct is to ensure that all planning activities and documentation are linked to the identification and confirmation of the business objectives. Access to the business objective provides the audit engagement team with the ability to easily facilitate the true process risk identification discussion as that discussion is driven by the business objectives.

Using the business objectives as the starting point for the true process risk discussion provides the auditor with access to the risk data without ever having to use the term *risk* in the discussion. The focus in this discussion with the business partners will be to ask them what barriers could stand in the way of achieving their business objectives. Any barriers discussed will provide the details of the true process risks that face the business operations team on a daily basis. Once the true process risks are documented, the auditor can transition to the corresponding business activities (controls) the business partner has put into place to ensure these barriers do not occur, or if they do, they are identified and addressed in a timely manner.

Utilizing the Beyond Audit methodology's planning approach (Three Pillars of Planning), internal auditors can efficiently facilitate critical risk and control planning discussions without ever using the "audit" words *risk* and *control*. That is why in Chapter 5 the focus was on the fact that the primary source of business objective identification and confirmation comes directly from the business partner. And that is also why Chapter 10 detailed the importance of communication and building a productive relationship with the business partner. The business partner will always remain the most critical member of the audit team and source of business intellectual property. Remember, in order to be effective in the internal auditor role, we need the business partner to be an active participant throughout the audit process.

Another example of a supporting statement for the precision category of the ARB states, "An audit dashboard is implemented to track and report on individual audit and departmentwide metrics (based on your current audit methodology) on a monthly basis." As discussed in detail in Chapter 9, in order for dashboard to effectively track audit performance metrics, it must be based on the existing audit methodology. The audit methodology sets the standards and corresponding requirements for the audit phase activities and associated documentation. It is impossible to create a dashboard without having a detailed audit methodology to establish performance parameters. However, once the audit methodology has been finalized and a dashboard has been created, it is one of the most effective methods to document, track, and communicate audit performance to the audit management team. The critical point to remember when developing the dashboard is that the detailed metrics must be linked to the primary audit phase requirements and deliverables for the dashboard metrics data to be actionable. The key point to remember regarding any internal audit dashboard efforts is to create the dashboard using the same planning techniques as in an individual audit by validating the objectives of the audit process and identifying the critical process requirements for the audit department to be successful in its execution of the audit methodology. The one word of caution related to the precision category relating to internal audit dashboards is the frequency of the dashboard reporting (typically monthly) is only effective in facilitating change when the data is kept up to date and identified gaps are addressed promptly upon verification. The precision category is based on diligent adherence to the audit methodology where execution targets have been established for each audit phase, audit template compliance is documented, and each phase of the audit process is actively monitored.

ARB Category Four – Data

The fourth category in the ARB assessment is data that represents the information being utilized in every phase of the audit, as well as in the annual risk assessment process. Internal auditors must recognize that data, in this instance, does not solely represent information that is obtained from writing and executing information technology programs. Data in the ARB includes intellectual property regarding the business process, business unit personnel tenure, processing volumes and dollar amounts as well as any business process indicators that are being tracked to effectively manage the business unit process being audited. The data objective states, "All available data types (documented and technology based) are utilized effectively to support the audit evidence." It is important for every internal auditor to recognize, especially in this instance, that generic terms incorporated into audit discussions are very often mistakenly used and interpreted incorrectly. When the term *data* is spoken or written during an internal audit engagement, all parties involved in that discussion or receipt of correspondence will immediately assume this "data" reference means the information was obtained through some form of technology software, program, or system download. Internal audit departments must alter their usage and assumptions when it comes to the term *data* because it is a much more comprehensive and inclusive term when used in an audit environment. In a discussion regarding the audit phases or completed work, there are a multitude of documents, meetings, interviews, technology programs, metrics, and reports (generated or received by the business unit under review), which could qualify as "data." The lesson to be learned in this category is that business unit data can be obtained and effectively incorporated into the audit process but does not have to come from a technology term. Auditors should look to gather any and all relevant information (data) pertaining to the business operation under review in an effort to continually build their business process knowledge and focus on the most critical deliveries of the process being audited.

One of the statements supporting the data objective in the ARB says, "Sufficient business documentation must be obtained to adequately support the audit engagement workpapers and conclusions." Even though it has been mentioned a couple of times already, reinforcement of this point can never be overstated. Internal audit departments must not only realize that the audit workpapers are the sole source of evidence to support their work, but also recognize that the workpapers are going to receive significant scrutiny to ensure they fairly represent the current business process environment. In order to pass that detailed examination from internal audit management and questioning from business operations management, the internal audit engagement team must obtain, document, and arrange *sufficient* documentation (data) to support their work.

The biggest challenge pertaining to the audit workpapers is always going to be the word *sufficient*. Internal audit teams are always debating how much information is sufficient and asking if we should keep looking for more evidence. This is another part of the audit process that the auditors should not overcomplicate. The more direct and simpler the question, the easier it is to answer. When it comes to the sufficiency point, remember the concept of ensuring the workpaper can stand on its own. Recall the critical components of a workpaper and how important it is to verify all those components are present to have the workpaper be independent and properly support the enclosed conclusion. Those component requirements are the same in this instance to ensuring the workpaper has the correct level of data to support the exceptions noted and the conclusions. The other point to keep in mind when developing and documenting workpapers is that every single individual who examines the workpaper documentation or reviews information derived from a workpaper did not have the benefit of examining any documentation or participating in any discussions related to the final communicated message. In that case, internal auditors must be diligent in how and what information is obtained, documented, and included in the workpapers so that any questions can be properly and sufficiently satisfied from what was obtained during the fieldwork and development of the final workpaper.

Another example of a supporting statement for the data category of the ARB says, "Effective data mining is utilized to provide the audit engagement team with the volume, dollar, and regional data so representative sampling techniques can be applied." There is no arguing that technology continues to advance at a rapid pace, and it is critical for internal audit departments to recognize and embrace the power and information generation that technology can provide. Throughout the audit phases, technology can provide data and direction when harnessed correctly. When any internal audit team is planning the audit of a business process, there is often an avalanche of information as well as transaction-level data that must be considered for the upcoming testing that will be completed during the targeted fieldwork phase. With that daunting task ahead, internal auditors must identify the most effective method to compile the complete population of data for the scope period and determine what data is the most critical and what data provides support. The challenge associated with this data dump of business-level information is that there has to be a verification that the total population for the scope period has been received and that there is no other data which should be included. Verifying an accurate and total population data download is difficult to do, and that is where the technology solutions can be so effective. Any time an internal audit team receives, retrieves, or downloads a business transaction population file (for the scope period), there must always be a validation that the information received is complete (accurate when it comes to the total number of transactions as well as the supporting information that was supposed to be included). For internal audit to ensure the population is complete, an independent technology program should be executed to determine the validity and completeness of the population before any further planning can be completed related to that information.

While there is no reason to doubt the veracity of the information provided by the business partner, it is always recommended to obtain confirmation of the data integrity to ensure that the information source is pure (best data available that accurately reflects business activity). Once the business activity data has been determined to be pure, any final planning can be completed, and the subsequent testing executed. With any technology, there are a couple of cautionary notes to be considered. First, for as all powerful as technology may seem, there is always a temptation during audit engagement planning and fieldwork phases to go bigger and deeper with the samples to be tested. There are even discussions of testing the entire population. These thoughts of bigger and all-inclusive testing may sound good, but they are a bad decision. Not only does going larger or testing 100 percent of anything require a significant time commitment (which was not in the original budget), but also, there is no justification that would support the need to test more than the documented sample. Sampling techniques, when executed properly, provide the rationale and adequate support for the testing results. Another cautionary note regarding technology is that there can be a risk associated with the internal audit technology process providing too much data regarding a business process. This can cause audit engagement teams to get preoccupied with all the data and lose the focus of the critical process steps that are supposed to be tested. Be mindful when technology is incorporated into the audit process and effectively incorporates the power of the software tools your team possesses to streamline the audit process and not burden it with an unnecessary amount of data.

ARB Category Five – Offerings

The fifth category in the ARB assessment is offerings that represent the type of services the internal audit department can provide to their business partners. These types of audit activities must be incorporated and properly documented in the audit methodologies as well as clearly known and understood by every member of the internal audit team. Additionally, each team member must be able to explain every service available to any business partner in a consistent manner. The offerings objective states that "objective focused risk-based audits represent the majority of the audit activity and are complemented with agile, continuous, culture, investigation, operational, and technology reviews." It is monumentally important that every auditor be aware of the services provided by the internal audit department and have a clear understanding of not only how to explain the details of each specific service to the business partner but also which service is the most appropriate to provide an independent validation of the corresponding business process control environment. There will be instances where an alternative type of audit may be more effective in a business process evaluation than a traditional risk-based audit. That is why it is so critical on every audit engagement that the business objectives be identified and validated (as discussed in Chapter 5) to determine the most effective audit methodology to apply. Even though the risk-based audit will be the most frequently used methodology to validate the business process, there will be instances where a continuous or agile audit may be more effective and efficient to validate the current business control environment. Always examine the business objectives of the related process coupled with previous and external audit activity to determine which audit approach is best suited for the current engagement.

One of the statements supporting the offerings objective in the ARB says, "The internal audit department's foundation is the risk-based audit methodology incorporating the objective, risk, and control (ORC) model." The good news here is that it does not matter what country or industry you work in or how big or small your internal audit department is, the ORC model is the most useful risk-based audit approach when planning an audit of any business unit within your company. As discussed in detail in Chapter 5, the ORC model provides the most effective approach to identifying and understanding the business operations objectives. This is the key to the ORC model due to the fact that the business objective, once identified, is used to facilitate the discussion to identify true process risk, which in turn is used to identify the corresponding controls. The significant challenge facing internal auditors in the planning phase of any engagement is having the dreaded risk-and-control discussion with the business partner. This meeting is so difficult because the business partner does not use the audit terms *risk* and *control* when discussing their own process and sometimes finds it hard to provide specific and detailed responses to the auditors' questions during this crucial interview.

The beauty of the ORC model is it changes the dynamics of the risk and control identification discussion with the client because it never mentions those two audit terms. The auditor's goal in this discussion is to focus on the business process and have the business partner discuss the daily business unit activities which must occur to achieve the business objectives. And without realizing it, the business partner has identified the true process risks and corresponding controls as the auditor facilitates the discussion using the business objectives as the starting point. To be successful with this approach, auditors need to turn every formal interview with the business partner into a conversation about the business process. In the same conversation, the auditor is also building and strengthening the auditor and business partner relationship. Embrace the ORC model and improve the effectiveness of your communication skills and audit engagement planning techniques.

Another example of a supporting statement for the offerings category of the ARB states, "For any business partner self-identification issues, internal audit reviews the data to determine the extent of the defect, data analysis, root cause, and proposed management action." Another major misconception regarding internal audit is that they were only created to go into every business processing area and identify any and all problems associated with the process and then make the business partner fix the issues. First of all, that is not an accurate statement and internal audit provides so many more services than just reviewing business processes. And for the record, internal audit does not evaluate business processes with the objective to identify breakdowns and errors. The objective of the internal audit process is to examine policies to ensure the business partner's established control environment is producing the intended outcome.

Additionally, as discussed in Chapter 10, another one of internal audit's objectives is to establish and foster ongoing, productive relationships with the business partner and in doing that can provide verification of issues identified by the business partner. However, any time the internal audit department performs a validation of data, there needs to be a formal process to ensure all required information is identified and reviewed to support the data. When proactive business partners reveal already confirmed business process issues, internal audit will work with business process personnel to discuss the issue detail, review the supporting data, and ensure the business team has a solid grasp on the issue and how to fix the problem (identified root cause and the required corresponding action). The key to any self-identified issue by the business partner is not that the issue was proactively communicated to the internal audit team but that there is evidence the proposed action plan has been implemented to address the identified issue. There are far too many instances of where an issue, identified by the business partner, did not receive any root cause analysis, or has a proposed management action that has never been implemented. While it is great to see business partners proactively engaging in the first line of defense with properly implemented review controls, the self-identified issue will never be corrected unless it receives the right analysis as to cause and a corresponding action plan to address the deficiency.

ARB Category Six – Value

The sixth and final category in the ARB assessment is value, which represents the recognized benefit that the business partner receives when any type of audit services are performed in their business unit. It is critical for the ongoing success of internal audit to be able to identify, confirm, and communicate a value to the business partner on every engagement. This value does not always have to come in the form of a dollar value savings, although that would be wonderful. Instead, the value could be in a process improvement recommendation, which would result in a savings of process time or a verifiable reduction of process rework. Believe it or not, value to the business partner could also be an independent validation that the business process is executing transactions successfully and that the existing control environment is generating the intended outcome on a consistent basis. Any one of the alternative value statements is a victory for both the internal audit and business process teams. The value objective states, "Internal audit delivers quality via root caused focused recommendations and partners with the business team to facilitate change with targeted action plans." Any time there is a discussion related to internal audit delivering value, it should be linked directly to improvement in the quality of the business process environment. All of the examples listed above regarding what value looks like will result in an improvement in business process operations.

As was stated in Chapter 10, internal audit's success is based on the strength of their business partner relationships and those relationships are the primary reason that internal audit can provide value to the business partners. Without successful relationships, the internal audit engagement team would never be able to access the information and data required to make recommendations that would improve the business process. Without the data, there would be zero value presented because the recommendations would be at such a high level that it would make no difference in the operating environment of the business process. The value category of the ARB is so vital to the success of the audit department because it is the point at which internal audit's success is based. If the internal audit department and its corresponding methodology cannot generate quality recommendations, there is no way that the business partners will see the value proposition in all of the work, time, and effort that was dedicated to the audit engagement. Internal auditors must remain diligent in their methodology requirements, even in this remote auditing environment, to ensure the quality of their work product never suffers.

One of the statements supporting the value objective in the ARB says, "The internal audit department does not present opinions or personal perspectives on audit engagements but relies on the business data to drive the message." In every internal audit definition, it states the audit engagements will be an independent and objective evaluation of the business process. In this instance, *independent* means that internal audit is totally separate and *objective* means that internal audit is unbiased to the work being performed. *Unbiased* is the key when it comes to staying focused on what the business-provided data is telling the auditors and where the data is taking them. In that description of audit, there is no place or justification for personal opinions, judgments, or subjectivity on the part of the audit engagement team. Regardless of what preconceived notions, thoughts, or conclusions may be in the minds of the audit engagement team, those opinions will not enter into the evaluation of the business process during an audit. The only opinion that matters in relation to the business process evaluation is the one based on the information, documentation, and data specifically reviewed and tested in the audit itself. The key when it comes to generating data supported conclusions on any audit testing is to ask yourself, what is the data telling me? The data is the source that will provide the direction and support for the final conclusion on the adequacy of the work. And remember to keep in mind that all independent readers of your conclusion only have the workpaper documentation to examine to determine whether they agree with the state conclusion. Before forwarding any completed workpaper documentation, ensure the data results have been validated with the appropriate business partner and a self-review of the workpaper has been completed. Ensure that the self-review includes a verification that the workpaper contains sufficient documentary evidence to support the conclusion.

Another example of a supporting statement for the value category of the ARB says, "Internal audit recognizes and understands the difference between action plan implementation and adoption and has created formal follow up procedures to confirm both before closing an open issue." As detailed in Chapter 8, there is a stark difference between action plan implementation and adoption and it is exceedingly difficult to initiate lasting change in any business process. Even though change is complicated because it requires work and commitment, it is possible to accomplish and it is up to internal audit to have a formal process to ensure that change not only happens but also gets embedded in the business process long term. The only way to ensure that the root cause of a valid, verified issue gets addressed is for internal audit to incorporate a formal process to conclude that the corresponding action has been properly adopted by the business process team. It does not matter what procedures are utilized to verify action plan adoption, as long as it can be confirmed. If action plan adoption does not occur, then the business process risk will continue to grow rapidly, only to be identified as a repeat audit issue in the subsequent audit engagement. As referenced in Chapter 8, the Beyond Audit methodology uses a continuous audit to validate action plan adoption. It is a simple, direct, and many times, nondisruptive process to verify that the action plan is still being used in the business process. In the remote audit environment, the continuous audit methodology is an excellent approach to incorporate into any internal audit department for action plan adoption.

 ## ARB CONCLUSION

Once the supporting statements have been read and scored for each of the six categories, all category scores are totaled to create the internal audit team risk profile score. As mentioned in the introduction to this chapter, the total score is then compared to the overall risk ratings of low, moderate, and severe. Each rating has a corresponding narrative and recommends the appropriate level of action to be taken to address the internal audit methodology opportunities for improvement. In addition to the explanation of the risk profile score, there are improvement suggestions for each one of the six categories. Remember when completing the ARB self-assessment to be certain to provide honest responses based on the current, documented audit methodology in your department. The ARB has been designed to evaluate the current audit approach and provide focused suggestions to strengthen the audit process and team.

12

How Good Is Audit?

T HERE HAS ALWAYS BEEN a desire in every job to exceed the stated expectations of your team and the internal audit department is no different. In the challenge for any and every time when striving for excellence or trying to become the best, there are no specific goals or standards set that would indicate performance excellence. The word most often used to describe excellent performance is *world-class*. When that term is spoken or heard, everyone thinks this must be the best of the best available and that should be the department's stated objective. There is only one problem with this term and the simple fact is that there are no established standards, documentation, or requirements to determine when a team, any team, has executed their job with such precision that they would be deemed world-class. The unfortunate fact is that, besides the Olympics, there is no way to determine with confidence that a team, in our case internal audit, is world-class. Everyone would agree that there are individuals that compete in the Olympics who have set records and are world-class in their respective sports. All would agree that Michael Phelps is a world-class swimmer with his gold medal achievements and that Usain Bolt is a world-class sprinter and possibly the fastest man on the planet. No arguments from anybody regarding those two gentlemen. But when it comes to internal audit, there will be no chance that your department will be on the podium receiving a gold medal for report writing or just hoping to make the podium for risk assessments. Those types of competitions and awards do not exist for audit departments and hopefully never will. However, there have to be methods or industry standards to determine that an internal audit department is not only doing their job, but also doing their job effectively and efficiently while improving business partner relationships, improving business process operations, and developing a strong internal team to execute the audit methodology responsibilities with precision.

The Beyond Audit methodology has established a set of standards for internal audit departments to use as a baseline in determining the effectiveness and efficiency of their operations as they strive to achieve excellence in all phases of their product delivery. As previously mentioned, there is no specific list of performance achievements or standards to define a world-class internal audit organization, but the Beyond Audit methodology has compiled 10 distinct characteristics in an attempt to document the requirements for precision execution via a self-review. The method in which these characteristics are reviewed is that each one includes supporting descriptive statements and then a clarifying question to assist the internal audit team in determining whether the department is represented by the supporting statement or if the department needs to address the identified gaps. The 10 characteristics are broken down into five specific hard characteristics and five specific soft characteristics. Each will be revealed and explained with the culmination of the discussion, concluding with a self-review and directive action to improve the internal audit operations. To provide background on this compilation of characteristics, it should be noted that this is not a list which was generated by an individual or a particular time in a specific industry. This information was researched and gathered over a two-year period from various industries from around the world. As a global facilitator, there was an opportunity to solicit internal audit departments in various industries in an effort to define the elusive concept of world-class. To accomplish this endeavor, during each training, keynote address, or conference speech over 24 months, the question was presented to attendees asking what they thought made an internal audit department world-class. As you can imagine, there were myriad responses, which were compiled with the most frequently given responses captured and summarized where applicable. Of course, there were more than 10 responses, but no one would sit and consider the top 31 characteristics of a world-class audit organization, and as a result you have the following 10 to consider.

INTRODUCING THE TOP TEN

Now that the background of how this information was identified and compiled has been explained, it is critical to provide a foundation before detailing the top 10. The foundation for this discussion is simple; the primary consideration prior to reading this is to ensure your internal department is dynamic (open and willing to change) and always striving for process improvements in their own operations. This is a critical point because, as previously discussed, there are too many internal audit departments who are executing audits with the intention of moving the coverage needle instead of trying to build a greater knowledge of the business operations being audited with the objective of improving the existing business processes. So, if your department is dynamic and you are proud to be a member of this internal audit team, then this discussion is specifically designed for your consideration, evaluation, and call to create tangible actions to improve internal performance. Most of the internal audit departments who openly embrace this self-review are the ones who are constantly looking to challenge their team members and trying to identify opportunities to improve on a daily basis. Discussion of the top 10 will begin with the 5 hard characteristics most often stated as the characteristics of a world-class audit organization.

1. Defined Audit Methodology

While there are numerous reasons and benefits to have a fully developed and communicated methodology for the audit department, there is an overwhelming desire from the audit staff to have an established methodology so that audit team members can understand the expectations for each phase of an audit. The methodology also provides auditors with the specific audit objectives, which makes it easier for them to explain the audit process to business partners. Remember that this documented methodology must include the mission statement and the audit charter, which will explain the internal audit role in the company as well as clearly state the organizational independence that internal audit must have in being able to report directly to the audit committee. This type of documentation clearly outlines the internal audit reporting line and should strengthen their ability to provide value-added recommendations that are recognized by their business partners. Additionally, the methodology must contain the detailed process that internal audit completes on an annual basis to review, evaluate, and triage the auditable entities within the company. This detailed process is completed to not only define the audit universe, but also generate the current year's internal plan listing the business processes which are scheduled to be audited. The audit plan is derived from a combination of factors including, but not limited to, risk scores, previous audit activities, how long it has been since the last internal audit, external partner reliance, and regulatory and compliance exposure. Once drafted, reviewed, and approved, the current audit plan can be communicated to both the internal audit team and executive management to keep them informed of the scheduled audit activity throughout the company.

There are always going to be questions surrounding how detailed an internal audit methodology document should be and how much of it should be shared as any one of the auditors describes the audit process to business partners. The answers to these common questions are simple. First, the audit methodology must contain the appropriate level of detail in order for any audit team member to be able to read it and clearly understand how all of the corresponding audit responsibilities and activities are defined and executed from the annual risk assessment to developing the audit plan up to and including audit committee reporting responsibilities. That is a large range of information that must also detail critical executables, including the audit phases, responsibilities, and corresponding templates required to be completed in an effort to compile the proper amount of supporting documentation for the conclusions. The methodology details regarding the annual risk assessment must include the scoring system to support the evaluation of the individual auditable entities, along with the steps incorporated to ensure the overall scores are consistently applied.

Additionally, the methodology must explain the specific steps and corresponding required templates that must be completed for each phase of an audit engagement to make sure any internal or external review will agree with the level of supporting documentation and reach the same conclusion. That level of detail should be included in the methodology so that any party inquiring about the internal audit process can clearly understand the objectives and services offered by the department. The second question related to how much of this methodology should be shared with business partners is to allow auditors to communicate the entire risk-based audit process or whatever audit service is being performed to inform the business partner that the audit department has a regimented approach for every audit activity and nothing is being executed without properly designed and specific documented objectives. This communication will allow the business partner to have some level of confidence in the audit activity taking place in their business unit. Internal audit already has way too many negative misconceptions about what they do and why they do it. So, being able to clearly explain the internal audit process details to a business partner can help clear up any mystery regarding an audit and immediately dispel any thoughts of negative intentions on the part of the internal audit department.

Once the review of these characteristics of the internal audit methodology has been discussed, the question to be answered is, "Does the internal audit department have a fully documented and communicated methodology?" Now, before giving any answer, the methodology reviewer(s) must verify that the methodology is documented, including the annual risk assessment process, a listing of all audit services offered, the documented process of each audit service along with the corresponding templates, the action item receipt, verification, adoption, tracking, and reporting process, and the audit committee responsibilities. If those details are documented, every auditor has received and read the internal methodology, and there is a formal communication to the internal audit team regarding changes to the methodology, then it is clear that the department has a fully documented and communicated methodology.

2. Business Process Knowledge

As has been mentioned in numerous chapters already, the most effective internal auditors are the ones who continually develop and build their business knowledge in an effort to increase the depth, detail, and value of their audit work. It is virtually impossible to execute internal audit work around a business process if the internal auditor does not understand the basic objectives and process requirements of the process being reviewed. Keep in mind, an audit can still be planned and executed without a detailed understanding of the business process, but the audit work will be executed at a general level and the results of that audit will be non-value-added and result in no real improvement in the business process operations.

There is always going to be a demand and requirement for internal auditors to solicit, obtain, build, and share business knowledge. This level of commitment from an internal audit team fosters the development of a strong team utilizing communication as the cornerstone of their department. However, the commitment required for this type of learning environment is an all-team commitment. There cannot be any member of the internal audit team who does not recognize the value of business learning and exhibit the effort required to continually build on their existing business process knowledge. When the entire team is focused on the learning aspect of internal audit, the internal audit department's reputation and credibility with the business partners, executives, and audit committee rise exponentially. But it cannot be stressed enough that this business process learning aspect is a 100 percent audit team member commitment. The success of this learning initiative relies on each auditor recognizing that there are business process details that not even the most tenured internal auditor knows or understands. The lack of understanding or knowledge realization should be enough to convince the auditor to realize that it is the business partner that is the process expert (not the auditor). Once that reality sets in, the auditor understands the only way to access the critical process details is to actively facilitate a discussion with the business partner to unlock the more intricate process requirements needed to achieve the business objectives on a consistent basis. Make no mistake about it, the current process details that the internal audit department understands are only the details that the business partner has decided to share with the auditor at this juncture of the internal audit and business partner relationship. All auditors must realize that their level of business process knowledge is exactly the level at which the business partner wants it to be. As auditors, they must strive to push the learning envelope to gain a greater understanding of the process requirements.

Recall from Chapter 3 when marketing the internal audit department was discussed. This aspect of creating an audit team, which is focused on building relationships through ongoing business process learning, must be part of that marketing. However, like any other aspect of marketing, just stating that the internal audit department is going to do something will not be enough. Most people know that anyone trying to convince another person of anything will say whatever it takes to sell it. With internal audit, there is close scrutiny of all audit activity, and the marketing of the department is no exception. If there is a mention that the internal audit team is dedicated to continually learning the business process, then the auditors are going to have to show evidence of that effort on every audit engagement. That is why stressing the point of 100 percent team commitment for business process learning is so critical to the success of the department.

Do not build a reputation for being all talk and no action. It is easy to say the team will do something but monumentally difficult to get the team to actually do it, especially at 100 percent. Stay focused on the learning aspect of internal audit from both an audit methodology and business process perspective. With that type of commitment, your internal audit team will be successful in their efforts.

Once the review of these characteristics of business process knowledge has been discussed, the question to be answered is, "Does the internal audit department focus on developing and building business knowledge on every audit engagement?" This question seems too simple and direct when in actuality it is not. It is one of the questions in this self-review where auditors will immediately respond *absolutely*, when in reality, that probably is not the case. Clearly consider the wording of this validation question, specifically the part about building knowledge on every assignment.

Two distinct concepts in this question must be emphasized and understood prior to providing an answer. The first is the word *building*; all auditors will attempt to learn the process in order to plan or execute the testing. However, there are many auditors who believe that they possess a sufficient understanding of the business process and that attempting to gather more business process details is probably not worth the time, effort, and headache to extract that information from their business partner. This is the exact type of auditor attitude that can result in critical process details being overlooked during the planning phase or missed during the fieldwork phase. The assumption of sufficient business process knowledge is a mistake, and any internal auditors who assume they understand the intricate details of the business process are doing themselves, the audit team, and the business partner a disservice. Do not make this mistake. Create a business process learning mentality of trying to learn at least one new aspect of the business each time you interact with the business partner. Commitment to this type of approach will result in internal auditors inherently and naturally asking detailed process questions without realizing it, and it will pay off in the long run from both an educational and relationship perspective.

The second word to consider in this statement is *every*; this is a reminder to the auditors that each engagement they participate in must have a business process learning aspect, including to increase the value of the audit objectives. If the internal audit department wants to be recognized as a value partner in the business, it must incorporate existing and newly acquired business knowledge throughout the audit process. So, remember to focus on the learning aspect of the business process while completing the audit methodology requirements. If there is a consistent commitment of learning throughout the audit department on every assignment and it is reflected in the audit results and strength of the business partner relationships, then you can be confident that the audit team is focused on developing the necessary business process knowledge.

3. Continuous Auditing

The most established internal audit departments provide tools and methodologies for the audit team to perform engagements in an effort to not only identify and confirm the business objectives but also provide process-focused recommendations to improve business process efficiencies. The days of internal audit being an extended oversight arm of the executive team are over (or at least should be), as internal audit is viewed as a critical third line of defense providing an independent evaluation of the control environment that governs the most critical business processes in the company. In order for an audit team to be successful in that incredibly difficult and demanding endeavor, it is going to take more than a basic risk-based audit approach. With the varying business unit requirements and deliverables, the internal audit department, during the initial planning of each engagement, must determine what is the most effective manner in which to validate the business process control environment with a confident level of certainty. The selection of what specific audit methodology to apply is based on the business process requirements, technical skills required, and audit time available. Also, if this particular audit was not on the original annual audit plan, there is going to be a consideration of who requested the audit and why. All of these factors contribute to determining what audit methodology would be best to achieve the corresponding audit objectives.

While there are numerous alternative audit approaches to be considered, continuous auditing is the one methodology that provides the effective validation of the control environment with the least amount of disruption to the client. Before discussing the Beyond Audit continuous auditing methodology, there are others to consider, such as limited scope, agile, operational, and performance audits. Each one of these audits has challenges, such as reduction in coverage, significant business partner commitment, or reliance on business process results. In any alternative auditing testing techniques, there are going to be challenges. And while continuous auditing is no different, it provides data-supported validation for the critical controls selected to verify they are producing the intended outcome of the business process requirements.

The challenge that comes with continuous auditing is that all controls in the business process are not being reviewed. The continuous auditing methodology only tests the controls determined to be stage gate controls. A *stage gate control* is a control for which, if it fails, there are only two possible outcomes; the business process comes to a complete stop or the business process produces an incorrect outcome. The focus of this type of review will hinge on the audit team's ability to accurately identify the most critical stage gate controls in the business process. The requirements of the continuous audit methodology are to examine and document the business process, identify the true process risk and corresponding controls, and select the stage gate controls to be detail tested. The controls are going to be tested on a recurring basis to validate that the business process is producing repeatable, reliable results.

The other distinction regarding continuous auditing is to recognize that it is not a monitoring tool that is being performed by internal audit in perpetuity for the business partner. That is not the objective of this testing methodology. Continuous auditing is an alternative testing approach that has a distinct start date and finish date. Remember that the internal audit department is part of the third line of defense and cannot be involved in the development, implementation, or execution of any business process activities that would include the monitoring of critical controls. The identified controls would be selected, testing would be developed, a sample source would be identified, and the corresponding testing would be executed and reported on as the methodology requires. All of the alternative testing methodologies to be considered are implemented to complement the risk-based audit methodology in an effort to increase the internal audit coverage and depth of the audit universe.

Once the review of these characteristics of the continuous auditing methodology has been discussed, the question to be answered is, "Does the internal audit department utilize any alternative testing methodologies to increase audit coverage?" This question in the evaluation of a world-class audit organization is more focused on being able to adjust the approach of the audit department to meet the specific needs of the business function under review. There will be instances where the business process itself requires an alternative testing methodology to determine the effectiveness of the business control environment. In the current remote operating environment for internal audit, the continuous audit approach is more effective for remote testing and provides a more in-depth analysis into the critical business controls over a longer period of time. This recurring audit testing allows the audit engagement team to examine and compile significant evidence (testing data) in determining the conclusion of control environment effectiveness. Regardless of the alternative testing approach implemented by the internal audit department, ensure that the corresponding methodology for the approach is documented and provides adequate supporting documentation for any conclusions made. Also, it is important to verify that the alternative methodology can be effective in a remote audit engagement scenario.

4. Implemented Dashboard

As detailed in Chapter 9, a fully integrated audit performance dashboard plays a critical role in keeping a pulse on the effectiveness and efficiency of the current internal audit methodologies. The dashboard itself, when implemented properly, provides valuable data to the audit management team pertaining to individual audits, as well as the annual audit plan status and departmentwide initiatives. The most valuable characteristic of an audit performance dashboard is that it is a true assessment of the team's understanding, execution, and compliance with the established methodologies. When a department dedicates the necessary time and resources associated with formalizing and documenting their audit methodologies, it is valuable to have an internal quality control check to confirm the effectiveness of the documented approaches and proactively address deviations from the standard when identified. As was mentioned in the detailed dashboard description (Chapter 9), the metrices created, tracked, and reported must originate directly from the audit methodology it is designed to evaluate. Also, it is critical that the audit methodology specifically identify and document satisfactory performance so the corresponding evaluation criteria can be properly built (listing achievable and reasonable goals) to evaluate the current period's performance.

Remember that the most important point when it comes to an internal audit dashboard is ensuring that the dashboard is not driving any auditor's behavior or performance. It must be stressed to the entire audit team to never rush or expedite any audit activity in order to make a state metric requirement. When the dashboard starts to impact and drive auditor behavior, the value of the dashboard metrics becomes useless because the individual metrics being tracked and reported on the dashboard do not reflect actual auditor performance or audit engagement compliance. This is quite a common occurrence with internal audit dashboards, as the objective of the audit team incorrectly becomes focused on meeting the dashboard metrics instead of understanding the business and providing an independent evaluation of the control environment. This type of behavior tends to go unnoticed until it is too late, and when it does occur, it usually is department-wide, as no one auditor assumes the attitude of never wanting to miss metric compliance. Do not let this happen on your internal audit team, and be sure to stress that the dashboard is designed to improve the audit process by tracking actual performance and data, and the information will never be used as a discipline tool regarding any auditor's performance.

High-performing internal audit departments understand the dashboard objectives and focus their specific metrics on the multiple aspects of their department, including team-specific metrics, which could include retention, development, or recognition; audit execution metrics such as audit elapsed time, report timeliness, and business partner communications; or quality metrics like client surveys and action plan implementation. Each of the specific metrics an internal audit department creates will be unique to that particular department and the corresponding audit methodology requirements being tracked. There are no required dashboard metrics or related criteria evaluation standards. This information will be developed by audit management based on the most critical aspects of their methodology components that they want to ensure are being completed as designed. This compliance will help ensure that the audit department produces a quality product consistently across the department. If and when there are metrics that identify less than satisfactory performance, the deviation from the methodology standard should be handled in the same manner as an identified business exception. The data will be confirmed and then a root cause discussion will be executed to determine what potential actions will be needed to address the gap. Remember when developing and maintaining the dashboard that it is a dynamic measurement tool that must reflect the current methodology requirements and be adjusted any time there is a revision to accurately reflect the changes.

Once the review of these characteristics of the dashboard has been discussed, the question to be answered is, "Does the internal audit department have a metrics dashboard to capture, evaluate, and track audit methodology key deliverables?" In regard to the top 10 characteristics of a world-class audit organization, this question may be the most direct to answer because your department either has a dashboard or does not, but it is one of the most critical for a couple of reasons.

First, if your department does not have a metrics dashboard, it is important to consider implementing one as soon as possible, as it usually provides unbelievably valuable performance data immediately. Even when an audit department appears to be performing well, completing audits, and moving the audit coverage needle every quarter, the dashboard tends to highlight individual aspects of noncompliance with the audit methodology that are being masked by the fact that audits themselves are being completed but not the way they were designed or with the required supporting documentation. The first few months of a newly implemented internal audit dashboard tend to be the most valuable since the metrics immediately highlight items that previously had been occurring and gone undetected. This is not a bad thing or reflective of poor team performance. Instead it should be viewed as the team being focused on getting audit engagements completed while becoming more disciplined in complying with the audit methodology requirements. The dashboard will help to identify methodology gaps, allow teams to tighten compliance with their existing methodology requirements or examine it for potential updates, and effectively prepare for any external quality review.

The other reason to consider when evaluating the dashboard question is related to audit departments who already have an existing dashboard or set of metrics that are being tracked. Check your process and verify that the current metrics accurately reflect the methodology requirements, the corresponding evaluation criteria is reasonable but challenging, the frequency of data capture and reporting is at least occurring on a monthly basis, and any actions needed are developed via a root cause discussion with the appropriate actions being tracked through implementation and adoption. If these two reasons are considered when discussing your internal audit's current dashboard status, your team will be in the right position to determine how to best implement or update their internal quality measurement tool. Consider how beneficial a methodology compliance tracking tool can be in the remote audit environment when there is not a significant amount of real-time oversight being provided to the audit team members who are executing the audit engagements.

5. Effective Technology Usage

There is no denying that in the current remote auditing environment there is a significant dependence on technology being incorporated into the audit process on a daily basis. Every single day, audit engagement information is being gathered, developed, documented, and shared among an audit team working on a current engagement. Now, consider the audit teams that do not have an automated workpaper database and are attempting to execute audit engagements remotely. In that scenario, it is going to be exceedingly difficult for audit teams to share information regarding the business unit being reviewed especially during the planning phase when communication of business process details is so critical. It will be nearly impossible for these audit teams to share information timely and they will probably have to perform a significant number of individual audits. While that is not an impossible scenario, it makes the audit process even more challenging than before and significantly impacts the review and approval process of audit workpapers. To be honest, this aspect of the world-class characteristics discussion (when it was created) did not consider a situation where internal audit teams would be separated and not be able to work in a central location or onsite with a business partner. The remote audit environment was not a consideration upon development of this type of internal review. However, given the current situation, it is a topic that must be noted and discussed. Therefore, internal audit departments who utilize an automated workpaper database must be even more diligent than before when it comes to the audit methodology and documentation requirements due to the simple fact that the other audit engagement team members are going to access this information, review the data, and create corresponding testing to evaluate the business process. At the end of the day, auditors must recognize the significant level of scrutiny and reliance other audit team members will be placing on the documentation that has been completed and uploaded into the audit database. In the remote auditing world, there is an immediate assumption that the information in the audit database for a particular project is accurate and factual and ready to be used in other phases of the audit. If your team is using an automated workpaper database, ensure that all documentation has been reviewed and has evidence of an approval prior to assuming the information included is accurate and ready to be shared. If there is no evidence of approval on the workpaper, contact the auditor responsible for the creation and discuss the documented evidence before relying on it in any other work or audit testing.

The original objective for including the effective technology usage characteristic in this review was focused on how internal audit incorporated their current available technology tools when executing an audit engagement. The specific reason for including the term *current* in this statement was to stress to audit departments that they should not use this to try and purchase more software but to determine any existing department software that could help them on their current project. Incorporating software usage in an audit could be as simple as using Excel or Access to help with data calculations, sorting, or sampling.

Too often, internal audit teams look for a specific technology that they believe will not only help them complete an audit engagement but also reduce their audit work time. Here is a news-flash for any auditor who believes that: It never happens that way. What *does* happen is auditors incorporate these technology tools to expand samples, create complex calculations, or attempt to test 100 percent of a population. All of those activities will cost valuable audit time and, when completed, will not result in any difference to the audit conclusions.

Once the review of these characteristics of the effective technology usage has been discussed, the question to be answered is, "Does the internal audit department effectively utilize their current technology tools to support their audit process?" The most important point to consider when answering this question is understanding the technology options available to the audit team and observing that the auditors properly apply the software where applicable and when appropriate. The audit team must be able to recognize the opportunities for efficient use to compile and analyze information, develop business process mapping, or accurately select testing samples. No matter how the audit department incorporates technology into the day-to-day operations, ensure it is being used to assist the audit team in completing the engagement requirements and not wasting valuable time attempting to use technology just for the sake of saying it was incorporated into the audit work. Audit departments must also realize that there is no technology solution available anywhere on the planet that will solve all of the problems of any internal audit department or business process for that matter. The technology tool is there to help auditors with their work and will always be as effective as the information being loaded into the software.

As mentioned in the introduction of this topic, the top 10 world-class characteristics are broken down into two sets of information, one represented the five hard characteristics discussed above and the other the five soft characteristics, which will follow. These characteristics represent concepts and skills that were mentioned most often during the solicitation of this information. The discussion of soft characteristics, or any soft skills, is based on subjective opinions of the audit departments solicited to provide input. There is no definite listing identifying all the most effective soft skills needed to be successful as an internal audit, but these represent ones that were not only the most frequently suggested but also proven to motivate audit team members and effectively drive results. Remember, the objective of this self-review is for audit departments to consider these topics in an effort to challenge their team to perform at a high level on every audit engagement. The top-10 discussion continues with the soft characteristics that help audit departments effectively execute the hard characteristics in an effort to build a world-class audit organization.

6. Visionary Leadership

Leadership is one of the most difficult soft skills to define, as every internal audit department would define this term in a hundred different ways. The best way to approach this topic is not to try and *define* leadership but to describe the characteristics that a leader would exhibit on a daily basis to each audit team member. First and foremost, a leader treats every individual audit with the same approach, respect, and discipline regardless of the audit experience or tenure within the team. Just like in the relationship discussion in Chapter 10, trust plays a major role in the success of a leader, as the leader must be viewed as someone who can be approached with any topic or provide guidance when solicited with every audit team member receiving the same amount of time and attention. That is how a leader treats all individuals on the audit team.

In order to accomplish this goal, the leader must be recognized as someone who has a mastery of the audit methodologies used by the department and a strong grasp of the business processes. It is with this foundational knowledge that the leader will be recognized as a strong internal audit asset whom the auditors can rely on to clarify a methodology question or provide guidance with a challenge regarding the business process. A leader will exhibit a willingness to help auditors when approached with any question or problem. A true leader welcomes this support and guidance role, which inherently results in the leader becoming a well-respected member of the internal audit team and trusted source. This level and recognition of respect helps foster the team environment and encourages other audit team members to actively communicate and share their knowledge with others.

These leadership skills are easy to describe and gain agreement but the skills will only be successful if the individual in this position is able to show that they are not just talking the talk but performing the same skills that they preach about to their teams. Too often, potential leaders believe they know how to build a strong team, which contributes on every project and assists other audit team members when challenges arise – but real leaders jump into action without being asked. This action shows their team that just talking about chipping in or helping out is not the same thing as actually doing it. Leaders who think they are successful because they are good speakers or always seem to be there to provide suggestions are fine, but real leaders exhibit strong tone from the top with corresponding actions to illustrate what needs to be done to be successful. The true internal audit leaders always put the needs of the team first and help individuals as the need applies.

Additionally, successful leaders are excellent at marketing the internal audit department and keeping the big picture in mind, which in the end is delivering value to all business partners within the company. Remember the discussion about marketing the audit department in Chapter 3 and how the success of that effort is based on the ability of the auditor to detail and explain how the audit process works? Leaders continual develop that message so it can be effectively communicated to business partners during every audit engagement.

Once the review of these characteristics of visionary leadership has been discussed, the question to be answered is, "Does the internal audit leadership team direct, advise, and share information effectively?" Keep in mind when responding to the soft characteristic questions that there is going to be a more subjective approach in determining an answer. However, when possible, try to identify specific examples where the soft characteristic was illustrated and use that information to formulate your response. Being a successful leader does not mean you are going to be friends with everyone in the audit department. The key to leadership is continual learning regarding the audit process and business operations, being open and adaptable to change, and being someone who can be counted on to provide guidance when requested. Leadership will be challenged on occasion to deliver a difficult message, provide critical feedback to a coworker, or make an unpopular decision. But to succeed, even in the midst of a difficult situation, is to ensure that the task you are executing is done based on confirmed, accurate information and the realization that this action will benefit the internal audit department in the end. And while the leadership team may have to make some challenging decisions, it is important that everyone on that team be open and adaptable to change if it benefits the internal audit team and the execution of their responsibilities. Remember, examining this question regarding leadership is not about judging decisions which were made or not made. It is about the leadership points discussed and how well the leaders within your audit department possess and exhibit these behaviors.

7. Change Agent

As described in Chapter 7, working with a business partner in an effort to convince them to implement an additional step or alter their current process is going to require the internal audit department to facilitate real change. The only way real change ever gets off the ground is if the auditors can become change agents. This additional role for auditors will require them to understand and effectively execute the Beyond Audit methodology *foundation four* to becoming a change agent. What this foundation four includes is (1) effectively facilitating a root-cause analysis; (2) partnering to identify a viable solution; (3) verifying the solution implementation; and (4) confirming the solution adoption. Let us briefly discuss these one at a time. Keep in mind that the success of all steps after the root-cause analysis is based on the information that was discovered in step one. The internal audit team must remain patient and diligent in the root-cause analysis to ensure they are using accurate information to complete the rest of the required steps to facilitate real change. When examining root cause, the auditor must work with the business partner and combine the auditor's risk and control knowledge with the business partner's process knowledge to determine why the particular business control tested is not producing the expected outcome on a consistent basis in the most effective and efficient manner. This analysis will be facilitated by the internal auditor using the condition statement, as discussed in Chapter 7. Remember to confirm the root cause and obtain agreement from the process owner so that both parties are on the same page to proceed to the next step of partnering for solutions.

The second step in the foundation four approach is to work with the business partner to identify the proper solution to address the confirmed deviation from the business standard which was revealed during the audit fieldwork phase. In this step of the process, the auditor will use their communication skills to explain the specific data identified during the audit testing and verified with the business team for accuracy and completeness. The strength of the data supports the issue and illustrates the need for a solution to address the deviation. The other supporting evidence the auditor can use is the draft audit report itself to provide background regarding the audit approach used in reviewing the business process where the issue was identified. To ensure the effectiveness of the suggestion solution (action plan) to address the issue, the audit should never be reluctant to challenge their business partner regarding the completeness of the suggested action if it does not appear on the surface to properly address the root cause which was identified and agreed to in the first step. Using the word *challenge* in working toward a solution means to discuss putting the action in place and talking through the effectiveness of the same and deciding if it can be strengthened in any way to ensure it has the desired impact on the business process.

The third and fourth steps in the foundation four approach are to verify implementation and confirm adoption of the suggested solution, respectively. Implementation is an interim step to be executed by the internal audit team when notified by the business partner that the solution has been incorporated into the business process. As part of the implementation verification, internal audit will examine documented evidence supporting the statement that the new process has been incorporated into the business process and is delivering the intended outcome. That is only half of the validation to ensuring that real change has occurred and the audit department was successful in achieving its goal. The second half is for internal audit to perform a second verification within six months of implementation to confirm that the business team has truly adopted the new process step or enhancement into their daily responsibilities, and again the documentation is provided and reviewed to determine that it has been effectively adopted by the business team. Once the final confirmation has occurred, the internal audit team can be confident that real change did take place. While it does not happen often, it is amazing when it does because it truly illustrates the value of the internal audit and business process departments working together to improve the process.

Once the review of these characteristics of change agent has been discussed, the question to be answered is, "Does the internal audit department have a formal, documented process to verify proposed action plans have been implemented and adopted?" This question is much easier to answer than the other soft characteristics discussed because it has a formal process associated with it. Every internal audit department has some form of action plan follow-up process to verify that the business partner's action plan, as stated in the audit report, has been implemented into the business process as described. The breaking point for most audit departments when it comes to being a change agent comes at the expense of a lack of a formal process of confirming the business process change by allowing some time to pass and then reviewing the business process change to ensure that it was truly adopted. If your audit department does not have any process to validate action plan adoption, consider enhancing your current audit methodology to include this step to strengthen the business process accuracy and efficiency.

8. Best Team

One of the most significant challenges in any internal audit department is to recruit and maintain true talent in their organization. While this is not just confined to the internal audit department, turnover on an audit team always tends to be higher than in any other business unit. To adequately discuss this topic, it is more effective to view the characteristics of the best team category in two distinct parts. The first part is the hiring standard of recruiting and maintaining skilled staff and the second part, just as critical, is the methods by which you assign and use your current resources. This category is not, and never will be, about how to remove existing team members, but focuses on the identification of team development, proper training, and effective deployment of team skills to adequately review the control environment of specific business areas.

Discussing the recruiting and maintaining of audit staff, the core foundation will be based on incorporating the knowledge from the learning maps for each level, which detail the core competencies and expected results, to identify corresponding candidates to fill particular audit positions. All potential candidates should receive the proper skills screening and if appropriate be interviewed by at least two current internal audit team members to ensure not only that the candidate can articulate examples of how they have conquered specific audit challenges in their current job, but also whether they fit on the current audit team. The characteristic to look for in an audit interview is always going to be the ability to confidently communicate and provide support for any perspective being discussed. How comfortably candidates are presenting themselves in an interview will provide an example of their communication skills and how well they could become a member of the team. There are many internal audit leadership teams who believe hiring an auditor is much easier than keeping one. However, if audit teams would incorporate the personal development plan process in unison with the learning map, it will be much easier to maintain your current team. Providing audit staff, at any level, with the roadmap to progressing through the department with the specific competencies, skills, and behaviors to be successful on the audit team keeps auditors motivated and focused on their own development. The audit management team must ensure that there is proper training available and opportunities to practice the developing skills. If the training is appropriate and on-the-job training opportunities are provided, the internal audit team will develop and build on their craft while participating on the assigned audit engagements. An important part of this successful development is to have internal audit leadership teams maximize their existing audit team's strengths and put their auditors in a position to succeed. The correct combination of skills on every audit is the key to effective execution of audits.

The second part of the best team category to consider is, how do audit management teams assign and use their existing resources? In order for any internal audit department to be successful, the management team must clearly know, recognize, and understand the combination of skills and resources that they have at their disposal to deploy on each audit assignment. The challenge that arises most often is that the skills required on audit assignments overlap projects and result in a shortage of a particular need being available for all projects currently in process. When this occurs, audit management must decide and triage the needs for that skill in the ongoing audits. Additionally, there must be an acceptance that if the skills needed for a specific audit are not available, the skill must be recruited or co-sourced to address the need. The critical point to remember when selecting the co-sourcing options is that while the need may be met in a more expedient manner, it will not be cost effective, and the particular skills obtained will leave the audit department the moment the assignment is completed. There is no retention or transfer of knowledge when it comes to a co-sourcing arrangement. So, while it might be effective to "rent" the skill for a particular audit, in the long run it does not increase the knowledge of your team or improve your audit product in the future. Co-sourcing is the appropriate decision when there is an immediate need to address a glaring gap in your audit team's existing skillset.

Once the review of these characteristics of best team has been discussed, the question to be answered is, "Does the internal audit department have fully developed learning maps for each level to effectively guide individual auditor development?" When considering this question, review the current audit department onboarding process and verify that it includes a discussion of the job responsibilities as well as a listing of the core competencies and expected results for the current job and an explanation of the progression of next steps. That type of discussion provides every audit team member with the performance details for their current level and the responsibilities and requirements for the next level in their development and progression opportunities within the department. Every internal auditor benefits from understanding the roadmap available to them and it keeps them motivated in the development of their own skills.

9. Communication Skills

As discussed, and detailed in Chapter 10, communication must be the cornerstone of every audit department and throughout every level. A good method to create a foundation and background for this characteristic would be to go back and review the highlights of the communication chapter and recognize how these skills play such a critical role in the effectiveness of every internal audit department. There is no aspect of the internal audit process that does not require successful communication in delivering a message; requesting business partner time, documentation, or data; and successfully executing all three audit phases. Remember that the communication skill requirement is a commitment for every audit team member and must be included in every audit position learning map to stress the vital role this skill plays. Being a good communicator requires a focus on listening, dedicated effort to share business and audit knowledge, confident and consistent description of audit services, and clear explanation of business issues that need to be addressed. Combining these characteristics of being a successful communicator with adequately preparing for every meeting or encounter with a business partner will increase the audit reputation and quality of audit product. Productive and effective audit departments are the ones that stress the importance of effective communication both inside and outside the audit department.

Once the review of these characteristics of communication skills has been discussed, the question to be answered is, "Does the internal audit department focus on effective communication throughout the audit process and stress the continual development of this critical skill?" Determining the adequacy of communication skills within the audit department should be one of the easier world-class characteristics to evaluate since it reflects how you view the effectiveness of internal audit communication, especially within the department. Also, consider how business partners throughout the company perceive, accept, and solicit internal audit activities, inquiries, reports, and assistance with projects. With these considerations, it will be simple to determine if your audit team is sufficiently focused on the communication skill requirements and development of same.

10. Transparency

Throughout the entire process of gathering this information in an attempt to define what *world-class* means when describing an internal audit organization, one response was consistently mentioned as a critical characteristic. There was also a significant majority, almost to an individual level, who believed this particular characteristic directly tied to the overall success of the internal audit department. *Transparency* in any process is a dedicated effort for the corresponding team members to accurately and effectively describe the process so that any business partner would clearly understand not only the steps being executed, but also the reasoning and importance of each individual step. The level of process and information sharing from an audit department regarding their process requires a dedicated effort to keep their business partner in the process information loop from the moment an audit is assigned up to and including the creation of the final report. It will be incredibly difficult to develop a successful internal audit and business partner relationship if there is no transparency between the two parties. The internal audit department should have no secrets from the business team and should provide them audit phase explanations as the audit progresses. This helps in the facilitation of the audit phases as well as the receipt of critical documentation, data, and intelligence required to complete the audit requirements. It is important for the internal audit team to remember that the business partner is a key member of the audit process and is needed throughout the audit process. As explained in Chapter 10, it is critically important to keep the business partner "in the know" regarding all audit activity in their area and ensure they have no doubts as to the purpose of why a particular process is being reviewed or what the testing for that process will include. Utilize the transparency characteristic to foster the relationship environment and continue to build the foundation of trust.

Once the review of these transparency characteristics has been discussed, the question to be answered is, "Does the internal audit department maintain transparency the audit process when dealing with the business partner?" While this may seem like a straightforward question, it may be difficult to answer because it will be based on feedback and observations from multiple audits and could be difficult to say definitively. In determining the level of transparency within your internal audit department, examine the department metrics related to audit phase completion, current year's audit plan status, report timeliness, and action plan implementation. If these specific metrics are performing well, you can be pretty confident that the internal audit team has placed a high value on being transparent with the client regarding all phases of the audit and all communications with their business partners as the level of transparency will directly affect internal audit's ability to complete audit phase requirements and action plan implementation in accordance with the established audit methodology.

CREATING AN ACTION PLAN

After completing this examination of the top 10 characteristics of a world-class audit organization, does that mean we are world-class if we are fairly good with these 10? The process of determining the effectiveness of your audit team will be based on your interpretation of how many of the 10 characteristics your department currently exhibits. Experience has shown that having the first five hard characteristics in place will result in success with the soft characteristics of the evaluation. But like any other process, there must be clear objectives and standards that all team members recognize are critical to the success of department operations. There is no formal scoring model that says that if an internal audit department has 60 percent of the top 10 characteristics, then it is a world-class audit organization. This self-evaluation does not work like that, nor was it intended to be a formal scoring model. At the end of the day, the world-class characteristics provide audit departments, regardless of your size, industry, or location, with a framework of attributes exhibited by the most successful audit operations in the world. And while some may not seem to fit your current department, examine your audit department objectives and determine if any of those could help enhance the services you currently provide to business partners in an effort to improve their daily operations to be more effective and efficient. Ensure that if and when you determine your department requires improvement related to any one of the corresponding 10 characteristics, the current status is evaluated, a root-cause analysis is completed to determine steps needed to improve the process, and an achievable action plan is developed and implemented. To confirm that an action plan has been properly incorporated into the audit methodology and/or supporting process, monitor the progress and improvement of the revised/new process and adjust the requirements as needed.

CHAPTER THIRTEEN

Focused on Learning

THE MOST IMPORTANT ASPECT of every internal audit department is going to be the continuing education, developing, and learning of the team members both from an audit perspective – more specifically, how their audit methodology is executed – and from a business knowledge perspective. And while both of these topics have been highlighted throughout this book, this chapter provides a deeper dive into the learning responsibilities of an internal auditor. As with any attempt to learn something new, improve on an existing skill, or try to master a technique, there must be a desire from the auditor to want to accomplish the objective. This type of learning is different than the continuing education that an auditor participates in when it comes to earning continuing professional education (CPE) or attending a conference. As all auditors are aware, you can attend and participate in these different learning opportunities, but they are not the same as having the desire and drive to build on a personal skillset and achieve a specific objective. And when you consider how challenging the audit environment has become, especially with the remote audit requirements, focusing on developing techniques and skillsets to assist in the facilitation of these audit engagements becomes an asset to any audit organization. There has been a significant increase in the demand for communication and relationship development skills since they are seen as the primary skills which directly benefit auditors in the remote audit environment.

To increase any audit technical skill, there must be an evaluation of the specific skill(s) identified in their development plan that must be improved on. Remember that the development plan is a document (discussed in Chapter 4) that is personal to each and every auditor and is completed based on the identified, discussed, and documented skills that the individual auditor must work on to be successful at their job level. Do not underestimate the value of the skills discussion related to the learning objective, because it assists in providing the auditor with particular examples of development opportunities and proposed solutions to address the learning gap. After the desired skill and corresponding value of improving it has been discussed and approved with your supervisor, the task of identifying a training event to address the learning opportunity must be identified. Examine each available training and pay close attention to the specifically stated learning objectives. Ensure that upon completing the training activity, the learning objectives will provide tangible knowledge, techniques, or tools that can be directly applied to the execution of your audit methodology. While there are no guarantees associated with training, too often auditors select a training based on location rather than the specific learning objectives, and that is a mistake. Another helpful tool in the selection of training is to utilize the Learning Map that corresponds to your job and provides the detailed listing of core competencies and expected results of your current position as well as the same level of information for the next level in your progression within the audit department. The training you select should be focused on the skills needed to be successful at your current and future job responsibilities. Always remember to keep the learning objectives as the primary reason for participating in any training event to facilitate the corresponding learning documented in your development plan.

REMOTE LEARNING

Keep in mind that the remote learning environment requires discipline and dedication on the part of the auditor because all of the training currently being offered is going to be done as a self-study or an online meeting room. While neither of those training venues provides the most effective learning environment, they still cover critical skills and techniques that can be beneficial if given the proper level of commitment and contribution on the part of the participants. But take it from someone who has been facilitating training for 30 years, it is difficult to get training attendees to stay focused, listen, and participate in the learning environment when it is being facilitated in person. Now imagine how much more challenging achieving the learning objectives becomes when the topics and techniques have to be learned via self-study or during an online meeting. These alternative learning environments create significant barriers to an effective learning environment and for the most part do not offer the ability to ask questions of the facilitator or significantly reduce the availability for same. The key to development of an auditor's skillset is always to remember that an auditor must take ownership of their business knowledge and audit skill development and document the specific needs to improve their performance. Development is a self-owned event and never more prevalent than in the current audit environment.

To assist auditors with their development, an excerpt from the Beyond Audit Training Learning Map outlines suggested training in basic skills to provide a solid foundation for auditors within the first few years of their audit career. Which topics apply to which auditors would depend on the current audit experience and skillset the auditor currently possesses. Table 13.1, an excerpt from the Learning Map, provides the suggested training, along with the corresponding topic and a brief description of the skills to be covered.

TABLE 13.1   Beyond Audit Training Learning Map

Course Name	Topic	Skills Description
Risk-Based Audit (RBA)	RBA overview	■ Business understanding ■ Objective identification ■ Risks defined ■ Controls defined ■ Three phases
Business Processing	Business process auditing	■ Defining flow auditing ■ Obtaining business procedures ■ Risk assessment ■ Control identification ■ Input, process, output
Beginning Auditor Skills	Audit foundation	■ Roles and responsibilities ■ IIA standards ■ Audit process model ■ Budgeting ■ Planning ■ True process risk identification ■ Control evaluation ■ Program development ■ Testing execution ■ Workpaper evidence ■ Reporting ■ Action plan implementation

(Continues)

TABLE 13.1 *(Continued)*

Course Name	Topic	Skills Description
Six Sigma Overview	Audit integration	▪ Six Sigma basics ▪ SIPOC ▪ Process breakdowns ▪ Targeted testing
Three Pillars of Planning	Planning RBA	▪ ORC methodology ▪ Objective identification ▪ Identify and rate risks ▪ Risk management ▪ Control evaluation
Interviewing Fundamentals	Learning business process	▪ Communication model ▪ RBA facilitation ▪ Questioning techniques ▪ Interview preparation ▪ Effective documentation
Flowcharting Basics	Document business process	▪ Understanding objectives ▪ Interpreting policies ▪ Symbols and techniques ▪ Identifying gaps ▪ Documenting controls
Risk Control Matrix (RCM)	RCM development	▪ RCM defined ▪ Component explanation ▪ Risk/control types ▪ Inherent and residual ▪ RCM development
Audit Program Creation	Audit testing development	▪ Audit objective confirmed ▪ Targeted testing ▪ Process validation ▪ Clearly written steps ▪ Sampling techniques ▪ Sufficient data obtained
Issue Identification	Detailing exceptions	▪ Confirm deviation ▪ Supporting evidence ▪ Associated exposure ▪ Identify and rate risks ▪ Likelihood and significance ▪ Business agreement ▪ Effectively document

(Continues)

TABLE 13.1 (Continued)

Course Name	Topic	Skills Description
Workpaper Evidence	Document the audit	▪ Methodology requirements ▪ Utilizing templates ▪ Workpaper components ▪ Required support ▪ Sufficient and relevant ▪ Stand-alone document
Issue Development	Completing an issue sheet	▪ Understand requirements ▪ Review validation ▪ Five component approach ▪ Effective development ▪ Issue communication
Flowcharting Basics	Document business process	▪ Understanding objectives ▪ Interpreting policies ▪ Symbols and techniques ▪ Identifying gaps ▪ Documenting controls
High-Impact Report Writing	Effective reporting	▪ RCM defined ▪ Component explanation ▪ Risk/control types ▪ Inherent and residual ▪ RCM development
Audit Program Creation	Audit testing development	▪ Know report purpose ▪ Report template usage ▪ Required fields ▪ Issue development ▪ Report ratings ▪ Writing keys ▪ Clear and concise ▪ Interpretation needs ▪ Self-view requirement ▪ Cold read process ▪ Practice writing ▪ Draft report
Communication Cornerstone	Effective communication	▪ Communication model ▪ Medium selection ▪ Active listening ▪ Delivering the message ▪ Driving with business data ▪ Supporting not defending ▪ Understanding audit's role ▪ Business partner relationship

Although the Beyond Audit Learning Map for beginning auditors provides an overview of the core competencies to effectively establish a foundation of critical learning during an auditor's introduction into a department, each audit team will have their own specific onboarding process and training suggestions and requirements for their own teams. This Learning Map can be used as a template for the development of core audit skills required to be successful in any department. Keep in mind that the remote auditing environment will necessitate greater focus on communication and relationship skills as previously mentioned. So, any time you have an opportunity to get exposure to those types of learning activities, take them. They will benefit you as you continue your audit skill development journey.

Always remember that the greatest asset an internal auditor can possess is a strong and ongoing development of business knowledge. Remember to always keep your business partner in the loop and never stop learning. Good luck.

Index